Women in the
Administrative Revolution

WOMEN IN THE ADMINISTRATIVE REVOLUTION

The Feminization of Clerical Work

by

Graham S. Lowe

UNIVERSITY OF TORONTO PRESS
Toronto and Buffalo

Published in 1987 by Polity Press in association with Basil Blackwell.

First published in North America 1987 by University of Toronto Press.
Toronto and Buffalo

ISBN 0–8020–2757–5 (cloth)
ISBN 0–8020–6686–0 (paper)

Canadian Cataloguing in Publication Data

Lowe, Graham S.
  Women in the administrative revolution

Includes index.
ISBN 0–8020–2657–5 (bound)   ISBN 0–8020–6686–0 (pbk.)

1. Women clerks – Canada – History.   2. Sexual
division of labor – Canada – History.   I. Title.

HD6073.M392C3 1987   331.4′8165137′0971   C87–094565–3

Typesetting in 10 on 11½ pt Plantin
by Columns Typesetting of Caversham, Reading, Berks.
Printed in Great Britain

This book is dedicated to my parents,
Amy Phyllis Lowe
and
Stanley Cathcart Lowe

Contents

List of Figures and Tables

Preface

In 1973–4 I worked in Toronto at a medium-sized general insurance company. After about eight months as a 'trainee', performing mindless clerical tasks, I was 'promoted' to claims adjuster. The women who showed me the ropes had no such escape route, despite their greater experience and seniority. Not that settling insurance claims resulting from house fires and automobile accidents held out great rewards. In fact, low salaries, poor supervision and meagre benefits were chronic grievances for male and female staff alike. Yet complaints were loudest among the women, trapped as they were in menial, dead-end jobs. Many quit after a while; staying to fight for a better deal was simply not considered a viable option. Or so I thought.

About this time, the Canadian Labour Congress launched its ill-fated white-collar unionization campaign in the private sector (public sector white-collar unionism was well advanced). The target was Toronto's huge finance and insurance industry. The CLC's slick advertising campaign featured 'Mary the Signed-Up Secretary' exhorting clerks to join the union. One day at coffee break the discussion got around to the new CLC union. Why not check it out, I asked? The suggestion seemed to fall flat. But when annual salary increases failed to materialize as expected, a union organizing drive erupted almost spontaneously. Management reacted first with shock, then they got tough. Ultimately their coercion and intimidation tactics undermined the confidence of the union supporters. Consequently the Labour Relations Board certification vote failed to gain the necessary majority. The spark of collectivism was snuffed out and it was back to business as usual.

The idea for the present study was germinated during this experience as an office worker. When I left the insurance company for graduate school, I had in mind a research project on the difficulties of organizing Canadian office workers, particularly women, into unions. Inspired by the 'classics' on white-collar workers by C. Wright Mills in the United States, David Lockwood and Bob Blackburn in Britain, and Michel Crozier in France, I soon realized that this was uncharted territory in

Canada. I would have to begin from square one. The resulting doctoral dissertation, completed at the University of Toronto in 1979, therefore dealt with the origins of the modern office in Canada and the creation of its female labour force. I saw this as the necessary spadework for future analysis of office employment relations. This dissertation forms the basis of the present book. A thorough study of white-collar unionism in Canada, I should point out, has yet to be done.

The book has evolved over the course of more than a decade. I have accumulated many debts along the way. Dennis Magill, Lorna Marsden and Noah Meltz gave me expert guidance during the initial research. The Canada Council helped support me by awarding a doctoral fellowship. My research was based almost entirely on archival materials. I am very grateful for the assistance provided by librarians and archivists in the following organizations: Bank of Nova Scotia, Sun Life Insurance, Manufacturers Life Insurance, Bell Canada, Canadian Pacific Railway, IBM, Imperial Oil, Massey-Ferguson, the Public Archives of Canada, and the Provincial Archives of Ontario and British Columbia.

Several chapters draw from previously published articles. Specifically, some of the data in chapters 3 and 4 were first presented in 'Women, work and the office: the feminization of clerical occupations in Canada, 1901–31', *Canadian Journal of Sociology*, 5 (1980), pp. 354-65. Much of chapter 6 first appeared as 'Mechanization, feminization and managerial control in the early twentieth-century Canadian office', in Craig Heron and Robert Storey (eds), *On the Job: Confronting the Labour Process in Canada* (Montreal, McGill-Queen's University Press, 1986). Chapter 7 is based on 'Class, job and gender in the Canadian Office', *Labour/Le Travailleur*, 10 (1982), pp. 11-37.

The book strives to go beyond my dissertation and these published articles in two important ways. First, I have written the book in a more comparative vein, hoping to add a new dimension to current scholarly debates about gender, work and stratification in Britain and the United States. Second, the book attempts to present a sustained argument about the causes and consequences of clerical feminization, something I did not set out to do in the dissertation.

The Department of Applied Economics at the University of Cambridge provided me with a stimulating intellectual environment in which to write the manuscript. Discussions with members of the DAE's Sociology Group and Labour Studies Group helped sharpen my theoretical focus on white-collar workers and labour markets. In particular, Bob Blackburn offered much encouragement as well as insightful suggestions on how to improve my arguments. Helpful comments on draft chapters were provided by Rosemary Crompton, Jill Rubery, Elizabeth Garnsey and John Thompson. Suggestions from the publisher's anonymous reviewers also were valuable in revising the manuscript. Shani Douglas, Anne

Mason, Sharon Metcalfe and Sue Moore of the DAE's office staff diligently processed the text. Tim Williams kindly provided editorial assistance. The Social Sciences and Humanities Research Council of Canada generously granted me a leave fellowship to undertake the project. To all of these individuals and organizations I owe an enormous debt of gratitude. I, of course, bear responsibility for any shortcomings which remain.

Graham S. Lowe
Cambridge, England

Introduction

This is a study of how clerical work was transformed from a strictly male dominated occupation in the late nineteenth century to the leading female occupation of today. Our point of departure is the simple observation that, in virtually all advanced capitalist societies, clerical jobs employ more women than any other single occupation and, further, that the great majority of clerks are female. Clerical work is the contemporary prototype of a female job ghetto. But casting our gaze back into the not so distant past, we discover that something very significant indeed has occurred in the office. No other major occupation has undergone such a dramatic shift in its sex composition, from exclusively male to predominantly female. Considering that the explosion of white-collar jobs since the early twentieth century is inseparable from the dramatic rise in female labour force participation, the office is a microcosm of the forces which have restructured the division of labour in society. Despite a burgeoning literature on women's work, the question of how current gender inequalities in the workplace originated has received surprisingly scant attention. Thus in order to understand better how employment opportunities and rewards are unequally distributed among men and women in our society, this study examines the origins and development of low-grade, low-paid, dead-end jobs for women in the office.

More specifically, I carefully attempt to dissect the causes and consequences of the feminization of clerical work. This process highlighted the growth and development of the modern office in Canada between the turn of the century and the onset of the depression. In 1981, over 52 per cent of adult women in Canada were employed outside the home. At least one-third of these – numbering in excess of one and a half million – were clerks. And even with massive advances in labour-saving office automation, employment projections point to unabaited clerical growth into the 1990s.[1] These trends have their roots in the late nineteenth century. The small counting house staffed by a couple of male bookkeepers and general clerks characterized this era of capitalism. But the rise of corporate capitalism had a profound impact on the nature of office work. As the counting house grew into a huge, multi-departmental bureaucracy, it was women – not men – whom employers recruited in droves. Modern office tasks became more fragmented, mechanized and routinized in comparison with the almost craft-like general skills and responsibilities of the old-fashioned male bookkeeper. The powerful convergence of economic, organizational and occupational changes which created a pool of cheap, malleable female clerical labour occurred in Canada between 1900 and 1930. Clerical work had all the trappings of a respectable male, white-collar, middle-class occupation at the turn of the century. However, by 1931 the rapid expansion of routine administrative functions had transformed the office. With 45 per cent of clerical jobs held by women, many areas of office employment had clearly become female domains. The foundations thus were laid for the gender divisions of today's office.

These trends, I shall argue, are by no means unique to Canada. The growth of a vast battalion of subordinate female clerical workers is a defining feature of all advanced capitalist societies.[2] While my central task is to present a fine-grained, historical account of the processes by which growing numbers of women were recruited into major Canadian offices, I have taken liberties in venturing some generalizations. By making strategic comparisons with Britain and the United States in particular, I attempt to show that clerical feminization is linked to broader trends of capitalist development. I have gone no further, however, than to sketch out the basis of a comparative analysis. By identifying key international similarities in the growth of the modern office and the feminization of clerical work, the foundations for a more encompassing explanation have been laid for the future.

But at the same time, a prominent theme throughout the study is how the specific characteristics of organizations – their product or service, size and location, managerial traditions, previous labour supply and employer recruitment patterns, market position, internal division of labour – help to explain variations in the timing, pace and pattern of feminization. In other words, the contingent nature of how, when and why changes in the means of administration motivated employers to break with tradition and hire women instead of men exposes the inadequacy of any explanation claiming to be universalistic. What we stand to gain from future international comparative studies is a clearer grasp of how national differences in the industrialization process, cultural values, managerial orientations and practices, women's economic roles – to name only some of the important factors which spring to mind – influence the structure of female clerical employment.

At its most general level, the complex interplay of forces that coalesced in the shift from male to female clerks constitutes nothing less than an administrative revolution. By locating the feminization process within the administrative revolution, we can account for the sharp growth in clerical employment after 1900 as well as fundamental alterations in job content and working conditions. The type of office tasks for which women were hired bore only superficial resemblance to those performed by the preceding generation of male clerks. For one thing, the small counting house gave way to huge, impersonal bureaucracies. For another, the clerical division of labour grew more specialized as machines, hierarchical structures and rationalized work procedures ushered in a new type of office. C. Wright Mills's description of the besieged male bookkeeper epitomizes the magnitude of these changes: 'his old central position is occupied by the office manager, and even the most experienced bookkeeper with pen and ink cannot compete with a high-school girl trained in three or four months to use a machine.'[3]

Mills's juxtapositioning of the male bookkeeper and the female detailed clerk is perhaps the most visible result of the revolution in administration launched in the late nineteenth century. There was no clear break with the past in the office, nor was there a precise point in time when the old office underwent a neat structural metamorphosis. The process was uneven and protracted. Furthermore, it remains incomplete given the vestiges of the old-style office still found in some firms. Life in the nineteenth-century office is difficult to document with any great precision. But we do know that Dickens's portrayal of Bob Cratchet toiling in dismal surroundings over Scrooge's ledger was not inaccurate of many of the counting houses in Victorian England. Scholarly research has documented wide variations in the circumstances of the nineteenth-century male clerk, especially regarding working conditions and career mobility prospects.[4] Bank clerks were undoubtedly the aristocrats of clerkdom. In contrast, clerks in small commercial establishments – places which largely escaped the administrative revolution – faced long and irregular hours, dingy and unhealthful conditions, low wages and bleak prospects. Typical of this sort of clerical employment would have been Manchester warehouse offices: 'sombre little counting houses, with a table in the centre, a raised desk in a covered recess where a clerk may sit on a high stool, some cupboards and an iron safe built in the wall'.[5]

Parallel evidence from the United States emphasizes the growing importance of administration with the ascendancy of corporate capitalism. During the early nineteenth century the offices of large American firms resembled the counting houses found in fourteenth-century Florence and Venice. Administrative staff usually included 'a handful of male clerks. There were two or three copiers, a bookkeeper, a cash keeper, and a confidential clerk who handled the business when the partners were not in the office. Often partners became responsible for handling one major function . . . The organization and coordination of work in such an office could easily be arranged in a personal daily conversation.'[6] In fact, the pre-Civil War office typically had a rudimentary division of labour: copyist, bookkeeper, messenger or office boy, and clerk.[7] All except the copyist, whose job was quite tedious, performed a range of skilled tasks and commanded a general knowledge of the firm's operations. Soon more specialized, semi-skilled jobs restricted to filing, billing, shipping and so forth arose. A major milestone in the development of modern clerical work was the introduction of the typewriter in the 1870s. This new technology opened the office door to women, but only enough for them to get a foot in. Not until the post-1900 economic boom did the office's male culture, paternalistic employer attitudes and traditional work procedures yield to the winds of change. Offices grew immensely, firms were restructured along bureaucratic lines, a hierarchy of authority emerged with professional managers at the pinnacle, administrative systems replaced *ad hoc* practices and, most crucially, in this cauldron of change the sex composition of the clerical labour force shifted decisively from male to female.

The active ingredients of the administrative revolution, based on the historical particulars of the Canadian case may be summarized as follows: the rise of corporate capitalism in Canada after 1900 precipitated a revolution in the means of administration. Two trends converged, transforming the nature of clerical work. First, the flood of paperwork generated by the expanding economy required growing numbers of clerks. Second, managers came to rely on the office as the nerve centre of administration. As organizations expanded, managers replaced traditional, unsystematic methods of administration with 'scientific' programmes founded on the rational concepts of efficiency in organizational operations and control over the labour process. By the end of the First World War, these trends had greatly magnified the scope and complexity of office procedures. But the burgeoning layers of administration became a source of inefficiency, threatening to undermine the managerial powers vested in the office. This sparked a surge of rationalization in major Canadian offices, particularly during the twenties. By the end of the decade, the typical large central office exhibited certain factory-like features. Work had become fragmented and standardized; hierarchy and regimentation prevailed.

Task specialization was fundamental to this revolution in the means of administration. As the burden of office work increased, managers found that clerks performing simple tasks repetitively were cheaper to employ, produced more and could be easily regulated. The new jobs created in this manner lacked the skill components found in the more craft-like work of the bookkeeper. Consequently, they were unattractive to middle-class male clerks expecting upward mobility and comfortable salaries. Employers were pragmatic enough to recognize the clear advantages of women's higher average education, traditionally lower pay and greater availability for menial tasks. A permanent secondary labour market of female clerks thus developed. Its emergence was buttressed by a number of socio-economic factors, such as the rise of mass public education, male labour shortages during the First World War, the gradual loosening of social norms regarding women's employment, and the fact that female wages were generally better in offices than in domestic or sales work. In short, a hallmark of the modern office is the replacement of the generalist male bookkeeper by an army of female workers. As women flooded into these subordinate positions which employers had defined as 'female', they became entrenched as the modern clerical corps.

This study finds its home in the growing camp of historical sociology, where the two disciplines join forces to help us make better sense of how contemporary circumstances evolved. As such, I have tried to strike a balance between sociology's quest for general theoretical explanations about social structure, on the one hand, and history's careful attention to specific events, individual actions and concrete contexts, on the other. Historians and sociologists alike seek answers to the question: 'how did it happen?'[8] We must therefore dispense with the notion that history and sociology are distinct scholarly enterprises.[9] This study attempts to contribute to a fruitful scholarly dialogue between the two disciplines by addressing issues of relevance to each. The flourishing of social history and, more specifically, the new working-class history since the mid-1970s now vividly documents the living and working conditions endured by toiling masses of the past. But most of this research has been slanted towards male manual workers; few studies have made the female clerk their focal point.[10] Within sociology, despite major advances in our theoretical understanding of gender divisions within the workplace and the labour market, few sociologists have explored the origins and development of these now deeply embedded sources of inequality.[11]

Indeed, the nature of women's work experiences only recently has become a legitimate research question within both history and sociology. An enormous scholarly black hole has thus begun to receive illumination, largely by the efforts of feminist researchers, over the past two decades. The present study of clerical feminization will hopefully cast more rays of light onto this important topic.

Broadly speaking, the research that I present below follows what Theda Skocpol lays out as the agenda for historical sociology: it asks questions about social structures or processes which are concretely situated in time and space; it addresses processes of change over time and explains outcomes in a temporal sequence; it focuses on the way individuals' actions and their structural contexts interact to produce intended and unintended consequences; and it highlights both the uniformity and the variation in particular social institutions and patterns of change.[12] This approach raises a number of issues which punctuate debates about history and sociology. Chief among these is the problem of agency – how intentional actions by individuals and groups shape and in turn are shaped by social institutions. Equally pivotal is the related issue of generalization. The sociological tendency to seek refuge in often deterministic general theories can grossly distort the erratic and contingent qualities of social change. Highly apropos is Ernest Gellner's observation that events are 'something more than contingency, something less than necessity'.[13] This clearly demands the combined skills of history and sociology. Indispensible, then, is the historian's eye for individuals' actions in their particular historical setting and the sociologist's grasp of the constraining influences of rules, regulations and conventions – in short, social institutions. This unity of perspectives yields a much sharper awareness of the historically concrete and dialectical nature of social structure and human action.

The concept of an administrative revolution is a convenient device for organizing into a meaningful whole the welter of factors associated with the transformation of the office and the feminization of its staff. The administrative revolution is not some abstract, internally driven process – nor can it be deduced from general principles. Rather, it is very much an *ex post facto* interpretation of specific historical developments. Yet while seeking to construct a historically grounded analysis of the changing office landscape, I also have sought out the basic contours of the feminization process. Of primary interest then is why employers required larger, more complex administrative systems and, furthermore, why they increasingly turned to women to staff the new jobs thereby created. Employers did not tread down a single, well-beaten path to modernize their offices. Why some offices survived as relics of the nineteenth century largely remains elusive. What I have provided is a rather more useful analysis of the variations in the feminization process among major employers within the parameters set by existing social, economic and organizational contexts. Also vital to the administrative revolution were the actions of managers. Each major employer faced unique constraints and conditions, albeit within the same overall economic environment. How organizations and their individual managers responded to the forces of economic development – by expanding their offices, streamlining clerical procedures, recruiting females – is critical to my account of how and when the transition from the old office to the new occurred.

I argue below that the modern office emerged in Canada between the turn of the century and the start of the depression. This periodization is, of course, to some extent arbitrary. I have chosen the years 1901 and 1931 to delimit the study's focus mainly because they coincide with occupational censuses which furnish much valuable data. More important, it was during these three decades that the die for the modern office was cast, tilting the sex ratio of male to female clerks decisively toward the latter. Subsequent decades witnessed developments which essentially elaborated upon these trends in clerical employment.

The meteoric growth of clerical jobs, the reorganization of offices into multi-departmental bureaucracies, the rationalization of clerical work by managers vigilant of inefficiencies and rising costs – these defined the administrative revolution which ushered out the traditional male bookkeeper with his pen and ledger book and marched in battalions of routine female functionaries. As is often the case in historical research, pieces of the puzzle are missing. In some instances, documentation is fragmentary or lacking because existing records are unsystematic or corroborative evidence is hard to locate. For instance, the role of clerks themselves in shaping modern administration is still largely an enigma. Unlike the well-documented responses of nineteenth-century artisans to the onslaught of the factory system, how male and female clerks either resisted or acquiesced to their changing living and working conditions remains uncharted terrain. Other research strategies may unearth this sort of evidence and add a valuable human dimension to the story presented below. Nonetheless, a fairly clear outline has emerged, admittedly sketchy in places, of the feminization process that became a major social force during the early twentieth century.

The first step in my research strategy was to document the growth of clerical occupations. Here I relied mainly on published and unpublished Canadian census data which, after 1901, provide increasingly detailed information about the subdivisions within clerical work, the occupation's changing sex composition and the industrial distribution of clerks. The decennial censuses are undoubtedly the best source of data for documenting occupational change. But they paint a very general picture. The truly provocative questions surrounding the causes and conse-quences of the feminization process are best answered by examining workplaces. This required the analysis of archival data from leading corporate and government employers. I therefore focused on changes primarily within the Bank of Nova Scotia, Canadian Pacific Railway, Bell Telephone Company, International Business Machines, Sun Life Insur-ance, Manufacturers Life Insurance, the Federal Government, the Ontario and British Columbia Provincial Governments, and Imperial Oil Company. These particular organizations were selected mainly because they were at the advancing edge of industrialization in early twentieth-century Canada. The obvious limitation, of course, is that other perhaps even more representative organizations lacked accessible archival data. Nonetheless, these case studies have allowed me to identify the recurrent patterns of feminization as well as major variations on these. Commen-tary from contemporary business journals and government publications helped to place the organizations studied on a larger economic canvas.

National periodicals such as *Industrial Canada*, the *Monetary Times*, and the *Labour Gazette*, as well as industry-wide management publications such as the *Canadian Textile Journal*, *Canadian Railway and Marine World*, *Telephone Gazette*, the *Journal of the Canadian Bankers' Association* and the *Proceedings* of the Life Office Management Association were indispensible in constructing a more general analysis of clerical feminization during the administrative revolution.

The overall interpretation to emerge is that, while each managerial decision to introduce office machines, hire more females as routine clerks, or to reorganize office procedures may have passed largely unnoticed, by the time the depression hit Canada in 1930 the cumulative effect of three decades of such changes had produced nothing short of a revolution in administration. The modern office was an organizational reality; women clerks had come to stay. But all of this pertains to Canada, raising relevant questions about international trends. Part of my research strategy entailed moving beyond the Canadian situation by drawing parallels with other advanced capitalist societies, especially the United States and Britain. In some fundamental ways Canada's economic development has been unique. Yet a remarkably common feature Canada shares with other major capitalist societies is, since 1900, a booming clerical sector increasingly comprised of women.

The book is organized in the following manner. Chapter 1 sets the stage for an analysis of the changing sex composition of the office workforce during the administrative revolution by critically examining theoretical perspectives on the feminization process. I also evaluate the historical interpretations put forward in the few existing studies of women's entry into American and British offices. In chapter 2, I explore the economic and organizational foundations of the administrative revolution. This chapter documents the turn-of-the-century emergence of corporate capitalism in Canada and the attendant revolution in the means of administration. The key argument advanced in the chapter revolves around the concept of control. Briefly, I argue that control over external markets, internal production processes and employees was the driving motive behind the rise in modern administration. Giant bureaucracies staffed by legions of low-grade, low-paid, increasingly female clerks became the regulatory hand of modern management.

Chapter 3 charts the growth of clerical occupations historically in Canada, showing how they have become the largest occupational group and the major source of employment for women. The feminization of clerical work is linked to the general rise of a new white-collar stratum in the labour force and the movement towards a service-based economy. A comparison of two prominent clerical employers in the financial sector shows, however, that the origins and early development of female clerical work varied according to the specific context of an organization. The chapter also locates Canadian clerical trends in an international perspective.

Chapter 4 is an in-depth investigation of the circumstances surrounding the initial recruitment of women as clerks and their eventual predominance in routine office jobs. Specifically, I document women's entry into banking, the federal civil service, and stenography jobs in Canada during the early twentieth century.

Chapters 5 and 6 deal with the organizational and technological dimensions of the modern office. The impact of these aspects of the administrative revolution on working conditions and the changing social situation of clerks are prominent themes. In chapter 5, I discuss various rationalization strategies used by management to expedite the processing of mountains of paper work generated by industrial development. The bureaucratic, multi-departmental office had a specialized division of labour with a more factory-like regimentation imposed on work activities than anything found in the counting house. Instrumental in the routinization of clerical tasks was their increasing mechanization. Chapter 6 focuses directly on the technological transformation of the office, emphasizing its importance to the recruitment of women. The administrative revolution also had significant consequences for the class position and general living conditions of clerks. Chapter 7 takes a close look at whether or not the factors reshaping the office led to a proletarianization of clerks as a social group. Here I attempt to show how the feminization process defies any simple interpretation along the lines of the proletarianization thesis.

A concluding chapter synthesizes the various stands in my analysis of how clerical work came to be the leading female job ghetto. It also addresses some of the unresolved issues raised in preceding chapters. Foremost among these is the question of how clerks responded either individually or collectively to the forces that changed their world.

1

Theoretical Perspectives on Clerical Feminization

The spectacular growth of white-collar occupations in advanced capitalist societies since the turn of the century has transformed their labour forces. One of the most visible features of a burgeoning white-collar workforce has been the shifting sex ratio of many jobs as more and more women entered paid employment. Of all occupations, clerical work's swing from 'male' to 'female' has been the most dramatic. The nineteenth-century office was populated mostly by men. Yet today clerical work is the largest source of employment for women and, moreover, is imprinted with all of the ideological trappings of femininity. Thus if one wishes to understand the dynamics of female job ghettos, clerical work is the ideal case study. Much can be learned about the origins and persistence of female labour force segments by investigating how clerical work became feminized.

The feminization process is vital to the rise of the modern office. Beginning in the late nineteenth century, a veritable administrative revolution gathered momentum in leading corporate and government offices in virtually all capitalist nations. Like the rise of the factory system and mass production, the exact timing, extent and form of the modern office varied according to specific countries and industries. But viewed broadly within the context of capitalist development, there can be little doubt that this transformation in administration signalled an important watershed. The hallmark of the administrative revolution was the creation of large, centralized office bureaucracies, coupled with the increasingly strategic role of administration in regulating all aspects of economic activity. The administrative revolution was both a by-product and a facilitator of the transition from the small-scale, entrepreneurial capitalism of the nineteenth-century to modern corporate capitalism. Within this crucible of economic change a huge new group of clerical occupations was forged. These jobs, in contrast to those in the old fashioned nineteenth century office, bore the stamp of managerial rationalizations, technology and bureaucracy. But perhaps most significantly, by the 1930s the Dickensian male bookkeeper had been largely eclipsed by a multitude of subordinate female functionaries.

The changing role of women in the administrative revolution can be illuminated by addressing four interrelated questions about clerical feminization. First, how did clerical jobs come to be defined as women's work? Second, what social and economic factors motivated employers to shift their source of labour supply from men to women? Third, in what ways do the characteristics attributed to female clerks as individuals – few career aspirations, tenuous attachment to the labour force, an overriding interest in office social life, low levels of skills and responsibilities – actually reflect the nature of the jobs into which they have been channelled? And fourth, did women displace men in existing clerical jobs or replace them in qualitatively different kinds of work? I shall address these questions first by critically evaluating the theoretical perspectives on occupational sex segregation found in the literature. Then I shall review the various historical arguments put forward to explain women's entry into British and American offices. This theoretical discussion sets the stage for a more comprehensive explanation of the origins of female job ghettos in offices as a by-product of the administrative revolution.

OCCUPATIONAL SEX SEGREGATION

The concept of a labour market is a convenient way of referring to the complex processes and institutions which influence, directly or indirectly, the purchase and sale of labour power. Market operations, determining who gets allocated to which jobs, have concrete results for individual men and women. This is why discussions of labour markets cannot avoid the larger problem of the unequal distribution of opportunities, income, power and status.

During the first half of this century the most prominent occupational division was between blue-collar and white-collar jobs, both occupied mainly by men. Yet during the post-Second World War period this has been overshadowed by a gender-based division of labour as women poured into the workforce.[1] To understand these gender-related inequalities it is necessary to examine how men and women have become segregated into unequal and non-competing groups in the labour market.[2] As Rosabeth Moss Kanter points out, gender has become the main locus of power and inequality within the office itself: 'managerial and clerical jobs are the major sex-segregated, white-collar occupations, brought into being by the development of the large corporation and its administrative apparatus. A sex-linked ethos became identified with each of the occupational groupings. Ideologies surrounding the pursuit of these occupations and justifying their position in the organization came to define both the labour pool from which these occupations drew and ideal images of the attributes of the people in that pool.'[3]

Two overlapping theoretical perspectives on labour markets have gained wide currency since the early 1970s. The dual labour market and radical labour market segmentation approaches share a view of the economy in which the characteristics of firms, by generating demand for certain types of workers, create primary and secondary labour markets.[4] Jobs in the secondary labour market are usually in smaller, labour intensive firms in highly competitive industries. Such jobs are not part of internal job ladders and therefore provide few advancement opportunities: wages are relatively low; there are few fringe benefits; the work environment often is unpleasant; workers are in a weak bargaining position, typically lacking union representation; tasks are routine and unskilled, making workers highly replaceable; and managerial control frequently involves heavy-handed discipline and threats of dismissal.[5] Primary sector jobs, in sharp contrast, are as 'good' as secondary ones are 'bad'.

According to the labour market segmentation theory first articulated by radical US economists, the rise of corporate capitalism has fragmented a once fairly homogeneous working class by segmenting the labour process within firms and, as a consequence, within the labour market.[6] Segmentation occurs when changes in productive processes lead managers to establish differential occupational characteristics, behavioural rules and working conditions. The main criterion shaping job requirements is the degree of stability the organization requires from the job holder.[7] Methods of obtaining the desired stability and commitment from employees are anchored in different systems of workplace control. Employers thus separate jobs requiring long-term employee commitment and integration into the organization from those that do not. Good salaries, generous benefits, pleasant working environments and access to internal career ladders are inducements to stability for incumbents of managerial, professional and technical positions. But for routine clerical and manual jobs, where workers are highly interchangeable, there is no reason for employers to offer expensive employment packages.[8] Hence the creation of a secondary labour market defined by little career mobility, part-time or short-term employment, minimal financial rewards, subordination and powerlessness.

Segmentation theory has sharpened our focus on how changes in the labour process within organizations are linked to unequal opportunities and rewards in the labour market. It reveals quite clearly that discriminatory practices on the basis of race, ethnicity, sex and age have become deeply imbedded into the occupational structure. But the model has failed to explain the origins of such divisions. This weakness is particularly glaring when it comes to female employment. Thus crucial questions pertaining to the origins and maintenance of job ghettos remain unanswered. A closer examination of two of the most prominent books by radical segmentation theorists, *Contested Terrain* and *Segmented Work, Divided Workers* amply illustrates this point.[9]

In *Contested Terrain*, Richard Edwards proposes three unequal market segments, each based on a different form of managerial control over workers. This may hold true of white, male workers, but Edwards himself admits that his model cannot fully account for differences based on race or sex.[10] He further concedes that the dynamics of gender divisions in work demand separate analysis. For one thing, they overlap market segments; for another there is gender discrimination within each segment.[11]

The general theoretical model of segmentation is elaborated in *Segmented Work, Divided Workers*, by David Gordon, Richard Edwards and Michael Reich. This book examines the creation of a segmented labour market in the United States – and the resulting political inertia among the working class – by tying these changes to long cycles of economic development. The authors do not claim to be able to slot all workers into one of three major labour market segments. But employed women are nonetheless a troublesome case, for they tend to concentrate in occupations, such as clerical work, which cut across all sectors. Indeed, women are more likely than men to be segregated more along occupational lines, regardless of whether their employer is a huge monopolistic corporation or a small firm struggling on the economy's fringe. Even core sector employers tend to recruit from the secondary female labour market for low-level office jobs, isolating these workers from the rewards of the internal labour market.

Critics offer a number of helpful correctives to these difficulties. While much of the American analysis has been at the aggregate level of industrial sectors, British research, notably by the Cambridge Labour Studies Group, has examined employment practices of small firms on the economy's periphery where many women work.[12] Findings from the Cambridge study suggest that women were paid low wages regardless of their job content. Moreover, females were systematically excluded from higher grade posts simply because males had traditionally occupied them. Many women's jobs were actually fairly skilled and demanding, contrary to segmentation theory's hypothesis about pervasive deskilling in the secondary labour market. This study thus shows, first, that employment patterns outside the core sector do not fit the segmentation model and, second, that labour supply factors, independent of demand, exert a major impact on the structuring of labour markets.[13]

The Cambridge researchers do not seek to explain the roots of a segmented labour supply. Rather, their major contribution is to document the ways in which market conditions, technology and unionization interact with workers' characteristics to determine earnings and job conditions.[14] Where females are concerned, it is imperative to move away from segmentation theory's preoccupation with employer-determined labour demand to consider how the supply and demand for certain types of workers interact. The Cambridge researchers reject a deterministic model of demand based on capitalism's 'need' for managerial control strategies. Instead, they emphasize the influence of the reproduction process on the labour market position of men and women. More specifically, the researchers argue that employers do have some discretion in making hiring decisions but within the context of certain constraints. Major constraints would include the type of production process, economic climate, size and interrelations of firms in the industry, government employment regulations, and institutions such as unions and schools that are linked to the labour market.[15]

But equally crucial are influences on labour supply. Especially important in this regard are unpaid household and community activities aimed at raising a new generation of workers and sustaining existing workers. To comprehend these social reproduction factors fully it is necessary to consider the concept of patriarchy.

PATRIARCHY AND WOMEN'S WORK

Clerical growth trends, which I document below in chapter 3, show that the labour market for office workers had its own internal divisions and, moreover, that female recruitment advanced at different rates depending on the particular employer. These variations in the general pattern of clerical growth cannot be reduced to economic forces alone. While it is not my intention to get drawn into radical feminist debates about patriarchy, it is nonetheless instructive to consider how the organization of gender relations and social reproduction within the family places women at a disadvantage in the labour market by providing a basis for male exclusionary practices. The concept of patriarchy, then, illuminates how women's labour market involvement is part of the larger canvas of family, social reproduction, male–female relations generally, and the social ideologies which confer legitimacy to different patterns of behaviour for members of each sex.[16]

Recalling Kanter's statement above, her portrayal of the male boss and female secretary captures the dialectic of male dominance and female subordination in the world of work. Viewed from the feminist perspective of patriarchy, job segregation is a mechanism for perpetuating male superiority over women. Because women are paid poor wages and relegated to low status jobs, their economic dependence on men is perpetuated. And so too is the unequal division of household labour, in which women perform most childrearing and domestic tasks – a situation which in turn contributes to their inferior labour market position.

Capitalist forms of work organization developed historically by incorporating elements of traditional forms of patriarchy – essentially a system of social and economic organization founded on male domination. Now capitalism and patriarchy mutually reinforce each other. Patriarchy, Veronica Beechey asserts, 'is of fundamental economic, political, and ideological importance to the capitalist mode of production.'[17] The concept of patriarchy is thus useful because it forces us to look beyond the purely economic motives of capitalists for hiring men or women. More specifically, it highlights the role of male employers, trade unions and workers in denying women access to better jobs and identifies the social ideologies which justify this exclusion as natural.

But how far can the concept of patriarchy advance our understanding of clerical job ghettos? On the one hand, Paul Thompson claims that the independent influence of patriarchical relations lies in management's use of femininity as a device for manipulating office employees. Male office managers have instituted 'systems of gifts, material rewards and "treats", which are not just "bribes" to conform, but a way of connecting to the dominant themes of consumerism, family and sexual attraction in women's lives.'[18] Kanter similarly shows how a 'masculine ethic of rationality' defined the role of managers in a manner which excluded women, who were considered too emotional, from top jobs.[19] In short, prevailing stereotypes of women are part of managerial control strategies in the office. Founded on assumptions about women being more oriented to pleasing others, more sensitive to the quality of their surroundings, more honest and less mercenary than men, these stereotypes are frequently internalized by women. Unwittingly, female clerks thereby reinforce their own subordination.

On the other hand, Fiona McNally's study of temporary female office workers ('temps') challenges the tenet that the subordinate position of women in offices results from male domination.[20] In the case of temps, 'neither the supply of nor the demand for such employees can be accounted for simply in terms of attempts by men to maintain a position of relative advantage in the labour market, or in terms of the discretionary attitudes of employers.'[21] Instead, McNally builds her analysis on the interaction between the objective conditions of clerical work and the constraints placed on women by family obligations and limited employment alternatives. Labour shortages in the permanent clerical sector were a strong influence shaping demand, she found. So too were the desires expressed by the temps McNally studied for flexible hours and varied working conditions, especially when they had young children to care for at home.

I would now like to attempt to tie together the strands of the above discussion. On balance it appears necessary to augment the labour market segmentation model, which describes the unequal structuring of work opportunities and rewards, with several other analytical concepts. The segmentation model is perhaps least helpful when it comes to being able to account for the historical origins of female job ghettos.[22] Critics of the model underline the contingent nature of employers' hiring decisions and, crucially, how these interact with the supply of female workers. In terms of what shapes supply, patriarchical relations in society, particularly embodied in the household division of labour, are very influential. And patriarchy not only manifests itself in the form of social values justifying the subordination of women in office job ghettos; it also reinforces the popular images of clerical work as a 'female' domain.

This labelling, or sex-typing, of jobs as either male or female is fundamental to the feminization process. By manipulating job characteristics such as experience, skills and educational requirements, as well as working conditions and remuneration, employers can tailor labour supply. For example, job requirements such as physical exertion, geographic mobility, or an unbroken work history immediately bar many women. Similarily, stereotypes of women as manually dexterous, patient, ineffectual supervisors, and secondary wage earners in a family have provided strong rationales for their restricted employment at the bottom of the occupational hierarchy.[23] Madden explains what has happened in this respect within North America: 'if job requirements are structured as to preclude part-time work, to require peak effort between the ages of twenty and thirty-five, or to require career continuity with one employer, that will never be a female occupation.'[24]

Strong norms have developed to exclude women from occupations socially defined as male. Conversely, sex-linked job requirements played a major role in labelling clerical work 'female only'. Such labels become firmly affixed. Once women are established in an occupation, their lower wage rates give employers little incentive to revert to higher-priced male workers. Discrimination consequently tends to be cumulative, reproducing in the female labour market the very attitudes and behaviours – such as weak job commitment and high turnover, both rational responses to poor employment conditions – which rule out women as candidates for better jobs.

But, in all of this, the initial erosion of barriers to women entering office employment remains rather sketchy. As a prelude to investigating how this happened in Canadian offices, I will now review the origins of clerical feminization in Britain and the United States.

Despite the overwhelming importance of clerical work as a source of employment for women, there have been remarkably few in-depth studies of its origins and growth. The classic studies of the working conditions and broader social circumstances of office employees, most notably Klingender's *The Condition of Clerical Labour in Britain*, Mills's *White Collar*, Lockwood's *The Blackcoated Worker*, Crozier's *The World of the Office Worker* and Blackburn's *Union Character and Social Class* do not explicitly address issues of gender.[25] Indeed their primary focus is the male clerk, although Blackburn does examine female bank clerks with respect to unionization. Moreover, Prandy, Stewart and Blackburn's recent sociological analysis of white-collar workers, while very comprehensive, is restricted solely to males.[26] Certainly one could argue that Kanter's *Men and Women of the Corporation* provides by far the most insightful analysis of gender stratification within the office. But it, along with Crompton and Jones's recent study of work deskilling and proletarianization among men and women in three British offices, concentrates on documenting present inequalities.[27] An historical perspective on how such inequalities emerged in the first place is, I would argue, long overdue.

CLERICAL FEMINIZATION IN BRITAIN

The recruitment of women into offices in Britain, which began slowly after 1870, was especially rapid between the turn of the century and 1911.[28] What accounts for the timing, industrial location and growth patterns of this feminization? Clearly factors influencing both the supply and demand for female office workers must be considered. On the supply side, a growing number of middle-class Victorian women, having lost the financial support of their parents or husband, or who remained single, were forced out to work after 1850. Wages for governesses, the most accessible employment for women from the better classes, fell due to an oversupply of educated women. Educational opportunities for women were beginning to expand, equipping growing numbers of them with basic office skills. This formation of a ready supply of potential female clerks coincided with a boom in trade and commerce. By the 1870s, some employers were slowly becoming receptive to the idea of hiring female clerks.[29]

One organization in particular led the way. The General Post Office, under the direction of a series of Post Master Generals sympathetic to the cause of female employment, was Britain's first major employer of female clerks. Indeed, the first female civil servant was hired in 1872 as a Post Office telegraphist, a new occupation yet to be sex-labelled. The Post Office saw some obvious advantages in employing women, recognizing them as quick, possessing a 'delicacy of touch' lacking among men, patient, not adverse to being sedentary, and from respectable backgrounds. And, of course, women were also cheap labour, which led some male postal employees to view them with considerable unease.[30] Not until the introduction of typewriters after about 1880 did women find their own niche. By the turn of the century the new office jobs of 'typewriter', short-hand writer and short-hand typist had become sex-labelled as female.[31] Victorian social morality only tolerated this new role for women on the understanding that it was merely something temporary until marriage. In fact, no married women officially were employed in the British civil service until 1946.[32]

What motivated Post Office management to pioneer the hiring of women as clerks? Whilst an unequivocal answer to this question eludes us, research by Cohn casts light on the difference between the Post Office and other industries.[33] The thrust of Cohn's analysis of varying rates of feminization is a comparison of two leading British white-collar employers, both centred in London. The General Post Office, as I have mentioned, was among the first organizations to hire large numbers of women. In contrast, the Great Western Railway remained a bastion of male clerkdom well into the twentieth century. More specifically, the GPO had a clerical staff that was over 40 per cent female by the beginning of the First World War; the railway did not even begin hiring females until 1906 and by 1933 fewer than one in every six of its clerks was female.

Cohn rejects 'cheap labour' explanations of clerical feminization, on the grounds that all economically rational employers would hire women if wage rates were the only difference between male and female workers. He points out that employer resistance to hiring women for office jobs also reflected sexist beliefs, social norms limiting male–female interactions in a place of business, and a general resistance among males to change the status quo of the office.[34] His empirical analysis leaves these issues aside, however, examining instead the economic structure of the firm. He tests the proposition that capital intensive firms can offset the costs of more expensive male clerks through savings due to new technologies and lower raw material and capital equipment costs. In other words, the structure of these firms means that they can afford to discriminate. Employers in white-collar industries, such as finance, commerce or the civil service, must live within a different set of constraints. Because clerical labour is their major overhead cost, these organizations will be more responsive to cheaper sources of labour. Cohn's quantitative analysis confirms that the intensity of clerical labour was much greater in the GPO than in the largely blue-collar staffed railway. Therefore more intense economic pressures were, Cohn argues, exerted on GPO management to reduce labour costs by hiring women.

Admittedly there is a certain logical appeal to Cohn's industrial organization thesis. But how generalizable is it beyond the particular circumstances of the railway and the Post Office that he examines? I have already noted that the personal attitudes of a succession of Post Master Generals, beginning in the 1870s, made them far more receptive to female employment than was the norm among managers. And even within white-collar industries, the variations in female recruitment patterns were sometimes substantial. My comparison in chapter 3 of female clerical staffs in two Canadian organizations, the Manufacturers Life Insurance Company and the Bank of Nova Scotia, will bring this into sharp relief. By 1911 in Britain, one-third of all commercial clerks were women (they formed 24 per cent of all clerks).[35] Yet women comprised only one-tenth of insurance clerks and were as scarce in banks as they were in railways.[36] Why the state sector, in contrast to most of the private sector, shifted earlier and faster to a female clerical labour supply remains unclear. Even by 1900 the proportion of female public sector clerical workers far outstripped virtually all other major industries in Britain. Equally important in creating employment opportunities for women in offices was the First World War.[37] Estimates place the number of women hired to replace men during the war at about 200,000, many holding onto their jobs after 1919.

CLERICAL FEMINIZATION IN THE UNITED STATES

In at least two respects there are outstanding similarities in the forces underlying feminization in Britain and the United States. In both countries, wartime shortages of male labour and civil service employment opportunities were very important. During the US Civil War in the 1860s, the federal Treasury Department was first to break the unwritten office employment code when it was forced into hiring women due to severe shortages of men.[38] Demand for clerks rose dramatically with vigorous post-Civil War industrial development. This demand far outstripped the supply of suitable male clerks, many of whom were opting instead for managerial or professional careers. Toward the end of the nineteenth century, American women were more likely than men to be high school graduates, thereby equipping them with basic clerical credentials. Other trends interacted with these changes to make clerical work the nation's major female white-collar job (ahead of nursing) by 1900.[39] This leading position was consolidated during the decade of the First World War, which further boosted female clerical employment, as it did in Britain. The introduction of the typewriter was crucial to this changing sex ratio in offices, as was the plethora of menial clerical tasks which had sprung up. Neither type of job had been previously staked out as a male preserve. This allowed women to make incursions into what, at least temporarily, was gender neutral territory.

There was also a class dimension to the birth of a new office labour force. Not until the 1920s did working-class girls succeed in escaping factory work for the cleaner, safer and more prestigious and remunerative office.[40] Even then they were restricted to the most routine and lowest status jobs. Opposite reasons kept educated, middle-class young women out of domestic or factory work. Employers did not just have cheap female workers waiting at their doorsteps; rather, the reserve pool of female clerical labour appears to have had all the appropriate class and educational pedigrees of male clerks. Sexist social norms prevented women from taking economic advantage of these characteristics in the labour market. For many males a respectable education and a decent family background were the stepping stones to a prosperous business career which often began as an office clerk.

Margery Davies devotes considerable attention to the heated debate throughout the 1870 to 1930 period over the morality of female employment outside the home.[41] Opponents advanced three different arguments: that woman's nature was somehow unsuited to clerical work; that women were depriving men of jobs; and that they were physically unable to perform such work. Actually the last of these arguments was double-edged. Part of the justification for restricting women to certain office tasks, such as typing or filing, was their allegedly more nimble fingers. And the fact that women displayed considerable dexterity in performing these tasks served to reinforce the stereotype. But all participants in the debate shared the fundamental belief that woman's natural role was to be a wife and mother. The same holds true for Canada and Britain. In concrete terms, only 5.6 per cent of female clerks in the United States were married in 1910 (at least officially).[42] Grace Coyle revealed the basic ambivalence of social attitudes towards female office employment when, in 1929, she observed: 'Employers and employment managers look with suspicion upon married women, although the basis for this attitude seems to rest less upon a scientific study of the relative efficiency of married women than on a commendable desire to defend the "American home" from subversive tendencies.'[43]

The role of technology in reshaping office employment certainly deserves close attention. Davies argues that the feminization of clerical work disguised its proletarianization.[44] Scientific office management had routinized and deskilled many office functions, observes Davies. This process was facilitated by the advance of mechanization.[45] By 1930, according to Davies, there were two classes of female clerks: a huge lower level performing routine, specialized and frequently mechanized tasks; and a smaller and more privileged upper tier, exemplified by the private secretary. Yet Davies cautions against placing too much emphasis on technology as the driving force of change.[46] However, another major study of US clerical workers argues that mechanization was the decisive factor in opening office doors to women.

Elyce Rotella uses the quantitative tools of the new economic history to explain why US women moved 'from home to office' in the decades between 1890 and 1930.[47] Rotella asserts that, by 1930, single women were exercising considerable independence regarding work decisions. This reflected the breakdown of the traditional family economy, which had depended heavily on women's unpaid work within the home. The clerical sector was at the centre of changing female work roles – just as I shall document for Canada in chapter 3. Almost one-quarter of new female (non-agricultural) workers were absorbed into clerical work during the 1870 to 1930 period. The initial burst of recruitment occurred during the 1880s, with a later and much greater surge between 1910 and 1920.[48] The expanding cadre of female clerks were more likely to be younger, native born, single and better educated than their sisters in other occupations. Rotella's statistical analysis of labour force data fails to account for the 'pace and pattern' of female clerical employment. This comes as no surprise considering the interplay of factors, probably too complex and numerous to build into her econometric model, on both sides of the supply and demand equation. What nevertheless emerges from Rotella's analysis is that the rapid growth of clerical occupations apparently was linked to steady increases in female labour force participation throughout the 1870 to 1930 period. The timing of clerical growth, however, reflected short-term fluctuations in demand, especially those resulting from technological changes between 1880 and 1910.[49]

The more fundamental question is why clerical work became feminized by 1930. Here Rotella relies on human capital theory to show how mechanization, particularly the rapid diffusion of the typewriter between 1880 and 1910, was decisive in shifting the demand from males to females. Why did employers not maintain the status quo and recruit men into the new detailed tasks created by office rationalization and mechanization? The answer, for Rotella, is to be found in relative productivity gains obtained through the employment of cheaper female labour. Mechanization and work rationalization measures, such as scientific management, essentially reduced the skill requirements of clerical work. Clerks no longer had to acquire firm-specific skills and knowledge through on-the-job training. Rather, general skills transmitted by an expanding public education system equipped women with the basic prerequisites prior to entering the office. Stated simply, mechanization lowered the unit cost of clerical output by reducing skill requirements which, in turn, shifted demand to cheaper female labour.

The distinction between firm-specific and firm-general skills is a key axiom in economist Gary Becker's human capital theory.[50] According to this perspective, workers entering the labour force already possessing basic general skills, such as shorthand or typing, are interchangeable among many employers. Moreover all firms stand to benefit from this enhanced worker productivity. It was mainly these technology-induced productivity gains, augmented by lower female salaries and justified through prevailing sex stereotypes, that Rotella sees as underlying clerical feminization. She elaborates:

> Mechanization and routinization reduced the specific skill component of most clerical jobs. Training in the new general skills could take place in schools where costs would be borne by the students (and by the public in the case of commercial education in public schools). Employers would be willing to hire women, despite their high expected turnover, for jobs in which the on-the-job training requirement was low. Since women's wages were lower than men's, women would be expected to completely dominate in jobs with the lowest firm-specific skill component. This appears to be the case in the most mechanical and routine jobs such as typing and filing which were rapidly taken over by women.[51]

The central weakness in Rotella's empirical test of human capital theory is that influential factors in the case of clerical jobs – such as ideologies regarding women's work, male workers' possible resistance to women entering the office, the impact of First World War labour shortages, and the general transformation of the clerical labour process through work rationalization and reorganization – are exogenous to the model. Also lacking is convincing evidence of the link between the changing skill requirements and task content in offices, on one hand, and the introduction of technology on the other. Furthermore, variations among employers in how women were incorporated into menial non-mechanized clerical jobs are not considered. Davies's research suggests that office machines *per se* were of secondary importance in creating particular jobs into which American women were hired. This issue will only be resolved by a thorough investigation of the general thrust of work rationalization and its convergence with the spread of typewriters and other office machines. At a more abstract level, it seems inconsistent that Rotella should adopt the human capital model as her theoretical framework, given her expressed interest in the creation of a gender-segregated clerical labour force and her emphasis on skill levels – all issues which fit rather more neatly into the competing paradigm of labour market segmentation theory. Rotella simply does not consider the segmentation perspective as an alternative explanation. Granted, Rotella sensitizes us to the changing skill component of clerical work. But her study falls short of offering a convincing explanation of how this was the *sine qua non* of US women moving out of the home and into the office.

CONCLUSION

Now is a good time to pause momentarily and take stock of the four questions posed at the start of the chapter. Essentially, I asked how clerical jobs came to be defined as women's work, why employers were motivated to shift their recruitment from men to women, how the natural qualities of female clerks as individuals actually were a reflection of the work they performed, and whether women displaced men in existing clerical positions or replaced them in new types of jobs. No definitive answers can be offered just yet. But I have tried to bring into focus a much clearer understanding of the causal web of supply and demand factors which underpinned the rush of women into the office.

Clerical work in Britain and the United States is a graphic example of a segregated, sex-labelled occupation for women. I go to considerably greater lengths below to document how this is especially true in the case of Canada. Labour market segmentation theory helps us to see how changes in the organization of work, managerial controls and task content are responsible for defining the appropriate labour supply. Once the workforce of a firm, or industry, is unequally structured along sex lines these divisions tend to take on a permanent form.

But in order to account for both the emergence and perpetuation of this rigid gender division of labour, it is imperative that we look outside the workplace. Patriarchal aspects of social relations, entrenched in virtually all social institutions but most importantly in the family, obviously have a direct bearing on women's subordinate position in paid employment. Ideologies which define what constitutes masculine and feminine spheres of activity have been effective tools in the hands of employers, and indeed male workers, to restrict women's employment opportunities. Large-scale economic and occupational changes, such as the ascendancy of corporate capitalism and with it an enormous white-collar service sector, are also basic themes in the story of feminization. So too are the labour shortages of the First World War which found many women thrust behind office desks, factory machines and store counters.

Broadly speaking, the economic and organizational forces of corporate capitalism underpinned the rising demand for clerks. However, to fully grasp why women, not men, were increasingly hired requires us to take account systematically of how the interaction of supply and demand factors gave rise to clerical job ghettos. The Canadian case studies of clerical employment presented below will illustrate how economic, organizational and ideological factors combined in different ways, thereby explaining more comprehensively than previous studies how, when and why women entered the office.

2

Corporate Capitalism and the Administrative Revolution

The purpose of this chapter is to situate the feminization of clerical occupations and the modernization of the office within their larger economic context. I locate these changes at the centre of what may generally be referred to as an administrative revolution that, to varying degrees, transformed major corporate and government organizations in Canada, the United States, Britain and most other western capitalist societies during the early twentieth century. Administrative systems and office personnel were an integral part of the new economic era that dawned throughout North America and Western Europe around the turn of the century. Information became a highly valued resource for the professional managers who took the reigns of corporate capitalism. Central offices thus became organizational nerve centres. They collected, processed, stored and communicated mountains of facts and figures indispensable for managerial decision-making.[1]

The most striking feature of the administrative revolution was the replacement of the small, informal nineteenth-century counting house run by a handful of male clerks by sprawling twentieth-century offices, where masses of women performed more routinized and narrowly focused clerical tasks as if on a paper-processing assembly line. C. Wright Mills's image of the modern office as an enormous high-rise file, spreading its regulatory tentacles throughout the economy, could not be more appropriate. 'The office,' Mills concludes, 'is the Unseen Hand become visible as a row of clerks and a set of IBM equipment, a pool of dictaphone transcribers, and sixty receptionists confronting the elevators, one above the other, on each floor.'[2]

The unifying theme of this chapter is, in a word, control. Control was the driving force behind the administrative revolution. The office as 'unseen hand' permitted managers to manipulate more carefully not only market forces, but also the entire production process including human labour. Administrative control exercised through the office increasingly demanded that the same principles of co-ordination, integration and rationalization be applied to clerical work – a crucial point that I will amplify below. But while the concept of control helps to illuminate the rise of modern administration and attendant developments in the clerical labour process, it is also fraught with several problems which deserve attention. Contemporary debates on the labour process revolve around the causes, consequences and historical evolution of various managerial control strategies. The monistic determinism of Harry Braverman's thesis of an all-embracing spread of management control through task deskilling, work degradation and diminished worker autonomy has prompted searches for sources of variation in the manager–worker dialectic. If one accepts John Storey's recent criticisms, the entire labour process debate is mired in theoretical quicksand. This reflects its inability to generate an overarching theory capable of incorporating the diversity of labour processes unearthed by empirical research.[3] I do not, however, take up the challenge to formulate a general theory of the labour process. My more limited contribution to this endeavour is to analyse systematically the nature of managerial control as it pertains to historical patterns in the clerical labour process.

The impetus for the administrative revolution can be found in three dynamics of economic development. The first incorporates the ascendancy of corporate capitalism, mainly due to the expansion of manufacturing and service industries. The second dynamic is organizational, embodied in the growth of huge public and private sector bureaucracies. The third dynamic, integrally connected to the first two, is the rise of a new professional class of managers whose quest for efficiency wrought far-reaching rationalizations in work processes, first in factories then later in offices. These three dynamics laid down the broad parameters for far-reaching industrial, organizational and occupational changes in Western capitalist societies from the late nineteenth century onward.

The details of how these trends were played out differed, of course, within each national context. At a very general level, however, the rise of modern capitalist economies rested on the twin pillars of thriving manufacturing and services sectors. Centralized bureaucracies became the standard form of work organizations. The blue-collar proletariat, prominent actors in the nineteenth-century industrialization process, eventually were overshadowed by expanding white-collar occupations. Foremost among these were office clerks and managers. These developments surfaced in Canada somewhat after their appearance in the United States, Britain or Germany. But once unleashed their dramatic effects soon became evident. Looking beyond the specifics of each national case, there can be little doubt that the interweaving of these changes produced the fabric of modern administration.

A corporate headquarters or the sprawling office complex of a government department is, from the outside, tangible evidence of the new-style office which gradually replaced the old, one-room counting house of pre-industrial capitalism. But behind the façades of these bureaucracies lie the most fundamental characteristics of the administrative revolution: a profusion of fairly routine clerical tasks; the accelerating rationalization of office procedures; a shift in recruitment from males to females; and a diminished social status for clerical occupations as a result. Indeed, the internal restructuring of the office which gathered pace after 1900 is most graphically illustrated in the feminization of its labour force. These dramatic alterations in the social character of the office workforce signalled deep-seated changes in the very substance of administration.

How, though, is clerical feminization directly connected to the rise of corporate capitalism? The crucial link is to be found in the new roles into which clerks were cast as the office assumed ever greater responsibility for exercising administrative control. Elaborate recording, communicating, filing, analysing and accounting procedures, so essential to the growing scale and complexity of business and government operations, formed the basis of modern clerical activities. Regulation of external market forces and control over internal work processes are what make the office inseparable from the functions of contemporary management. Indeed, with the rise of the modern corporation a widening array of detailed managerial functions were parcelled into specific tasks and delegated to clerical underlings. Without an extensive and efficient army of clerks, top management would be hamstrung. To invoke a physiological analogy: 'Management, the brain of the organization, conveys its impulses through the clerical system which constitutes the nervous mechanism of the company.'[4]

Internal changes in administrative structures and processes affected office working conditions, technology and job content. The generalist male bookkeeper no longer fitted into the more fragmented and standardized division of labour. These internal developments in administration coalesced with larger social trends which increased the availability of women for paid employment. Hence by the end of the 1920s, the female office clerk formed a prominent new social group in many of the leading Western capitalist societies.

Centralized bureaucratic organizations, the development of coherent managerial philosophies and practices, and the rapid growth of a pool of female clerical workers are, in short, the hallmarks of the administrative revolution. But as David Lockwood would be quick to remind us, 'there is no sharp dividing line between the counting house and the modern office.'[5] True enough, the evidence that I present shows that the transition was gradual in Canada, the United States and Britain. And there are no compelling reasons not to believe that this probably is the case in other advanced capitalist countries which I have not examined in this study. Certainly in Canada the essential features of modern administration were plainly evident in major manufacturing and service organizations by 1930. Small-scale offices run by a couple of male general clerks and bookkeepers were becoming relics of an earlier phase of capitalism. In other words, the onslaught of corporate capitalism from roughly 1900 heralded the beginnings of a revolution in the means of administration. I now turn to consider the specific details of this in one country, Canada.

THE DEVELOPMENT OF CORPORATE CAPITALISM IN CANADA

Canada embarked on the road to industrialization later than Britain or the United States. The nation's colonial legacy as a staple producing hinterland exerted a strong influence on the timing and character of its economic growth.[6] Canada was a late industrializer. Early signs of industrialization were evident by the 1870s, even earlier by some accounts, with the emergence of the factory system of production. But progress was slow; not until the opening years of the twentieth century did industrialization surge forward. By the end of the First World War the economic importance of industry surpassed that of agriculture.[7] By then the small-scale local enterprises of the post-confederation era had given way to huge corporations in key manufacturing and service industries. The present distribution of the gross national product was firmly established.[8] In short, Canada was catapulted into a trajectory of wholesale economic and social change that also set in motion a revolution in administration.

Canada's movement from entrepreneurial to corporate capitalism was comparatively unique in some respects. Of central importance in this regard is the dependent nature of its industrial development. This is a point that I shall not dwell on, other than noting that today a lack of economic independence is part and parcel of Canada's integration into the American economic empire.[9] By tracing the roots of this problem we discover that, despite achieving nationhood in 1867, Canada retained earmarks of colonial dependency.[10] The Conservative government's 1879 National Policy presented a three-pronged development strategy based on the construction of a transcontinental railroad, agricultural settlement on the western plains, and a protective tariff to stimulate domestic industry. This formula for industrialization relied on British financial capital, Canadian resources and, increasingly into the twentieth century, US industrial capital and know-how as active ingredients.

The industrial revolution had reached Canada around the time it achieved nationhood in 1867. Factories producing domestic consumer goods, textiles, iron and steel products, vehicles and agricultural implements more than doubled their output between 1870 and 1890.[11]

But for a variety of reasons, both internal and external, industry was still mainly small-scale and low technology in 1900. Economic growth indicators clearly point to the first ten or 15 years of the twentieth century as a watershed. Examining the growth of real gross national product in Canada and the United States from 1871 to 1920, the major burst in the US GNP occurred at the start of this period (3.3 per cent average annual increase, 1871–80) while for Canada a similarly strong performance happened 1900–10 (3.2 per cent average annual growth rate).[12] Canadian levels of investment in machinery and equipment, construction, and new inventory – crucial for most theories of economic growth – underwent a substantial jump after 1900.[13] Moreover, there were some distinctively Canadian features in the industrial structure that emerged. For example, most significant in the period 1896–1914 was the remarkable growth of a primary iron and steel industry – a key economic sector that was already the backbone of the American, British, German and several other European economies. The delay in this sector's maturation resulted largely from the importation of rails during nineteenth-century railway building, rather than their domestic production as in the other countries just noted.[14]

A major stimulus to economic developments which finally bore some of the fruits of the 1879 National Policy was the 'wheat boom' of 1900–13. It was the opening up of Canada's western agricultural frontier coupled with bumper wheat crops that helped fuel the growth of manufacturing and service industries. '"Modern industry",' write Brown and Cook, 'grew out of the demands of a booming agricultural economy for more extensive transport and communications facilities, for new railways, new and improved roads, bigger lakes grain carriers, refrigerated ocean steamers and the machines and tools needed to produce them, and a host of other sophisticated manufactured products.'[15] The pace of development accelerated during the First World War. By the end of the war, a solid basis for a modern industrial society was in place.[16] Interrupted by a brief post-war recession, expansion proceeded briskly until 1929. Industries of the second industrial revolution – automobiles, pulp and paper, nonferrous metals, chemical products, electrical equipment – flourished.[17] New production technologies and management systems significantly boosted productivity among industrial workers. Economic activity became concentrated in large, bureaucratically organized corporations. In short, by the end of the 1920s corporate capitalism was well entrenched.

Influential in the development of the manufacturing sector was US direct investment. At the turn of the century, Canada hosted 100 American manufacturing branch plants; by 1934 there were 1350.[18] Canada's old colonial dependence on Britain was being replaced by close links with corporate America.[19] Even by the start of the First World War most US industrial giants were operating in Canada, earning it the dubious distinction of having more US subsidiaries within its borders than any other nation in the world.[20] In some respects this spillover was a by-product of close geographic proximity, but Canadian industrial policy also opened the door to American firms in manufacturing, as well as in the resource sector. The spillover of US industry into Canada was mainly responsible for introducing American corporate organizational forms and managerial ideologies and practices sooner and faster than was the case in other industrial nations.

Another important manifestation of the Canadian pattern of industrial development was a relatively large and dynamic service sector prior to the rise of manufacturing industries, which normally generate a demand for services. Financial services, insurance, transportation and commerce emerged out of the colonial staples economy and became the power base of a dominant commercial elite.[21] Late nineteenth-century economic performance is distinguished more than anything by an impressive growth of services.[22] Indeed, services accounted for the largest sector gain in value added as a percentage of GNP throughout the last half of the nineteenth century. The post-1900 wheat boom probably stimulated as great a demand for services as for goods. Farm credit, transportation and settlement of immigrants, administration of an expanding young nation, the commerce of grain exporting – these, as well as other services demanded by manufacturers, created huge white-collar bureaucracies in major urban centres across the country. This robustness in services was subsequently sustained. In the mid-1960s Canada and the US became the first countries with service-based economies.[23]

THE ECONOMIC IMPACT OF THE FIRST WORLD WAR

The war of 1914–18 contributed significantly to Canada's industrialization process. Simply put, the demands of military production, coupled with labour shortages, precipitated social and economic changes more quickly than would otherwise have occurred.[24] Manufacturing industries received a tremendous boost, with production and profits soaring to new heights.[25] The service sector also was further invigorated. This was especially noticeable in government, where bureaucracy swelled to handle new rules, regulations and administrative procedures dealing with consumer prices, rents, wheat marketing, rationing, coal, public welfare and labour relations.[26] The imposition of direct taxation during the war and nationalization of two transcontinental railways in the early 1920s gave the state a far more active role in economic affairs. 'The war,' reported a Royal Commission some years later, 'had wrought many profound changes in public finance, in the economic structure of the country, in social conditions, and in the public conception of the role which governments ought to play in society.'[27]

The significance of the wartime labour crisis cannot be overestimated, especially in the case of office clerks. I document in chapter 4, for instance, how the acute shortages of male workers by the end of 1915 converged with rising demand for new occupational skills, such as typing and stenography, to induct huge numbers of women into the labour force. Many leading firms broke with tradition and actively recruited women after conscription was imposed in the fall of 1917.[28] By the end of the war, over 30,000 women worked in munitions factories, 8,000 worked in banks, between 5,000 and 6,000 were civil servants and legions of others performed what previously had been regarded as men's jobs.[29] Women also assisted the war effort through their work in voluntary organizations. Old fashioned views about women's work were challenged and public opinion began to accept that perhaps women had a right to earn their own living and, indeed, could make vital contributions to the economy. Although the female munitions factory workers returned home after 1919, many of their sisters in clerical jobs had earned themselves a permanent niche in the office. This direct involvement of women in the war effort strengthened the arguments of the female suffrage movement, which achieved victory in May 1918 when all women over age 21 were granted voting rights in federal elections.

THE RISE OF LARGE-SCALE ORGANIZATIONS

The centralized bureaucracy was the organizational form most compatible with an expanding industrial economy. Workplaces in late nineteenth-century Canada tended to be small, rudimentary in their organization and lacking any coherent management strategy. As late as 1890, four out of five manufacturing firms employed fewer than 75 people.[30] Sun Life Insurance Company, later to dominate the insurance world, then had a head office staff of 20.[31] More typical would have been the office of Imperial Oil's Winnipeg branch, which looked like this in 1883: 'A single room (upstairs) size about 14' x 18', one roll top desk for the manager, a high desk and stool for the writer, a table, sofa, box-stove, a half cord of wood piled up in the corner and as a final touch – one pair of hip-length boots.'[32]

The forces of industrialization unleashed around 1900 dramatically altered the organizational framework of business and government. Fundamental to the administrative revolution was the ascendancy of large corporate and government bureaucracies. The centralization of planning, co-ordination and information processing in offices can be traced back to the early twentieth century. As in most other advancing industrial nations, by the 1920s big business and big government – organized hierarchically and regulated by elaborate systems of administrative controls presided over by professional managers – dominated the Canadian economy. There were, however, important organizational differences cross-nationally. For instance, managerial hierarchies arose in Germany and America during the 1880s and 1890s, in Britain during the 1920s and in France not until after the Second World War. Canada followed just behind the United States in this respect, being more advanced than Britain and most of Europe.[33]

The spread of the joint stock form of industrial ownership and the consolidation of production into larger units facilitated massive organizational changes. The joint stock company became the principle vehicle for corporate expansion and management after 1900. Canada's first such firm was A. T. Galt's Sherbrooke Cotton Mill, established in 1844, but this was the exception until the rapid industrialization of the early twentieth century.[34] Absolutely crucial to the development of corporate capitalism, and hence new forms of administration, was the corporate merger movement. There were two big merger waves, one peaking in 1909–12 and the other in the late twenties. The pre-First World War merger movement saw 247 companies consolidated through 57 mergers; from 1923–9 there were 228 mergers absorbing 644 firms.[35] Approximately 40 per cent of all merger activity between 1900 and 1948 was focused in the 1925–29 period. The end result was a concentration of economic control to a handful of huge enterprises in leading industries.[36] Merger activity was actually stronger in Canada than the United States where, by 1929, half of all non-banking corporate wealth was controlled by 200 firms.[37] It was frequently American subsidiaries which dominated key Canadian industries. For example, by the end of the First World War, Imperial Oil Ltd, a branch of the Rockefeller's Standard Oil empire, had cornered the petrochemical market and employed a staff of 6,000.[38] And the Canadian automobile industry was synonymous with the American 'big three' – General Motors, Chrysler, Ford – by the 1920s.[39]

The forces of industrial consolidation and concentration were equally potent in the service sector. The banking industry grew in leaps and bounds after 1900, yet between 1916 and 1925 the number of banks fell from 30 to 11.[40] Telephones and other key utilities came under the control of giant monopolies such as the Bell Telephone Company. And the two national railways emerged as Canada's largest employers: the combined workforces of Canadian National and Canadian Pacific numbered a staggering 129,000 in June 1931.[41] Similarly, civil service ranks in municipal, provincial and federal governments literally exploded, from 17,000 in 1901 to 108,000 in 1930.[42]

Perhaps the record of Sun Life's astounding growth best exemplifies the way bureaucracy inevitably spawned huge central offices populated by numerous clerks. Sun aggressively swallowed up competitors on its way to conquering international life insurance markets. By 1930, after 14 acquisitions in the preceding four decades, Sun Life's Montreal headquarters employed 2,856.[43] It only seems fitting that we turn to T. B. Macaulay, President of Sun Life in 1905, for insights regarding what propelled organizational change during this era:

> Institutional success is but another name for growth, and corporate growth implies expansion – the absorption and concentration of wealth – and wealth, as we all know, is the power that rules and controls men and relations . . . To life insurance, concentration of wealth is an absolute necessity. A life insurance company should be a perpetuity, and its wealth should accumulate with the increase of the amount at risk.'[44]

THE GROWTH OF ADMINISTRATION IN MANUFACTURING

The rapid expansion of factory administration was one of the more obvious and, for many managers, problematic consequences of industrialization. The disproportionate increase in administrative employees – supervisory and office workers – relative to production workers was a standard feature of manufacturing industries throughout capitalist economies. Among the first to investigate this phenomenon was the German sociologist Emil Lederer. In a 1912 study Lederer attributed the growing ratio of administrative to production workers (A/P ratio) in manufacturing to the process of corporate concentration. Lederer argued that the high proportion of office staff in German finished goods industries reflected their advanced technologies, rationalized organizational structures and use of American business methods.[45] Generally speaking, the rising A/P ratio is a surrogate measure for the emergence of bureaucratic forms of organization and the delegation of management authority to subordinate administrative workers.[46] Also decisive was the rising productivity in manufacturing through labour saving technologies and more efficient production methods. According to C. Wright Mills these advances had a pervasive impact on white-collar work: 'as the proportion of workers needed for the extraction and production of things declines, the proportion needed for servicing, distributing and co-ordinating rises.'[47]

In more precise terms, there were 10.9 administrative staff for every 100 production workers in US manufacturing and mining between 1905–11. Similar figures for Canada and Britain were lower, at 8.6 and 7.6 respectively, perhaps suggesting less advanced forms of administration in these countries. However, by the early 1930s Canada had surpassed the US to attain probably the highest A/P ratio in manufacturing and mining in the industrialized world. Canada, the United States and Britain then had A/P ratios of 16.9, 15.4 and 11.3 respectively.[48]

In the definitive study on the topic, Seymour Melman investigates the impact of industry and plant size, type of corporate organization, operating costs, product type and age of the firm on the A/P ratio in US manufacturing between 1899 and 1947. He discovers that the only variable having any significant effect is size. Interestingly, size is negatively related to administrative growth, with larger firms having lower A/P ratios. Melman concludes that administrative staff are integral to newly created managerial control functions:

> The explanation of the rather homogeneous increase in the administrative type of overhead will be found, we suggest, in the growing variety of business activities which are being subjected to controls, both private and public. As administrators have sought to lessen the uncertainty of their prospects, by controlling more of the factors which determine the advantage of their plants or firms, they have attempted to control, in ever greater detail, production costs, intensity of work, market demands for products and other aspects of firm operation. Following this hypothesis, the evolution of the business process towards the expansion of controlled areas of activity by management comprises the basis for the addition of administrative functions and, thereby, the enlarged administrative staff.[49]

The crux of Melman's thesis is that administration developed as a mechanism of control. While empirically limited to manufacturing, his argument nonetheless has important general ramifications for clerical work. Clerks comprise the bulk of administrative employees. Early specialized staff functions relied heavily on cost clerks and production control clerks. These clerks were indispensable for the application of managerial methods that first appeared in US factories at the end of the nineteenth century. Indeed, factory clerks aided the work rationalization process: 'higher management would be able to regain control of their expanding, more specialized operation . . . through administrative systems operated by such new staff positions.'[50]

The creation of the factory system relied on a variety of strategies for cutting production costs and promoting efficiency through task specialization. But extreme task specialization had dysfunctional consequences. Administrative solutions thus aimed to 'recouple' organizations by establishing better systems of co-ordination and control. Specifically, this brought into practice inventory and production controls, formal job descriptions, the line–staff form of organization, open information channels up to top management and clear lines for delegating authority downward. By the turn of the century these administrative schemes were being adopted by leading North American firms. Clerical ranks thus began to swell as the office became the hub of modern administration.

Cost accounting was one of the standard responses to the administrative problems of industrialization.[51] David Landes considers cost accounting, and later 'scientific' management techniques, the administrative sequel to mechanized factory production.[52] Machines were efficient, predictable and readily governed by management; industrial organizations were subject to the same rigors by accounting systems that allowed management to predict and regulate future production costs. It was this logic of control which became the leitmotif of modern management. Braverman describes how the manufacturing office thereby came to resemble 'a paper replica of production' where each step in the manufacturing process was 'devised, precalculated, tested, laid out, assigned and ordered, checked and inspected, and recorded throughout its duration and upon completion.'[53]

The office also functioned as the 'unseen hand' in service industries by manipulating external market forces as well as the internal dynamics of the work process. Service organizations lack the convenient yardstick of the A/P ratio to measure the burden of administrative costs. Yet managers became increasingly vigilant in this regard. The mounting volume of paper, endless rows of clerks and expanding responsibilities stretched traditional office procedures to the limit. This eventually forced sweeping rationalizations in clerical work. An insurance executive amplified the heightened concern in the 1920s about cumbersome and costly clerical staff: 'Office administration is not a job by itself. We are in the insurance business, and office administration, scientific office administration, is merely one of the tools to help us carry on the insurance business more efficiently.'[54]

THE NEW SCIENCE OF MANAGEMENT

A key ingredient in the transition from entrepreneurial to corporate capitalism was the ascendant power of the salaried manager. The rise of large-scale organization was synonymous with centralized managerial hierarchies. The nature of management authority, and how it is exercised, has been at the core of organizational theory since Max Weber proposed his model of bureaucracy.

Research by business historian Alfred D. Chandler Jr. provides the most penetrating account of how, after 1870, professional managers became the 'visible hand' of American business, replacing elusive market mechanisms. Chandler argues that a centralized, departmentally based structure was the institutional response to technological progress and expanding consumer markets in the United States after 1850.[55] The traditional 'rule of thumb' approach to management was replaced by 'scientific' administrative systems. Higher productivity and profits, lower costs, and reduced decision making uncertainty could be more effectively achieved through careful managerial co-ordination. Rapid industrialization in the United States after 1870 brought together two trends: the development of large, increasingly complex factories and the entry of trained engineers into management positions.[56] This convergence initiated a drive for more methodical approaches to management. Observing the British case, Sidney Pollard traces the roots of modern management even further back, to the early industrial revolution:

> Basically, the range of the problems of management was the same in all industries that had to deal with them for the first time during the industrial revolution: labour recruitment and training, discipline, control over production, accountancy and accountability were the ingredients of a science which varied only in detailed application not in principle, as between different sectors of the economy.[57]

The new breed of managers who took command of corporate capitalism enlarged the scope of managerial concerns beyond technology to include the manipulation of social and organizational aspects of production. Around the turn of the century the relative pace of technological change slowed. Employers therefore had to search for other means of maximizing their firm's potential. The pioneers of factory management were often engineers who had been promoted into positions of authority. They laid the groundwork for the rigorous scientific management of Frederick W. Taylor. Time study methods, piece rate payment schemes, and closely regulated tasks largely devoid of skills and responsibilities reduced growing numbers of blue-collar workers to automatons. Employees were viewed as mere cogs in the productive machinery, motivated solely by economic self-interest.

A contrasting approach was advocated by industrial reformers, early personnel 'experts', and other forerunners of the human relations movement. This managerial orientation emphasized the importance of the 'human' factor in the production process. Yet no single strategy dominated. Rather, employers often combined elements of both approaches to suit their particular needs. The common thread was a quest for greater efficiency, higher productivity and a more compliant and co-operative labour force.[58] While the finer strategic details varied from industry to industry and organization to organization, by the 1920s the foundation of contemporary management was solidly established on the guiding principles of efficiency, co-ordination and control.

Modern business practices emerged as administration became a specialized function in American factories during the last quarter of the nineteenth century. From then on, managers in both the United States and Canada waged a running battle against sources of inefficiency in work organization. Managers also confronted what many saw as the more serious problem of recalcitrant workers with collectivist impulses. Capitalist industrialization had redefined the Hobbesian problem of order as the 'labour problem'. A search for solutions to the labour problem captivated much early twentieth-century management thinking.

The early factory engineers attempted to sweep away vestiges of traditional management with the new brooms of 'system' and 'method'. Formal, centralized controls gave managers greater direct influence over a factory's daily operations and its workforce. Recognizing that a lack of organizational co-ordination created an 'administrative vacuum', managers set out to 'put "method" into shop management' through administrative systems.[59] The engineers, known as 'systematic managers', mainly advocated production and inventory control systems to achieve horizontal integration, cost accounting to establish vertical integration, and wage incentives and bonus plans to boost labour productivity and cut unit costs.[60] The factory manager thus assumed a central role in overall production. According to an editorial in a prominent engineering journal, by 1900 there were visible signs in Europe and North America of 'an awakening in everything related to workshop administration, including organization, cost-keeping, [and] provision for depreciation of plant . . . These subjects are appearing in prominent journals on both sides of the Atlantic. It is beginning to be appreciated generally that success in engineering work, commercially considered, depends very greatly upon the manner in which problems of shop administration are treated.'[61]

The American engineer, Fredrick W. Taylor, extended and disseminated the innovations of the systematic factory managers. Taylor's name became synonymous with scientific management – a set of reforms based on new tools, work methods and organizational arrangements designed by Taylor and his disciples to heighten the efficiency and speed of machine shop production. By the time of Taylor's death in 1915, his doctrines had gained wide popularity in Canadian and American management circles, although their impact was less profound in Britain and Europe.[62] The crucible of 'progressive' managerial practices was unquestionably the United States. In fact, by the First World War an 'efficiency craze' had infused the entire American progressive era.[63]

Taylorism pushed the division of labour to the limits of specialization, reducing workers' skills and discretion and tightening management's grip on each step of the productive process. Despite scientific management's high public profile, the full-blown Taylor system was implemented in fewer than 200 firms.[64] Yet it is difficult to overestimate the influence of the general management principles embodied in Taylorism. For as Judith Merkle observes, internationally scientific management is 'one of the most pervasive and invisible of the forces that have shaped modern society.'[65] Similarly, John Kelly calls the detailed job descriptions, planned work flows, systematic stock control and careful unit accounting of Taylorism the 'bedrock' of contemporary management because these are now universal features rather than strategic choices.[66]

THE RISE OF MODERN MANAGEMENT IN CANADA

Despite the obviously indispensable role of managers in the industrialization process, the exact nature of their goals and strategies have received little attention in Canada. The administrative revolution, and the attendant growth of a female clerical workforce, are organically connected to new forms of organization and management. The ferment of post-1900 economic change in Canada helped to shape a consensus among an increasingly self-conscious group of professional managers regarding solutions to the most urgent organizational, production and labour problems. By the 1920s management had become institutionalized through professional associations, employer groups, business journals and specialized staff functions in public and private sector organizations. The ideological beacon of the management movement rested on a common understanding of the need to implement 'progressive reforms' to increase production efficiency, reduce costs and regulate how workers perform their jobs. An underlying motivation was the achievement of a harmonious partnership between capital and labour. By the early twentieth century a repertoire of solutions to the problems of factory and shop management were readily available. During the 1920s these same principles found their way into the offices of Canada's leading corporations and government bureaucracies.

The sweeping rationalization of production launched at the end of the nineteenth century in the United States spilled over into Canada. Closer economic links with the American industrial system meant that Canadian managers, when faced with standard problems of co-ordination, inefficiency and labour, naturally turned an eye southward. Paul Craven argues that 'the reliance on imported technique characteristic of the staples economy extended to techniques of business organization as well. Canada's managerial revolution, in a word, was imported from the United States.'[67] Craven explains that there were three conduits through which Canadian managers acquired the latest American administrative practices: direct foreign investment when management policies were dictated by American head offices; the hiring of American managers or 'efficiency experts'; and trade organizations and journals. Increasingly after 1900, influential national business publications such as the *Monetary Times* and *Industrial Canada* began to articulate a coherent view of the major challenges facing management. In addition to scientific management, the various solutions discussed in editorials and articles incorporated costs accounting, welfare work and vocational training. Publications aimed at specific industries, such as the *Journal of the Canadian Bankers' Association*, the *Canadian Textile Journal* and *Canadian Railway and Marine World* carried similar features.

Clear signs of the development of management can be found in the rise of industry-based associations. As early as 1901 the Canadian Manufacturers' Association was encouraging its members to develop a united front to counter the threat of unions.[68] By 1922 the CMA was throwing its full support behind the industrial council form of company unionism.[69] Likewise, by the mid-1920s the annual meetings and publications of the Canadian Telephone Association, the Canadian Bankers' Association, the Insurance Institute of Toronto, and the Life Office Management Association dealt in-depth with labour and organizational problems. The Life Office Management Association, for instance, was jointly founded by Canadian and American life insurance companies in 1924 to further scientific office management in the life insurance industry by pooling experiences and information. LOMA achieved considerable success, judging from the reforms found in its Canadian members. Indeed, an official of a large business machine company told the 1928 LOMA convention 'that no other line of business has surpassed the life insurance business in adopting the latest business machines, equipment and office methods. Such a progressive tendency has naturally exercised a great influence on the character of your administrative methods – simplifying and standardizing them to a marked degree.'[70]

It is plain to see that factory-type rationalization measures were being adapted to the office. The new management practices that I have described became increasingly institutionalized in Canada after the First World War. Professional associations sprung up, reflecting the growing specialization of managerial functions within administration. For example, a Cost Accountants' Association of Canada was organized in 1920 to further the 'new science of cost accounting.'[71] The growing stature of accountancy was already evident in the Dominion Institute of Chartered Accountants, founded in 1902. In 1908 a Canadian Accountants' Association was organized by those engaged in accounting and office management for large corporations.[72] Another good illustration of the diffusion and institutionalization of new styles of management is the Employment Managers' Association (later renamed the Industrial Relations Association). Founded in Toronto in 1920, this association pursued the following aims: 'to promote and foster interest in employment and industrial relations problems in Toronto and elsewhere; to discuss problems of employees, including selection, training, management and working conditions; to encourage closer cooperation between industrial relations executives and to work with municipal and governmental bodies to bring about close cooperation concerning employment problems.'[73]

The economic boom ushered in with the twentieth century presented Canadian businessmen with a welter of perplexing managerial problems. Many of these problems were common to large, complex organizations. Initial solutions centred around the reorganization of factory production. Industrialists were counselled to emulate the 'model factories' which began appearing during the first decade of the century.[74] *Industrial Canada* advocated 'economy in production', advising manufacturers to introduce labour-saving devices.[75] And as early as 1907, discussions of the model factory underlined the office's administrative role. A well-organized office, divided into executive, recording and sales branches, and employing accountants, bookkeepers and, of course, clerks to record and analyse all costs would, it was argued, facilitate efficient production.[76]

Taylor's brand of scientific management had developed a clientele in Canadian industry by the start of the First World War. The Lumen Bearing Company of Toronto had adopted the Taylor system by 1911. As an official of the firm explained, 'efficiency management is the biggest problem in manufacturing today.'[77] The company's rationalization programme included time-study by experts in order to determine piece work rates and the elimination of job planning by mechanics. The results no doubt attracted considerable attention from other employers when casting production jumped from 28 to 65 units per day. The Canadian Pacific Railway scored one of the more notable successes in the application of Taylorism.[78] H. L. Gantt, a close associate of Taylor, was hired in June 1909 to reorganize locomotive repair work at the railway's Angus Shops in Montreal scientifically. Gantt's reforms included a piece work payment system, job routines set down on instruction sheets, standardized tools, an elaborate scheduling method for repair work, and the physical reorganization of the shop.[79]

Tangible increases in output and control over labour gained wide publicity for scientific management. In 1911, H. L. Gantt told Canadian manufacturers about 'the straight line to profit'. Preaching that 'scientific management is the new gospel of industrial progress', he urged businessmen to slash unnecessary costs rather than raise prices. This was a fundamental axiom of the Taylor system. Gantt then struck a keynote in modern management theory: 'To eliminate this blind by-play with chance and substitute methods based on technical inquiry and proved [sic] results, is the task of scientific management. Every element in a business should come under this searching inquiry, from shop to office. And whenever it strikes, it means the elimination of waste time, waste energy, waste materials.'[80]

If manufacturers and other businessmen harboured lingering doubts about these new approaches, they may well have been won over by the three articles F. W. Taylor himself published in *Industrial Canada* during 1913. Beyond Taylor's job redesign formulas lay a new vista of harmonious labour relations in which an enlarged economic pie could yield bigger pieces for all. Scientific management, asserted Taylor, demanded a 'complete mental revolution' among workers and employers alike. He explained:

> The new outlook that comes to both sides under scientific management is that both sides may soon realize that if they stop pulling apart and both push together as hard as possible in the same direction, they can make that surplus so large that there is no occasion for any quarrel over its subdivision. Labour gets an immense increase in wages, and still leaves a large share for capital.[81]

In short the 'labour problem' would be solved once and for all.

As in the United States and elsewhere, Canadian manufacturers preferred to remedy organizational and labour inefficiencies through a battery of reforms rather than wholesale adoption of the unwieldy Taylor scheme. Piece work payment systems were especially popular. These allowed management to control production output, to relocate decision-making regarding production from the factory floor to the front office, and to reduce labour costs.[82] In 1921 the *Labour Gazette* reported on commonly used methods of wage payment.[83] Many of the incentive systems discussed had been devised by Taylor, Gantt or Emerson, the three foremost American scientific management experts.

Part and parcel of quantifying labour time and calculating wage costs was the introduction of mechanical time recording devises. Employee time recorders were introduced into Canada in 1902 as an accurate way to measure labour costs and worker productivity.[84] By 1915 the International Time Recording Company of Canada, the major distributor of these clocks and a predecessor to IBM, listed 50 large Canadian organizations among its customers. After the First World War IBM successfully marketed this equipment in offices. The firm's sales pitch argued that 'office help is expensive: and one of the largest overhead items. [It] should be measured and checked as carefully as light, heat, power, rent, etc.'[85]

Reducing labour costs was a top priority for businessmen, and time recorders were but one weapon in management's cost cutting arsenal. As the *Monetary Times* elaborates: 'Cost systems are an essential part of modern scientific business management. For the capital invested in a business proves just as efficient as are the brains employed to handle it; and the best guide for brains is analysis. That is the function of a cost system to give the manufacturer a detailed knowledge of his business – and to give him this detailed information regularly and automatically.'[86] Canadian managers became well aware that 'the secret of efficiency, after all, is costs.'[87] Cost accounting arose out of the attention given to the subject of costs by early British and American industrial engineers seeking more skillful management techniques. An early textbook on the topic claims that 'organization, management and cost accounting are so intimately related that it is almost impossible to consider them separately.'[88] Cost accounting records all manufacturing, marketing, distribution, administration and other costs. Analysis of these data allows management to regulate what each component of the production process contributes to final profits.

The spread of cost accounting in Canada paralleled post-1900 industrial growth. Extolling the 'practical value' of cost accounting, *Industrial Canada* argued in 1903 that the new science provided overall managerial control in addition to reducing expenses.[89] General economic prosperity and expanding national markets heightened competition among corporations. Cost accounting thus offered two main advantages: accurate cost estimates of planned production; and a critical appraisal of the effectiveness of managerial techniques, production methods and labour efficiency. Cost accounting was readily integrated with other rationalization strategies. After the First World War cost accounting became an established part of Canadian administrative practice. Indeed, banks often made the implementation of a cost system a condition for extending credit. Observing this trend, the *Monetary Times* concluded that 'soon the concern will be rare which does not use a cost system of some kind or other.'[90]

Welfare work, or industrial betterment, was a complementary technique for grappling with the 'labour problem'. The welfare work movement's concern with human factors in production makes it a forerunner to the human relations approach, which has dominated personnel management in the post-Second World War period. As such, it embodied quite different assumptions about worker motivation and employee relations than the utilitarian rationality of scientific management. Turn-of-the-century welfare work schemes gave way to modern personnel management during the twenties.[91] The human element in this approach was especially important in offices, where the efficiency measures of the Taylorites were only partly applicable. An insurance executive, speaking in 1927, expanded on this point:

Personnel management has made great strides in the field of training workers. There is a great opportunity and responsibility for each [insurance] company to train and develop its clerical workers by carefully thought-out methods of instruction. A number of years ago the outstanding figure in business in general was the industrial engineer whose entire time was occupied in developing new machinery and new systems. The present day business is not so much in need of new machinery and new system as it is in the development of 'Human Beings'.[92]

The Canadian welfare work movement derived much of its inspiration from the American experience. The publicity John H. Patterson attracted when he introduced a model welfare scheme in National Cash Register's Dayton, Ohio, plant did not escape Canadian businessmen. Americans were leading the way in the field and by the end of the First World War the 'welfare secretary' of Patterson's era had been established as a new profession – the personnel manager.[93] In one of the first public discussions of welfare work in Canada, *Industrial Canada* argued that 'pleasant surroundings are conducive to the economical production of good work, while at the same time they attract a much better class of working people.'[94]

Welfare work had a strong ideological affinity with the ideas of the urban reformers and other middle-class progressives of the time. Attractive looking factories with well-manicured lawns and healthful working conditions were thought to induce higher moral standards among workers and hence reduce class tensions. Pension plans, employee share ownership plans, company newspapers, cafeterias serving subsidized meals, athletic facilities, educational programmes, and medical departments were tangible results of the welfare work movement. Profit-minded employers justified these expenses on both moral and pragmatic grounds. The real advantage of the plans, however, lay in reducing overt employee discontent which detracted from productivity. *Industrial Canada*, for example, 'found that care for the physical, intellectual and moral welfare of . . . employees had a direct return in increased output and better work'.[95] Here the goals of welfare work and the various other forms of modern management converged. Indeed, at Williams, Green and Rome, an Ontario manufacturer of shirts, collars and cuffs, humanitarian features aimed at achieving industrial harmony through improved conditions of work were part of a comprehensive scientific management system.[96]

Usually the 'welfare secretary' who ran company welfare plans was a counterbalance to the stop-watch wielding efficiency expert. By 1910 firms at the vanguard of the movement had established welfare departments headed by these new specialists.[97] Welfare work and scientific management may be thus viewed as complementary pro-grammes. In management circles a consensus emerged, defining both as useful measures for countering labour and organizational problems. Factories were at the forefront of these innovations, but larger offices had started adopting similar measures by the First World War.[98] It was not uncommon in industrial corporations for office employees to receive vacation plans, pensions, sickness and disability benefits, and other 'welfare' schemes before their blue-collar counterparts in the same firm.

Whether producing goods or providing services, bureaucracies increas-ingly faced problems requiring multi-faceted solutions. The Consolidated Mining and Smelting Company, to give one example, established a comprehensive plan in 1930 based on the 'co-operative principle'. Included were efficiency measures, such as wage incentives and employment aptitude tests, as well as welfare provisions, ranging from pensions and insurance, to a home building fund and a safety department.[99] A survey conducted in 1928 by the federal Department of Labour revealed that scientific management was widespread among a sample of 300 manufacturing firms and public utilities.[100] Interestingly, the study's definition of scientific management encompassed joint industrial councils and other industrial relations plans and welfare work, as well as aspects of Taylorism.

By transforming the social relations of production, the factory system escalated the potential for class antagonisms. Employers intent on expanding production and reducing costs sought methods of minimizing any conflict between labour and capital that might undermine these goals. Labour remained the wild card in the mounting stakes of productivity and profits. American managements' assault on the evils of worker 'soldiering' (laziness) and the collective power of trade unions found parallels in Canada.[101] But an equally important ingredient in solutions to the labour problem, contributing directly to the development of modern management, was the attempt to co-opt labour into formal regulatory structures. During the First World War joint industrial councils became the vogue in Britain, the United States and Canada. A 1918 Canadian Royal Commission on Industrial Relations endorsed the concept as a way of 'promoting harmony and better relations between employers and employees'.[102] Major organizations such as Bell Canada, Imperial Oil and International Harvesters were first on the band wagon, in 1919, with others following in the 1920s. The spirit of these early councils lives on in the form of company unions and the Japanese-style corporate cultures of today.

Canada's home-grown contribution to modern management was William Lyon Mackenzie King's pioneering work in industrial relations. King championed the scientific investigation of organizational problems and greater co-operation between capital and labour. He epitomized the new school of technocrats who applied 'science' in the interests of industrial progress. As Canada's first minister of labour, King legislated disputes resolution procedures based on an ostensibly objective investigation of the facts by government conciliators. And as an internationally renowned labour relations expert, he provided the American capitalist John D. Rockefeller with an enduring formula for company unionism.[103]

THE ADMINISTRATIVE REVOLUTION

Using broad brush strokes, I have painted the backdrop to the administrative revolution which transformed the office landscape between 1900 and 1930. Three themes dominate the canvas: the creation of a twentieth-century industrial economy founded on the twin pillars of manufacturing and services; the growing dominance of large, centralized bureaucracies as work organizations; and the ascendancy of a new breed of professionals, the modern manager, with a mission to rationalize organizational life. These interacting trends surfaced with considerable impact in Canada in the early twentieth century. In addition to the stimulus of expanding markets and rising demand for a greater variety and sophistication of goods and services, Canada's administrative revolution was energized by two other sources. One was the already well-developed service infrastructure built around the commerce and finance of colonial staple industries. The other was the importation of US manufacturing systems, organizational forms and managerial policies. The interweaving of these economic, organizational and managerial forces gave rise to modern administration.

The growth of clerical employment can be traced therefore to the expanding scope, scale and complexity of business and government operations. Equally important, however, was the creation of new administrative functions in order for managers to deal with the ensuing problems of co-ordination, integration and overall control. The mixed bag of scientific management strategies demanded precise data on production, costs, markets and numerous other business variables. According to Nelson, 'factory clerks were an essential accoutrement of scientific management.'[104] Administrative systems eventually replaced the *ad hoc* methods of nineteenth-century management, if indeed it received any attention at all. The central office acquired a crucial economic role: 'it is through clerical channels that management communicates and co-ordinates.'[105]

It was not long, however, before the office itself was experiencing the upheavals of work rationalization. Administration came to be recognized as a cost burden and a source of inefficiency by the very managers who relied on the office to exert control over other components of the organization. The following comment on F. W. Taylor's factory planning department, made before the US Senate hearings on scientific management in 1912, underscores this point: 'The clerical overhead necessary for these elaborate systems makes overhead charges exceedingly great, and it is a question whether the increased productivity of the workmen in the shop . . . is sufficient to pay for all this non-productive labour which has been added.'[106] It thus comes as no surprise that by the First World War, the principles of efficiency management were being applied to the office. William H. Leffingwell, the leading proponent of scientific office management, wrote in 1917 that 'many business men, after analyzing the remarkable results secured by applying Frederick W. Taylor's system of scientific management in factories, have asked whether or not similar betterments could not be obtained in offices with the system. Their questions can now be answered, for the main principles of the Taylor system have actually been adapted and applied in office work.'[107] Taylor's ideas formed part of a wide range of strategies used by management to achieve greater cost-effectiveness in administration. The crux of my argument, in short, is that in order for administrative control to be exercised by management through the office, the same principles increasingly had to be applied in the office itself.

The rationalization of the office occurred essentially in one of two ways. Sometimes office tasks and procedures were restructured as a result of general organizational reform. Offices are an organic part of all economic units, so they would not escape from a plan to streamline an unwieldy bureaucracy. This is evident in Bell Telephone's introduction of a functional departmental structure in 1910. Bell employees were reminded that 'failure to recognize the true place of organization as the hand-maiden, the servant of administration, must tend, especially where the business conducted is large and complex, to unnecessary output or misappropriation of energy.'[108]

The second form rationalization assumed was a direct attack on clerical procedures, often on the heels of a rapid expansion of clerical staff. In these circumstances, traditional office structures and work procedures quickly became obsolete. This applied especially to the service sector. For example, insurance managers agreed that organizational reform was their first priority at the founding meeting of the Life Office Management Association in 1924. In fact, LOMA's main purpose was to counteract inefficiencies in the office through 'correct organization and administration of . . . clerical activities.'[109] Often accompanied by mechanization, these forms of rationalization resulted in a more fragmented and routine division of labour.

On a final note, I admittedly do not focus on how clerks' responses to their working conditions may have influenced management's reform initiatives. The reason for this, quite simply, is the lack of any well-documented resistance, either overt or covert, among Canadian clerks during the period under investigation. I address this lacuna in the last chapter through a discussion of clerical unionism. In a related vein let us for now consider a major strength of the present study. Beyond documenting the impact of the administrative revolution on clerical work – an aspect of occupational change about which little is known – I contextualize the decisions made by managers to recruit particular types of clerical employees and, further, to reorganize clerical labour processes. These managerial actions ultimately defined the contemporary office.

The evidence I present below reveals considerable diversity in the patterns of clerical growth and administrative change. No hidden logic propelled these developments, nor did managers move automatically down a unilinear track of reform. Only by paying close attention to the particular historical circumstances of an organization, can we accurately interpret the factors underlying the evolution of its workforce and labour processes. In this respect, the concept of administrative control advanced above helps us to locate the strategic choices of managers within the broad parameters of existing social ideologies and practices. In the next two chapters I examine the factors which influenced an early twentieth century managerial decision of critical importance to the contemporary office: the increasing recruitment of females as clerks.

3

The Growth of Clerical Occupations

The staid world of the clerk was thrown into turmoil after 1900. When the depression hit in 1930, clerks were the largest and fastest growing occupational group in the booming white-collar sector. The typical nineteenth century clerk, a skilled male bookkeeper hunched over his ledger in a small counting house, had been eclipsed by an army of female clerks. It is impossible to understand the explosion of clerical occupations without taking into account rising female labour force participation. Indeed, nowhere is the trend towards female employment more pronounced than in the office. By 1986, 55.1 per cent of all females in Canada 15 years of age and older worked outside the home for pay. This signals fundamental changes in the labour force since the late nineteenth century, considering that in 1891 only 11.4 per cent of the female population (10 years of age and over) were gainfully employed. The surge in female employment has been especially marked since the Second World War, but its origins can be traced back to the early years of the century.

This chapter will trace the growth and development of clerical occupations in Canada. Today the clerical sector is the quintessential female job ghetto. According to the 1981 census, there were 1,513,000 female clerks in Canada. Moreover, 34 per cent of all employed women perform some kind of clerical job and 78 per cent of all clerks are female.[1] Subtle gender role stereotyping and rigid labour market structures have channelled women into office employment – far in excess of their 42 per cent share of the total labour force. The gender segregation of the labour market is underlined by the fact that, next to teaching, clerical work was the most common occupational destination of Canadian female university graduates with bachelor's degrees in the 1970s.[2] Once in the office as clerks, women tend to be trapped there unless, of course, they leave the labour force altogether. Regardless of their educational credentials, promotion into a managerial career is still unlikely for most female clerks.[3]

CLERICAL OCCUPATIONS WITHIN THE CANADIAN LABOUR FORCE,
1891–1971

The most complete record of occupational change in Canada is found in
the decennial censuses. In addition to helping us to trace the historical
patterns in clerical employment, the censuses document the increasing
subdivision of office labour. As the Canadian economy became more
industrialized and dominated by large corporations, census categories
were modified to reflect the growing assortment of specialized administrative tasks. In post-confederation Canada, when industry was still at an
infant stage, clerks did not constitute a separate occupational group.
Accountants and bookkeepers, who numbered 2,302 in 1871 and 4,555
in 1891, and stenographers, who first appeared in the 1881 census 72
strong, were the full extent of the clerical workforce.[4] The ensuing three
decades fundamentally transformed industry and commerce. Thus the
1921 census records, for the first time, specific clerical occupations such
as shippers, proofreaders, weighmen, accountants, postmen, bookkeepers, stenographers, office appliance operators, and basic clerks. The
clerical division of labour documented in 1921 has been elaborated and
refined in subsequent censuses.

One of the first things to determine when studying an occupational
group is its relative share of the labour force. Accurate long-term
occupational trends can only be discerned using a consistent occupational
classification scheme. This I have done for the 1891–1971 censuses by
using the 1951 census definition of clerical worker as a basis for
standardization.[5] Table 3.1 shows that the number of clerks in Canada
increased from 33,017 in 1891 to 1,310,910 in 1971. During this period
the proportion of the total labour force engaged in clerical occupations
rose from 2.0 per cent to 15.2 per cent (table 3.2). Clerical workers are
now the largest occupational group in Canada.

Clerks spearheaded the expansion of the white-collar sector of the
labour force. Table 3.3 indicates that, with the exception of the 1921–31
decade, the growth rate for clerical occupations has consistently
outstripped increases in the total labour force. The clerical growth rate
peaked at 109.3 per cent during the 1911–21 decade. This was followed
by another period of intensified growth from 1941–51.

The 1911–21 boom in clerical jobs largely was a delayed reaction to the
tremendous expansion of the population, and hence the labour force, in
the preceding decade. The Canadian population increased by 34.2 per
cent between 1901 to 1911, mainly due to a huge influx of immigrants.
This coincided with an even more spectacular expansion (52.8 per cent) of
the labour force. Throughout the years from 1891–1921, clerical jobs
proliferated at a much faster rate than the labour force. But the fact that

Table 3.1 Number of workers in the labour force and in clerical occupations, by sex, Canada, 1891–1971*

	Total labour force	Total clerical	Male clerical	Female clerical
1891	1,659,335	33,017	28,307	4,710
1901	1,782,832	57,231	44,571	12,660
1911	2,723,634	103,543	69,820	33,723
1921	3,164,348	216,691	126,114	90,577
1931	3,917,612	260,674	143,037	117,637
1941	4,195,951	303,655	151,439	152,216
1951	5,214,913	563,083	243,900	319,183
1961	6,342,289	818,912	315,252	503,660
1971	8,626,930	1,310,910	407,515	903,395

* Data adjusted to 1951 census occupation classification.
Source: Occupational Trends in Canada, 1891–1931 (Ottawa, Dominion Bureau of Statistics, 1939), table 5; Noah M. Meltz, *Manpower in Canada, 1931 to 1961* (Ottawa, Queen's Printer, 1969), section I, tables A1, A2, A3; 1971 Census of Canada, volume 3, part 2, table 2.

Table 3.2 Clerical workers as a percentage of the labour force, by sex, and males and females as a percentage of clerical workers, Canada, 1891–1971*

	Total	Male	Female	Males as a percentage of clerical	Females as a percentage of clerical
1891	2.0%	2.0%	2.3%	85.7%	14.3%
1901	3.2	2.9	5.3	77.9	22.1
1911	3.8	3.0	9.1	67.4	32.6
1921	6.8	4.7	18.5	58.2	41.8
1931	6.7	4.4	17.7	54.9	45.1
1941	7.2	4.5	18.3	49.9	50.1
1951	10.8	6.0	27.4	43.3	56.7
1961	12.9	6.9	28.6	38.5	61.5
1971	15.2	7.2	30.5	31.1	68.9

* Data adjusted to 1951 census occupation classification.
Source: Calculated from table 3.1.

Table 3.3 Percentage increase each decade in the population, the labour force and clerical occupations, Canada, 1891–1971*

	Population	Labour force	Female Labour force	Clerical occupations	Female clerical workers
1891–1901	11.1%	10.4%	17.7%	73.3%	168.8%
1901–1911	34.2	52.8	53.3	80.9	166.4
1911–1921	21.9	16.2	34.0	109.3	168.6
1921–1931	18.1	23.8	36.0	20.3	29.9
1931–1941	10.9	7.0	27.1	16.5	29.4
1941–1951	21.8	26.1	39.7	85.4	109.7
1951–1961	30.2	22.4	51.3	45.4	57.8
1961–1971	18.3	33.6	68.2	60.1	79.4

* Data adjusted to 1951 census occupation classification.
Source: Occupational Trends in Canada, 1891–1931, table 5; Meltz, *Manpower in Canada,* section I, table A1; 1971 Census of Canada, volume 3, part 2, table 2; *Canada Year Book, 1974* (Ottawa, Information Canada, 1974), table 4.1, p. 160.

the peak in the clerical growth trend lagged behind the labour force as a whole suggests that industrialization, fuelled by the wheat boom and western settlement early in the century, was a necessary precondition for the development of modern administration. This seems to support the contention that clerical growth was directly tied to the rise of corporate capitalism.

The rate of clerical growth slowed to 20.3 per cent during the 1921 to 1931 decade. The twenties was a time of consolidation and rationalization in offices, when the army of clerks recruited in the preceding decade was moulded into an efficient cadre of administrative functionaries. As I document in later chapters, the twin forces of work rationalization and mechanization made significant headway in large corporate and government offices during this period. Clerical expansion tapered off even more during the depression of the thirties, though not as precipitously as total labour force growth. Clerical ranks again swelled during the Second World War decade. After a lull during the fifties, an upsurge in office jobs occurred during the 1960s mainly due to general labour force expansion.

In brief, clerical occupations have steadily increased in numbers since 1891, with concentrated surges between 1911 to 1921 and 1941 to 1951. The tremendous wave of recruitment during the First World War decade established clerks as the major white-collar group in the labour force. In 1911 they constituted only 3.8 per cent of the labour force; by 1921 this had jumped to 6.8 per cent (table 3.2). In sum, the growth of clerical occupations clearly signals the trend towards white-collar employment and a service-based economy.

THE ENTRY OF WOMEN INTO CLERICAL OCCUPATIONS

An outstanding feature of occupational change in twentieth-century Canada is the growing proportion of women entering the labour force. This feminization trend has been concentrated in a small number of occupations, the most important of which is the clerical group. Strictly male dominated at the turn of the century, by 1941 the majority of clerical jobs were held by women (tables 3.1 and 3.2). The pace of feminization was quickest from 1891 to 1921, with the growth rate for female clerks exceeding 166 per cent in each of these three decades (table 3.3). In absolute numbers, this meant a jump from 4,710 female clerks in 1891 to 90,577 by 1921.

The second major invasion of women into the office happened during the 1940s, and accounts for the general increase in clerical employment during this decade. The entry of women into clerical jobs is more a reflection of clerical growth patterns than of the overall expansion of the female labour force. Except for the inter-war years, women entered clerical jobs at a much higher rate than other occupations. In other words, the growth of clerical occupations can be attributed in large part to rising numbers of women flooding into the office.

Women increasingly became the main supply of labour for the burgeoning offices of an industrializing Canada. Consequently, the percentage of all employed males engaged in clerical occupations inched up only slightly from 2.0 per cent to 7.2 per cent over the entire 1891–1971 period. In contrast, the proportion of female workers holding clerical jobs rocketed from 2.3 per cent to 30.5 per cent over the same period. Not surprisingly, it was during the 1911–1921 and 1941–1951 growth surges that the clerical group increased its share of the total female labour force most sharply. Thus as employers hired additional clerks, they hired women.

Figure 3.1 demonstrates the impact of feminization on the overall growth of clerical occupations. It compares the actual number of male and female clerks in 1971 with what these numbers would have been had the occupational and sex composition of the labour force remained constant since 1901. The chart confirms that clerical growth far outstripped increases in the labour force. Moreover, it establishes beyond any doubt that most clerical gains are attributable to the influx of females into the office.

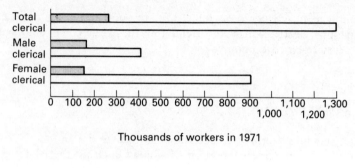

Thousands of workers in 1971

Number of clerks in 1971 if occupational structure were identical to that of 1901

Actual number of clerks in 1971

Figure 3.1   Changes in the clerical sector of the Canadian labour force, by sex, 1901–71*

* Comparison between actual distribution in 1971 and distribution calculated on basis of 1901 occupational structure, standardized to 1951 base.

THE CHANGING INDUSTRIAL DISTRIBUTION OF CLERKS

Sir Wilfred Laurier, who was prime minister when the twentieth century dawned, expressed the heady public optimism of an expanding nation when he proclaimed that the new century belonged to Canada. Certainly the booming agricultural economy in the west and the dynamism of central Canadian industry during the first three decades provided substance to Laurier's vision. This echoes my argument in chapter 2 that the rise of corporate capitalism precipitated the growth of offices and, in turn, the escalating demand for clerical labour. To flesh out this claim empirically, it is useful to identify the industries in which clerical growth was most heavily concentrated during the formative years after 1900.

Research by Marvin McInnis documents a massive shift in employment away from agriculture toward service industries between 1911 and 1961.[6] It is within this broad restructuring of the labour force, typical of all advanced capitalist societies, that the creation of a modern clerical workforce has its roots. Detailed evidence of the industrial distribution of clerical workers between 1901 and 1931 (see tables A1–A3 in the Appendix) reveals a concentration of growth in four industries: manufacturing, finance, trade, and transportation and communication. Over a longer period, from 1911 to 1961, the most rapid expansion of clerical employment is found in manufacturing, followed by trade, finance, then government.

The 20 years from 1911 to 1931 account for the most dramatic alterations in the industrial location of clerical jobs. Table 3.4 gives a breakdown of net clerical growth by major industrial sectors in this period. By combining manufacturing, finance, trade, and transportation and communication we can account for over 85 per cent of all new clerical jobs created. The table understates the importance of clerical jobs in the public service. Staff cuts and departmental consolidations after the First World War resulted in a net reduction of clerks during the 1920s. But in the two decades up to 1921, almost 13 per cent of all new clerical posts were created in the state sector.

Two changes highlight the entry of women into clerical occupations. The first concerns the creation of a gender-based division of office labour, whereby women were channelled into the newly created jobs at the bottom end of the office hierarchy. Typing is perhaps the best example of a strictly 'female' office job. For reasons which I document in the next chapter, the introduction of typewriters in the late nineteenth century created new vocational opportunities for women; by 1911 they occupied fully 85 per cent of all stenography and typing jobs. The second aspect of growing female clerical employment is its concentration in a few industrial sectors. By 1931, three industries – manufacturing, finance, and trade – each employed over 20 per cent of all female clerks. When government and community and business services are added to this group, over 80 per cent of total female clerical workers can be accounted

Table 3.4 Increases in clerical occupations by major industry, Canada, 1911–31*

	1911–31	
	Net increase, No. of clerks	%
Manufacturing	51,743	34.5
Transportation & communication	21,165	14.1
Trade	23,412	15.6
Finance	31,333	20.9
Community & business service	12,688	8.5
Government	6,496	4.4
Construction	3,004	2.0
Sum of all increases	149,841	100.0

* Data adjusted to 1951 census occupation classification.
Source: Calculated from table A1 (see Appendix).

for. The industrial pattern of female clerical employment thus reinforces my general argument about the importance of feminization for the development of clerical occupations.

Taking a closer look at this feminization process, it is interesting to note that the proportion of all clerical jobs held by women increased from 22.1 per cent in 1901 to 45.1 per cent in 1931 (see table A2, Appendix). Only two industries had more than 6 per cent of their clerical positions filled by females in 1901 (trade and manufacturing had 22.7 per cent and 16.5 per cent respectively). Yet by 1931, trade, finance, manufacturing and the service industries each had over 40 per cent of their clerical jobs performed by women. The most dramatic shift in the sex composition of clerical work occurred in the financial sector. Women held less than 1 per cent of clerical posts in banks, insurance companies and other financial institutions at the turn of the century. However, by 1931 the exclusive male right to these jobs had all but vanished.

VARIATIONS IN CLERICAL FEMINIZATION WITHIN FIRMS

Even in organizations at the advancing edge of corporate capitalism one can find considerable variations in the rate of clerical feminization. The trend towards recruiting more women into offices was, in short, far from uniform. The type of business activities, ideologies about appropriate male and female economic roles, the geographic location of a firm, its clientele – these are some of the factors accounting for inter-organizational differences in recruitment patterns. For example, public sector occupations such as nursing, teaching and librarianship became acceptable employment for educated, middle-class women well before clerical work did.[7] In the latter part of the nineteenth century, beliefs about women's position in society were modified to accommodate their employment, until marriage, in jobs consistent with their traditional roles of caring for the sick and infirm, nurturing the young, and guardians of culture. But in the world of business women were thought to have no proper place. These ideological barriers began to erode around the turn of the century. By the end of the 1920s the employment of women in low-grade, low-paid clerical jobs had been firmly established on the assumption, of course, that upon marriage they would retreat into the home.

The financial sector, as one of today's major clerical employers, offers an interesting case study of variable feminization patterns. Archival data from two representative firms in this sector, the Bank of Nova Scotia and the Manufacturers Life Insurance Company, provide a more finely grained analysis of the clerical labour market between 1911 and 1931.

In the bank's Ontario region branches and Toronto general office, the number of women rose from nine in 1911 to 114 by 1916. The severe labour shortages during the First World War paved the way for the now ubiquitous female teller. In 1911 there were all of two women, both stenographers, in the bank's 103 Ontario branches. Most of the women hired during the war were classified as 'emergency staff', a palatable justification for their intrusion into the male domain of the bank branch. Many of these women were displaced by returning veterans. Not until the late 1920s did bank management finally accept women as a regular source of clerical labour. By the onset of the depression, women filled just over 30 per cent of clerical posts in the bank's Ontario region. However, the co-ordinating functions of the head office spawned a higher proportion of routine clerical jobs and, consequently, more women were employed there (29 per cent in 1911, 75 per cent in 1916 and 50 per cent in 1931).

In sharp contrast, the early growth of large, centralized bureaucracies with many specialized clerical tasks greatly enhanced female employment opportunities within the insurance industry. The Toronto head office of the Manufacturers Life Insurance Company also recruited women to replace enlisting males during the First World War. But the trend to female clerical employment predated the war and, moreover, ascended steadily throughout the 1911 to 1931 period. In 1911, women already held 41.8 per cent of all clerical jobs in the insurance firm, compared with only 8.6 per cent in the bank. The war pushed females into a majority position in insurance clerical jobs; by 1931 they occupied 64 per cent of these posts. These differences between the two firms, reflecting broader patterns in their respective quarters of the financial sector, are outlined in table 3.5 (also see tables A4–A6 in the Appendix). What stands out, in particular, is that while feminization in bank branches proceeded slowly, both the bank's and insurance firm's head offices had a majority of female clerks by the middle of the First World War. Organizational factors – notably size, division of labour, work content, functions and goals – obviously had some bearing on the type of employee recruited.

Table 3.5 Females as a percentage of the clerical staff, Bank of Nova Scotia (Ontario branches and head office) and Manufacturers Life Insurance Company, 1911–31

	1911	*1916*	*1921*	*1926*	*1931*
Bank of Nova Scotia (Ontario)	8.6%	40.7	36.0	27.5	30.4
Manufacturers Life Insurance Company	41.8%	58.4	52.2	52.3	55.2

Source: Calculated from tables A4 and A6 (see Appendix).

RECENT TRENDS IN CLERICAL EMPLOYMENT

So far I have traced the development of modern clerical occupations, highlighting the rapid feminization of these jobs which occurred after 1900, but especially between 1911 and 1931. There are strong historical continuities in these trends, as I will now show by examining clerical work during the 1971 to 1981 decade. The enormous magnitude of the clerical sector makes it the primary source of female employment in Canada today. Whether this remains the case, however, in the face of the micro-electronics revolution presently transforming the office is the subject of considerable controversy.[8]

Just how homogeneous is the clerical group of occupations today? This question is central to the debate, sparked by Braverman,[9] about the routinization of clerical jobs due to managerial rationalizations and the introduction of office technologies. Typically, the term 'clerk' is utilized in an all-encompassing manner, without regard to the specific functions performed. Yet according to the Standard Occupational Classification[10] scheme used in the Canadian census, the clerical workforce consists of individuals performing a wide range of office tasks: stenography and typing; bookkeeping and account recording; office machine and electronic data processing equipment operating; material recording, scheduling and distribution; library, filing and correspondence work; reception, information, mail and message distribution; as well as a residual category for 'other' clerical and related occupations. Turning to table 3.6, here I provide a detailed account of the relative importance of these specific clerical functions over the 1971 to 1981 period.

Table 3.6 confirms that clerks perform a diversity of office functions. In 1971, about 35 per cent of female clerks were secretaries or typists, underlining the continuing importance of this traditionally female job in the modern office. The second largest concentration (around 29 per cent) of women was in bookkeeping and account recording jobs. The remaining types of jobs employed considerably fewer women. Interestingly, only 4 per cent of all female clerks operated office machinery or electronic data processing equipment in 1971. Despite the rise of the 'automated office', this figure changed little in the subsequent decade. Concerning the sex ratio in each of these job categories, stenography and typing was almost exclusively female, while only one – material recording, scheduling and distribution – had less than a majority who were women. This one exception results from the location of these jobs in manufacturing industries, areas generally regarded as 'men's work'.

A number of noteworthy internal changes occurred in the clerical division of labour during the seventies. By 1981, the clerical group of occupations employed 34 per cent of all women who worked for wages –

Table 3.6 Growth of female clerical labour force, Canada, 1971–81

	1971			1981			Change 1971–81	
	Number	Women as % of all workers in occupation	% of all female clerks	Number	Women as % of all workers in occupation	% of all female clerks	Number	%
Total female labour force	3,053,095	34.6	—	5,000,270	40.8	—	1,947,175	63.8
All clerical occupations	940,180	68.4	100	1,702,515	77.7	100	762,334	81.1
(Clerical as % of total female labour force)	(30.8%)			(34.0%)				
Stenographic and typing	326,890	96.8	34.8	475,125	98.6	28.0	148,235	45.3
Bookkeeping, account recording	268,565	74.9	28.6	633,285	85.2	37.2	364,720	135.8
Office machine and EDP equipment operators	37,980	73.1	4.0	76,340	77.2	4.5	38,360	101.0
Material recording, scheduling and distribution	23,730	15.2	2.5	59,230	24.0	3.5	35,500	149.6
Library, file and correspondence clerks	28,830	80.8	3.1	43,725	85.0	2.6	14,895	51.7
Reception, information, mail and message distribution	99,190	64.2	10.6	169,925	72.0	10.0	70,735	71.3
Other clerical and related occupations*	154,990	55.6	16.5	244,870	73.7	14.4	89,880	58.0

* Mainly includes the following occupational categories: collectors; claim adjusters; travel clerks; ticket, station and freight agents; hotel clerks; general office clerks; supervisors in the preceding categories.
Source: 1981 Census of Canada, Population, 'Labour Force-Occupation Trends', vol. 1, National Series, catalogue 92–920, table 1.

up from 30.8 per cent a decade earlier. More specifically, there was a drop in the proportion of women in stenographic and typing jobs. Simultaneously, a sizeable jump occurred in the relative numbers employed as bookkeeping and account recording clerks. This now is the largest detailed clerical job, employing more than 37 per cent of all female clerks.

A summary of the major changes in female clerical employment is presented in the two right-hand columns of table 3.6. The first thing to note is that clerical occupations as a whole grew at a faster rate than the female labour force – 81.1 versus 63.8 per cent – over the 1971–81 decade. Regarding clerical tasks, the greatest increases were registered in material recording, scheduling and distribution (149.6 per cent); bookkeeping and account recording (135.8 per cent); and operators of mechanical and automated office equipment (101 per cent). In terms of absolute gains, the largest concentrations of new clerical positions were in bookkeeping and account recording, and stenography and typing. Despite the acceleration of office automation, the actual number of clerks working more or less full-time with machinery is not that substantial. It is quite likely, though, that many of the additional clerks employed keeping books and accounts probably use computers in more limited capacities. Significant, then, is the relatively small number of clerks who, in the words of C. Wright Mills are 'the most factory-like operatives in the white-collar world'. [11] Probably a good share of the work done by pool typists is defined by regimented and standardized conditions. But it seems that a minority of typists work in pool arrangements. The most likely pool jobs are those of typists and clerk-typist, which made up only 26.3 per cent of the entire stenographic and typing category in 1971, declining to 21.8 per cent by 1981.

The number of secretaries and stenographers rose from 1971 to 1981, enlarging their share of the stenographic and typing group from 72.9 to 77.2 per cent. Certainly many of these tasks are machine related. But it is also true that these clerks maintain some responsibility and variety in their work by performing other general office duties. Historically, stenography provided status and economic rewards on a par with the traditional female professions of nursing and teaching, as I document in later chapters. And as Rosabeth Moss Kanter's study of the corporate secretary reveals, rather than having their working conditions shaped by the typewriter, this small and fairly privileged group derives certain 'perks' through informal, particularistic relationships with their male bosses. [12] In short, the full impact of technology and scientific management is not felt in all quarters of the office. It is usually the case that typewriter-based clerical jobs are organized into a fixed hierarchy. On one hand, pool typists face factory-like conditions but, on the other hand, private secretaries are relatively advantaged compared with other female workers. Just how radically the skills and responsibilities found in secretarial work will be diminished through automation remains an open question.

OCCUPATIONAL SEX SEGREGATION AND CLERICAL JOB GHETTOS

It should now be evident that the labour force is structured, or 'segmented', along gender lines. This occupational sex segregation, whereby women have been clustered together in a small number of predominantly 'female' occupations, goes a long way toward explaining inequalities in rewards and opportunities. Clerical occupations are the prime example of what can be called a 'job ghetto'; that is, jobs with a high concentration of women and where relatively low wages, poor working conditions and limited advancement opportunities are the norm. Such jobs are traps, their very conditions creating a vicious circle. Poor wages and routine tasks tend to produce the kind of work patterns – high turnover, weak job commitment and limited aspirations – which reinforce employers' discriminatory attitudes and perpetuate the inequalities inherent in existing labour market structures.

There are essentially two types of job segregation.[13] Horizontal segregation refers to the concentration of men and women into different occupations – women are office clerks, while men are in skilled manual crafts. Vertical segregation is found within a single job category, employing both men and women, but where men hold the more interesting, responsible and remunerative positions. Female school teachers and male school principals are an example of vertical segregation.

There is abundant evidence of both types of sex segregation in Canada, especially with regard to clerical and office jobs. It is quite remarkable just how stable gender segregation has been over time. Since the early 1900s, clerical work has replaced domestic employment as the major female occupation. Recall that by 1981 fully 43 per cent of all employed women were clerks. Taking a broader perspective, one discovers that eight of the 21 occupations listed in the 1981 census employing over 1 per cent of the female workforce fell into the clerical category.[14] Stenographers and typists alone comprise 10.1 per cent of the total female workforce. The social definition of stenography and typing as exclusively 'female' is virtually complete, considering that women fill 98.7 per cent of such jobs.

Horizontal sex segregation has decreased somewhat over this century, yet the concentration of women into clerical occupations has steadily advanced. It is interesting to note, for example, that the fastest growing female occupation during the 1970s was that of electronic data processing equipment operator, the automated version of a traditional clerical job. Furthermore, there is already a discernible trend toward vertical segregation within 'high technology' office jobs. Women are assigned the routine tasks of preparing and entering ('keying') data, while men have staked out the higher status and more lucrative technical and professional jobs, such as programmer and data analyst.[15] In other words, the decades old sexual division of office labour is now being perpetuated in a new guise by automation.

A COMPARATIVE PERSPECTIVE

I am now in a position to examine Canadian clerical growth trends within the comparative context of other major capitalist societies. Of central importance is the relative uniqueness of Canadian trends, for this will tell us how representative they may be of developments in female clerical work elsewhere. Clerical employment is a main indicator of rising female labour force participation rates. Canada's female labour force participation rate is now over 55 per cent, similar to the United States and surpassed by only Sweden of all the major industrial countries. Clerical activities are essential in all capitalist societies, thus accounting for between 16 and 18 per cent of all employment by the early 1980s in Canada, the United States, Britain, Australia and West Germany.[16] And as in Canada, by far the vast majority of clerks in these other countries are female.[17]

A more focused examination of Britain and the United States reveals cross-national similarities in the historical development of clerical work. The rise of the modern office, and with it the rocketing demand for clerks, is most accurately interpreted as part of the industrialization process. Recall from chapter 2 that Canada was a 'late industrializer' with a colonial legacy of dependence on Britain and, increasingly after the First World War, integration into the American economic empire. Consequently, its transition to corporate capitalism lagged behind Britain and the United States. Yet proximity to the United States resulted in the early penetration of American multinational firms into the Canadian market. American management methods, administrative systems and organizational structures were imported through branch plants, as well as widely circulated management journals and professional management associations. However, when making these comparisons it is important to bear in mind that the massive flow of immigrants to Canada, the United States and other white settler states exerted a major impact on labour force developments. This important exogenous factor was absent in Britain and the rest of Europe, from where most of the new world immigrants came.

Turning first to Britain, clerks comprised less than 1 per cent of the total labour force in 1851. Their employment share gradually expanded to 4 per cent by the turn of the century, rising further to 16 per cent of all full-time workers by 1979.[18] There were only 15 women enumerated as clerks in the 1851 census. Two decades later there were 1,412 female 'commercial' clerks, pioneering what would soon become a major social trend.[19] By the turn of the century women occupied 18.1 per cent of all clerical jobs. This upward trend steadily accelerated, pushed by the jump in female employment during the two world wars. At the start of the 1950s, women finally comprised the majority of clerks. This watershed was reflected in the fact that, in 1951, clerical occupations had grown to encompass 20.4 per cent of women and 6.4 per cent of men in the labour force.[20] This pattern has endured: in 1984 these figures were 30 per cent and 7 per cent respectively.[21] As in Canada, the concentration of women varies according to specific clerical jobs, with sex-typing being most pronounced in the typing, shorthand and secretarial category (about 99 per cent female).[22]

Shifting our attention to America, the first women entered offices during the Civil War in the 1860s.[23] Clerical occupations registered a staggering growth rate, due mainly to rapid business expansion toward the end of the nineteenth century. More specifically, clerical occupations grew by 784 per cent between 1870 and 1900, out of all proportion to the 125 per cent rate for the labour force.[24] The greatest surge in female recruitment was between 1880-90, with a ten-fold increase from 7,000 to 76,000 (or 5 per cent to 18 per cent of the clerical labour force).[25] Stenography and typing, in particular, quickly became defined as appropriate women's employment. Women comprised 40 per cent of this group in the early days of the typewriter around 1880. Yet by 1930 stenography and typing jobs were almost exclusively (that is, 95 per cent) female. By contrast, at that time women made up half of all bookkeepers, cashiers and accountants and only 35 per cent of 'general' clerks.[26] Feminization occurred earlier and more rapidly in the United States than in either Canada or Britain, given that females held 30.2 per cent of all clerical jobs at the turn of the century and 52.5 per cent in 1930.[27] In the early 1980s there were almost 20 million clerical workers in America, 80 per cent of whom were women.[28]

Overall, the basic contours of clerical growth and feminization are similar in Canada, Britain and the United States. It was the social and economic forces of capitalist development that made the office and its clerks a central feature of twentieth-century corporate and state bureaucracies. Such changes were hardly unique to Canada. The comparative data I have presented document, however, important national variations in the emergence of a modern clerical workforce. Clerical occupations in the United States employed a larger share of the labour force, and proportionally more women, by 1930. By then over 52 per cent of clerks were women; in Canada and Britain women came to hold a majority of clerical jobs in 1941 and 1951 respectively. Furthermore, the rapid expansion of US and British offices and the shift in female labour had been launched by the end of the nineteenth century, even earlier in the United States. Not until the First World War era did a similar phenomenon occur in Canada.

These differences aside, the outstanding feature of the transformation in clerical work was the dramatic movement from an all-male to a predominantly female labour force. Yet surprisingly little attention has been directed at the origins and development of the clerical feminization process which, as all of us can see, has left an indelible mark on the contemporary office. In the next chapter I take up this issue, using three case studies to illuminate the conditions underlying the initial recruitment of women into the office.

4

Clerical Feminization in Banks
The Civil Service and Stenography,
1900–30

This chapter provides a detailed analysis of the conditions under which clerical work became feminized. I am primarily interested in why employers began hiring increasing numbers of women for specific clerical jobs after 1900. To illuminate how this happened in the office, I will probe the interplay between the sex labelling process, at an ideological level, and the erecting of structural barriers in work organizations and the labour market which restrict female employment. The general pervasiveness of the female takeover of the clerical sector tends to mask equally interesting variations among major white-collar employers. That feminization did not progress in a steady and uniform way is already well established. I therefore will concentrate below on some of the situational factors behind these inter-organizational differences. At all stages in the feminization of an office, female stereotypes and gender role ideologies are influential. Indeed, patriarchal values are very much double-edged. Used to exclude women from the office until the late nineteenth century, the same general beliefs about women's qualities and their appropriate role in society were conveniently rephrased into justifications for their ghettoization in designated office jobs.

This chapter will focus on the transitional period, marked at either end by the dawning of the twentieth century and the onset of the depression in 1930, when the sex ratio in clerical work tilted permanently toward women. My intention is theoretically to integrate the most useful concepts identified in chapter 1 into a coherent analysis of the origins and development of feminization. Specifically, labour market segmentation theory will provide insights regarding the unequal structuring of the office work force; the concept of patriarchy will cast our attention on the crucial role of gender relations and supporting ideologies in the society; and the notion of sex labelling will explain how newly created routine clerical tasks came to be defined as women's work. The three case studies presented – a bank, the civil service, and the occupation of stenography –

underscore the continual interplay between the workplace and society and, equally crucial, between corporate capitalism and patriarchy. These case studies document how employers utilized nineteenth-century gender ideologies to exclude women from offices initially. Then in response to fundamental changes in administration, particularly a more complicated and specialized division of clerical labour, management invoked the early twentieth-century versions of these ideologies to justify hiring women into this new clerical substratum. I also will show how the actual timing and rate of feminization was influenced by differing combinations of economic, organizational and ideological factors.

WOMEN ENTER BANKING

Canadian women began making their presence felt in business offices during the 1880s. Jean Scott was thus prompted to write in 1889 that 'it is in office work more particularly that women of late years have displaced men.'[1] Old attitudes were also showing signs of adapting to women's emerging role in administration, for as Scott went on to observe, 'women seem as fitted [sic] for this work as men, and have proved as competent where the work was not too severe.'[2] Some basic prerequisites for women's entry into office work were present by 1890. Women were becoming more available for employment outside the home for relatively cheap wages. And within the office, changing skill requirements could be met by a high school education, increasingly attained by women, rather than through a traditional apprenticeship. Yet the tide was slow to turn; women consequently were not found in many offices until the new century.

The financial sector was a major employer of female clerks by 1930. Between 1901 and 1931 women's share of clerical jobs in finance shot from 0.8 per cent to 49.6 per cent, but this trend was far from uniform. I have already sketched the contrasting feminization patterns in banking and insurance. Sun Life, Canada's leading life insurance company, appointed its first female clerk in 1894; by 1911 many departments had 'an army of typewriters', in addition to a central typing pool, all operated by women.[3] But for a variety of reasons, mainly related to the organization and nature of the business, banks were rather reluctant to allow women into their staff fold. Indeed, it was the shortage of suitable male employees during the First World War, coupled with a rapidly expanding demand for banking services, that ultimately paved the way for the now ubiquitous female bank clerk.

Severe labour force disruptions during both world wars directly influenced the sex ratio of many occupations. Some scholars have argued that, far from transforming the economic role of Canadian women, the First World War merely created a temporary influx of women into the world of men's work.[4] At a very general level this view may be accurate, particularly with respect to manual work, but it plays down the importance of the war for clerical occupations. In many offices, the war served as a catalyst that triggered lasting shifts in the balance of the sexes.[5] The more enduring effects of the war on clerical occupations can be explained by the fact that shortages of male clerks developed at a time when rapid growth and major structural readjustments were occurring in offices. Office bureaucracies grew large and complex in response to the administrative demands of corporate capitalism. Efficiency and control were emerging as the guiding principles of management, and clerical tasks were rationalized to achieve these ends. The war provided opportunities for women to establish themselves as the most economical labour supply for these new routine clerical tasks. Many big employers responded to the prospects of lower salary overheads, and a more easily regulated workforce, by altering their clerical recruitment strategies.

The impact of the First World War on clerical employment opportunities for women was not even across all industries. In Montreal, for example, munitions plants hired numerous female clerks to help administer war production as well as regular business.[6] On the other hand, Montreal's post offices employed mainly female clerks in 1914 and the war brought about little change.[7] For the Manufacturers Life Insurance Company the war merely tilted the balance in favour of women, something which probably would have happened anyway. In banking, however, the war precipitated fundamental changes. Banks traditionally considered the ideal clerk to be a young 'gentleman' from a solid middle class background. When Canadians of this description were scarce, the banks recruited in England and Scotland. But acute shortages of male bank clerks during the war forced a reconsideration of tradition-bound staffing policies. The proportion of female clerks in the Bank of Nova Scotia's Ontario region leaped from 8.6 per cent in 1911 to 40.7 per cent in 1916. The war had shattered old hiring restrictions. Even with post-war readjustments, women still held over 30 per cent of these positions by 1931. Underlying the pattern of feminization in banking is the issue of social class. Simply put, bankers preferred to hire a middle-class female than an educated working-class male. The ideal junior clerk was one who had social respectability in the community, could be implicitly trusted with other people's money and had the qualities that, one day, could make him a senior bank executive. This highly individualistic employment philosophy was redolent with middle-class values. The inherent class ideology was so pervasive that eventually it cut across sex lines, drawing in young women from 'good' backgrounds.

Bankers' conservative attitudes towards the employment of female clerks were reflected in employment practices. But such practices were to undergo dramatic changes, as wartime labour shortages combined with an increasingly complex administrative division of labour to incorporate women into the clerical labour supply. Women were a rarity in turn-of-the-century banks. One of the largest Canadian banks employed only five women in 1901.[8] A major stumbling block was the entrenched belief that only male clerks and tellers could create the public confidence necessary for a successful branch operation. One branch manager, when faced with his first female employee in 1901, 'discussed with the head office in all seriousness the availability of having a screen – a good high one, too – placed around her to shut her off completely from the observation of the public.'[9] A *Monetary Times* editorialist proclaimed in 1907 that women in banking will remain a controversial issue, although he allowed that they may have a useful contribution to make.[10] After all, he pointed out, do not women handle the family finances? It appears that US banks may have had a more liberal stance regarding female employment. The mobility of women into positions of 'cashier or higher' south of the border offered role models for business-minded Canadian women.[11]

Prior to the war women tended to fill stenographic and secretarial positions, which by then was socially acceptable even within the banks, and menial head office jobs involving no public contact. One bank, for example, employed 350 female stenographers and 273 female general clerks in 1916, yet only seven women held teller positions in branches. But rapidly increasing male enlistments left banks seriously understaffed by the end of 1916. The *Journal of the Canadian Bankers' Association* wrote in an editorial that with the 'invasion of banking affairs by women . . . the question as to whether [they] are to gain a foothold in banks is past the state of discussion.'[12] As the war effort escalated, banks had little choice but to deploy females in the branches. Table 4.1 documents that 9,069 male bank clerks had enlisted by early 1919.[13] This figure represented 40 per cent of total Canadian bank staff, and at the same time women were performing 37 per cent of these jobs. Vacancies thus existed in all clerical positions, not to mention the many new jobs created by expansion. The sudden diffusion of females throughout the clerical hierarchy is described by one women who herself took advantage of these opportunities:

> The posts open to women in a bank are, of course, both stenographic and clerical, and on the former it is unnecessary to touch. In the head offices until quite recently the proportion of clerical openings was small, but it is rapidly increasing and affording, as the business of each bank expands, in the way of special openings calling for special ability. In addition to the ordinary run of clerical positions, women have been employed for the past few years in the branches of at least some of our leading banks in collection departments and on the ledgers; yes, on the ledgers . . . Since the outbreak of the war, women have been filling

Table 4.1 Female employment and male enlistments in Canadian banks, February 1919

Bank	Whole bank				Toronto		
	Total staff	Total women	Stenographers	Total enlistments	Total staff	Total women	Stenographers
Commerce	3,520	1,400	400	1,704	555	215	60
Montreal	2,200	1,200	200	687	260	150	30
Nova Scotia	1,304	516	90	612	236	112	28
British North America	750	269	50	300	46	22	2
Toronto	850	300	70	400	210	75	20
Molsons	725	200	50	250	60	25	10
Nationale	600	15	3	45	—	—	—
Merchants	1,500	500	125	750	54	15	3
Provinciale	380	20	4	25	—	—	—
Union	1,700	650	—	850	100	36	11
Royal/Northern Crown	3,800	1,700	450	1,150/220	275	130	40
Dominion	900	266	71	436	350	109	28
Hamilton	750	250	50	310	80	35	15
Standard	826	316	68	228	214	76	20
Hochelaga	800	100	20	100	—	—	—
Ottawa	575	165	40	288	32	7	1
Imperial	1,035	439	80	518	267	129	37
Home	267	109	15	111	92	42	9
Sterling	237	101	11	70	70	36	6
Weyburn	70	15	4	15	—	—	—
Totals	22,757	8,521	1,801	9,069	2,921	1,214	320

Source: Bank of Nova Scotia Archives, Canadian Bankers' Association Correspondence, File 42, Citizen's Repatriation League. 'Digest of Information Furnished by Banks to the Association's Representatives in the Business Council of the Citizen's Repatriation League, February 1919'.

positions both as clerks and as heads of departments which were formerly held by men . . . In fact, the only two posts which are not at present occupied by women in a greater or lesser proportion are those of accountant and manager.[14]

Bank managements reluctantly adjusted both their attitudes and hiring practices to the realities of the wartime labour market. In 1916, Bank of Nova Scotia branch managers were officially directed, for the first time, to replace enlisted male clerks with women. Head office officials soon complained, however, that 'most of our managers have made little or no effort to secure assistance from that [women] or any other source', urging the managers 'to endeavour to get young women who have some knowledge of bookkeeping or office work.'[15] Senior officials recognized that the scarcity of male clerks would likely continue. This situation made bankers face the possibility of placing women into previously male dominated jobs: 'We might just as well realize at once that the services of young women will have to be utilized for ledger-keepers, and at the smaller branches for tellers, so that attention should be paid to their training with this kind of service in mind.'[16] Yet many managers were unwaivering in their conviction that the male clerk was essential for their business. When the federal government imposed conscription in the fall of 1917, the banks unsuccessfully attempted to exempt their male clerks on the grounds that these employees possessed special qualifications and performed a vital role in the economy.[17]

Bankers began to acknowledge the merits of female clerks, tempered by the understanding that after the war most would return to their natural callings of homemaking and motherhood. The economic necessities of the war clashed with the traditional social norms governing female conduct. This created a dilemma for women. Many of the recently hired female clerks in banking and other industries proclaimed their intention to remain employed 'not merely as the assistants of men but as their equals in service and remuneration'.[18] Yet numerous other women demured in the face of this challenge, thus fulfilling the prophesy of one female supervisor in a large bank that, 'with the return of peace scores of girls will joyfully lay down their pens and return to their homes.'[19]

The immediate post-war boom carried wartime feminization into the twenties. The *Monetary Times* reported in 1919 that 'Canadian banks are busier than ever before, and by their policy of opening many new branches at the present time they are able to absorb their returning employees and still retain some of the temporary [female] help.'[20] The expansion of bank hierarchies pushed numerous former male clerks into supervisory positions. The recession in the early twenties resulted in many branch closures, and curbed the hiring of both men and women for a time. Some women competently performing as tellers or ledgerkeepers were kept on, as were the typists, stenographers, and machine operators whose jobs had acquired a female label. A few banks even had set up women's departments after the war. The female managers of one such department emphasized that women would only succeed in banking by 'playing a woman's part'. She went on to argue that women improved the work atmosphere, had intuition in credit matters, were good with female clients and had sound judgement – all assets for bank employers.[21] Women had become institutionalized as a secondary labour market for specified clerical jobs. When the economy picked up later in the twenties, banks therefore recruited women instead of men to fill these positions.

Changes in the clerical labour process, especially in large branches and head offices, tended to undermine the intent of the banks' time-tested recruitment and training procedures. Curiously, bankers actually considered male juniors cheaper to hire than women. As the *Monetary Times* explained:

> women do not cultivate 'mobility' which is such a characteristic part of Canadian banking. Again, they are not suitable for very small branches, where the employees act to a certain degree as protectors. Moreover, they do not respond to opportunities for promotion as readily as men, who are in the business as a life work. They have not so large a capacity for work as the average male, and consequently more clerks are necessary.[22]

The emphasis here on career development is important to note. It appears that when an organization has an internal career ladder that extends from the bottom to the top of its occupational hierarchy, the short-term economic advantages of hiring cheaper females – who until very recently have been deemed unsuitable for banking careers by the male establishment – is considerably diminished.

According to this view men were an investment because they ultimately contributed more to the bank by working their way up to responsible positions.[23] However, growing functional specialization and work rationalization during the twenties increased the number of dead-end, routine clerical jobs. The general clerkships, which had previously provided a training ground for aspiring males, shrunk in number. The modernization of administrative structures created a 'good deal of discontent among the younger men who . . . enter the banking service at low salaries with the expectation of rising to more responsible and highly paid positions'.[24] Managers therefore began to rely more on females to fill the lowest clerical levels, placing male recruits in career-path positions. A two-tiered internal labour market was thereby created: a tightly circumscribed one for women in non-supervisory clerical jobs, and a career track that groomed men for managerial positions.

The segmentation of the banks' clerical labour supply into male and female components was facilitated by discriminatory job requirements. Justifications for this sex-typing of specific jobs were made on the following ideological grounds:

Woman has manifestly been designed by nature as a complement, not as a substitute for man. If society has put her under certain political disabilities, her creator has put her under certain physical disabilities. Even independently of the curse of Eve, the average woman cannot calculate on her ability to work continuously with as well-grounded confidence as the average man, while in bodily strength she cannot compare with him. On the other hand, she excels him in delicacy of touch, in lightness of step, in softness of voice.[25]

This type of attitude condoned occupational and wage discrimination against women as they moved into the office. Women were expected to have certain inherent disadvantages, preventing them from pursuing male occupations. Yet, on the other hand, they were endowed with those typically feminine qualities considered useful in a small range of subordinate occupations. In this way patriarchal values reinforced the discriminatory work arrangements that became the basis for office work.

The unequal gender division of labour has been long based on the assumption that women are inferior to men. Initially this limited women's sphere of activity to the home and enforced their economic dependence on men. Jean Scott observed in the late nineteenth century that 'married women in Canada do not seem to go out to work as long as their husbands are able to support them.'[26] Strong social sanctions prohibited the employment of married women, so that in the early twentieth century approximately 90 per cent of the women in the Canadian labour force were single.[27] Women tended to internalize these prevailing norms. According to a 1930 article on women in business, because women saw their jobs 'merely as a fill-in before marriage', their 'business efficiency' was diminished.[28]

Women thus became trapped in a vicious circle. Prejudicial employment rules and traditional family values helped lay the groundwork for the sex labelling of many new office jobs. The jobs defined as suitable for women were more often than not monotonous, dead-end and unrewarding. Male assumptions underlying occupational discrimination – a woman's weak labour force attachment and lack of career aspirations, her primary role of homemaker and mother, and the equating of criteria for business success with male traits – turned into self-fulfilling prophesies. Women reacted to their relatively disadvantaged working conditions by limited work commitment and high leaving rates, thus providing supporting evidence for the negative stereotypes which initially helped to channel them into routine and constraining jobs. Ironically, women seeking employment in the early twentieth century usually were somewhat better educated than men. This was an added bonus for employers. But how was the discrepancy between women's lowly occupational status and often superior education rationalized? Part of the answer is found in the ideology surrounding women's social roles.

The 'cult of domesticity' required that women, as the transmitters of culture to children, should have an adequate stock of knowledge.[29] The growing number of women entering the secondary clerical labour market had to balance the demands of the world of work with those of home and family. Encouraged to gain specialized clerical skills by enrolling in one of the numerous business colleges, yet all the while knowing her destiny was in 'the happy seclusion of a home',[30] the young women in the 1920s faced a basic quandry. Mary Vipond explains: 'They were encouraged to gain a good education and to find a stimulating career, but then to turn their attention solely to housework, husband and children when they married. They were encouraged to be independent and self-sufficient before marriage, but warned that in order to find and keep a husband they must become docile clinging vines.'[31]

Expectations of finding a 'stimulating career' were shattered for most employed women by the harsh realities of the unrewarding office jobs in banks and elsewhere they held for a few years prior to marriage.

THIRD DIVISION CIVIL SERVANTS

The treatment of women in the Canadian federal civil service is one of the more blatant examples available of how some major employers used sophisticated bureaucratic measures to corral women into the lowest occupational grades. Beginning in the late nineteenth century, the flow of women into the lower ranks of the Ottawa 'inside service' steadily mounted, mainly for two reasons. First, there was the attraction of relatively high government salaries that accounted for rising female applications. Second, the introduction of entrance examinations in 1908 shifted the basis for appointments away from patronage toward individual merit. The result, as one expert on the Ottawa bureaucracy concluded, was that 'when opportunities were made available, as in the Ottawa civil service, women flooded in.'[32] This strongly suggests that the low rate of female labour force participation in the early twentieth century was more a function of meagre employment opportunities than a lack of interest among women in working. The Civil Service Commission, however, viewed the feminization trend with trepidation and was determined to control it carefully.

Women initially entered the civil service in response to a general demand for clerical labour. The Commission therefore resorted to rules, regulations and legislation to create separate male and female clerical streams, largely by confining the demand for female labour to specific tasks. There is no question that the inequality of opportunity built into the civil service bureaucracy in the early twentieth century created a cheap female labour reserve for the lowest clerical jobs.[33] The federal civil service is presently the largest employer of women in the country, most of them clerks. Going back in time, we discover that in 1868 only one woman was in its employ – a housekeeper.[34] By the early 1880s, there was a handful of female civil servants working in 'very subordinate positions.'[35] Yet even the bottom clerical ranks, considered stepping stones to a civil service career, were reserved for men. The very idea of a female clerk perplexed the Civil Service Commissioner, as his 1881 report attests:

> Whilst we see no reason whatever why female clerks should not be quite as efficient public servants as men, we are forced to confess that there are several obstacles in the way of their employment which we fear it will be very difficult if not impossible to overcome. For example, it would be necessary that they should be placed in rooms by themselves, and that they should be under the immediate supervision of a person of their own sex; but we doubt very much if sufficient work of similar character can be found in any one Department to furnish occupation for any considerable number of female clerks, and it would certainly be inadvisable to place them in small numbers throughout the Departments.[36]

While in 1885 there were fewer than 20 female clerks in all departments,[37] by 1891 women had been accepted as a permanent part of the service, albeit in minor positions. In fact, officials even agreed that they were as efficient as male clerks.[38] Estimates in 1908 placed the number of women among the 3,000 inside staff at 700.[39] This prompted a contemporary observer to assert that 'this army of clerks have [sic] come to stay.'[40] The Civil Service Commission envisioned an unmitigated disaster if this invasion of women continued. All-female departments, it was feared, would create administrative chaos and inefficiency. More- over, the preponderance of women in the lower echelons of the service (the training grounds for male bureaucrats) produced a scarcity of potential management talent. The Commission's solution to the trouble- some 'women problem' was simple and direct: regulate their numbers and restrict them to only certain routine clerical jobs.

The Commission moved in 1910 to limit appointments in the first and second divisions to men. This left only the third, and lowest, division open to women. Further restrictions, aimed at preventing a female monopoly, were introduced within the third division by a strategy of sex labelling. This is plainly revealed in the Civil Service Commission's 1910 report:

> The following are some of the reasons which render it inexpedient for women to be employed in certain branches of the Service, even in the Third Division. In the first place, there is certain work incidental to clerical duties, as in the handling of large registers, carrying of files and books up and down ladders, etc., which on physical grounds is not suitable for women. There are other positions in which, from time to time, the clerk may be called upon to travel considerable distances from Ottawa, alone or in the capacity as secretary or assistant. For obvious reasons, male clerks are required in positions involving such duties. There are, in addition, many special features connected with the work or location of individual offices which render the employment of women, to a large extent, impracticable.[41]

The new rules required women who passed the qualifying exam for the second division to take a position in the third. And temporary clerks had to pass typing and stenography tests, skills rare among males. Furthermore, occupational segmentation was advanced by allowing department heads to designate jobs 'male' or 'female' for recruitment purposes. Women therefore became stenographers and typists; men became general clerks.[42] These measures had the desired effects, although the Commission did not consider the problem of women's employment solved satisfactorily until two additional changes had been made. First, the 1918 Civil Service Act empowered the Civil Service Commission to limit job competitions on the basis of sex.[43] Second, in 1921 married women were barred from permanent posts with exemptions permitted only for those who were self-supporting or if other suitable candidates were unavailable.[44] Married women already in the service were forced to resign and reapply as temporary workers at reduced salaries.

Through its sex labelling practices, the government created a stable supply of clerks which it could tap as needed. Restrictions on hiring women gave rise to a caste-like system of employment under which the female civil servant had an officially defined inferior status. Inevitably these women came to expect only a few years of employment, no advancement opportunities, and lower salaries than men. The unequal structuring of job opportunities had the effect of marginalizing women, relegating them to a secondary labour market. This tenuous status sometimes had rather severe ramifications: 'When jobs became scarce, women, especially married women, were treated as a marginal group with less right to employment than men.'[45] The experience of the female civil service clerk supports my contention that the effects of sex labelling are self-perpetuating. Kathleen Archibald's contemporary study of the civil service concludes on this very point: 'If this were merely a matter of past history, it would be of interest only to historians. But these early discriminatory policies were a resounding and still redounding success; they accomplished their purposes so well that their effects are still in today's employment structure.'[46]

THE CASE OF STENOGRAPHY

The story of the female civil service clerk starkly portrays how some major white-collar employers devised bureaucratic ways of channelling the demand for clerical labour into separate male and female compartments. Straining under the weight of voluminous paper work and aware of an abundant supply of suitable female workers, Ottawa officials constructed tight civil service entry and promotion procedures so that women were routed into the lowest status positions. Faced with this official form of discrimination, women had little recourse but to adapt. So they entered government offices as typists or routine clerks. This sort of segregation preserved certain entry-level clerical jobs as training grounds for males, thereby keeping open their mobility channels. At the same time, there was a mounting burden of administrative details that could be performed by women at reduced cost. This neatly avoided any direct competition between females eager for respectable government jobs, and young men seeking a good training ground to launch their careers.

The occupation of stenography presents a rather different path to feminization. During the very early stages of the typewriter's evolution, women gained an accepted place in this occupation. Strictly speaking, stenography and typing jobs were not feminized; almost from their inception they were defined as women's work. What distinguishes stenography from other clerical tasks in the late nineteenth and early twentieth centuries is new technology. Technological change is a driving force in the division of labour, casting old jobs into obsolescence and forging new ones in their place. Save perhaps the male copyists, who used pen and ink in the tedious chore of transcribing correspondence, there was no antecedent to the typewriter. As a brand new technology it was more or less gender neutral. For a variety of reasons related mainly to the growing supply of educated, middle-class young women and ideas about feminity which lent themselves to the task of typing, women quickly became entrenched.

Even while the typewriter was evolving technically into a piece of essential office equipment, women had established a beach-head. Only in the last decade of the nineteenth century, at least 15 years after its origin, did modifications which allowed typists to actually see their work transform a rather cumbersome invention into a practical business device. But speculation of imminent changes in the office was already evident in the business community. The *Montreal Daily Witness* heralded, as early as 1879, a 'new industry' based on typewriting. The newspaper warned that male copyists and shorthand writers 'have formidable rivals in the girls who can use the new typewriter machine for they charge six cents a hundred words for their work and can produce it much more rapidly than the swiftist penman'.[47] Still in its infancy, the occupation received an early boost through special courses to train women in typewriting skills. One of the first of these in North America was launched in 1881 by the New York City YMCA for 'genteel young ladies'.[48] Because stenography required training beyond the standard secondary school curriculum at the time and, moreover, lacked obvious status or economic advantages, male clerks did not perceive it as very attractive.

Female stenographers were often pioneers, clearing a path for more women in future to enter offices. For instance, in 1898 the Manufacturers Life Insurance Company employed two female clerks, both stenographers.[49] By the turn of the century lingering doubts over women's expertise at operating typewriters had been laid to rest. To be sure, 80 per cent of all stenographers and typists in Canada were then women. Virtually all new recruits into stenography and typing were women, so that by 1931 about 95 per cent of such jobs were held by women. Stenography was cast into a female mould during its formative stage. Two implications followed from this. First, rarely did female stenographers or typists displace men already in a clerical job. And second, this early dominance was virtually guaranteed. With the march of technology picking up pace in offices after 1900, it would be women, not men, who were hired to operate these machines.

The sex labelling of stenography is a fascinating example of how the changing economic role of women was complemented by some very traditional notions of feminity. The office environment was clean and safe and the job of typing not too arduous physically. But perhaps it was the development of stenography outside the mainstream of male clerical occupations that made it so accessible to women. Victorian ideals of feminity were invoked to allay concerns about this new job disrupting the status quo of home and family. One Ontario business college, keen to recruit young women into its courses, took the following approach in its 1892 catalogue: 'as stenographers and typists [women] have special qualifications in neatness, taste, deftness of action and quickness of perception and there is no line of industry to which they are better adapted . . . possessing nimble fingers, nervous and delicate organs and being quick to hear, think and comprehend.'[50] It is not entirely clear just what women's 'nervous and delicate organs' contribute to their competence as stenographers. Yet comments such as this lay bare the duplicity of turn-of-the-century morality: the same line could be thrown up in opposition to women's employment outside the home.

Less ambiguous is the use of moral rhetoric to assuage male anxieties that women would pose a competitive threat in the clerical labour market. Ideology was a necessary accompaniment to the structural segmentation of the office workforce. North America's leading exponent of scientific office management, William Leffingwell, deftly intertwines female personal attributes with the objective characteristics of routine clerical jobs:

> a woman is to be preferred for the secretarial position, for she is not averse to doing minor tasks, work involving the handling of petty details, which would irk and irritate ambitious young men, who usually feel that the work they are doing is of no importance if it can be performed by some person with a lower salary. Most such men are also anxious to get ahead and to be promoted from position to position, and consequently if there is much work of a detail [sic] character to be done, and they are expected to perform it, they will not remain satisfied and will probably seek a position elsewhere. Women, on the other hand, while by no means unambitious, are tempermentally more reconciled to such detailed work, and do not seem to judge it from a similar standpoint.[51]

Leffingwell's message is that by nature women are only suited to subordinate office jobs, leaving the more onerous tasks of management to men. But women of the early twentieth century operated within the realm of what they perceived as possible. While no doubt some were dissatisfied with their subservient role, for most women it is likely that the comparatively high status and salaries of clerical jobs ameliorated the situation. Status and pay must have been an inducement to the ready supply of female clerks and stenographers. I shall document in chapter 7 that, with the exception of professions such as teaching, educated young women from respectable families would have been hard pressed to do as well outside the office.

Stenography raises deeper questions regarding the way in which gender ideologies, technology and industrial changes converged to draw women so quickly and completely into particular office jobs. Untangling the complex web of causes and effects is a daunting task. From a more speculative angle, it appears that the spread of typewriters relied on an emerging supply of educated young women whose employment in stenography jobs did not violate social norms. Initial demand fuelled supply and over time public beliefs were recast as rationalizations for women's expanded economic role. As more women entered stenography, the labelling process brought a stronger articulation of its essentially feminine nature. This had the effect of reinforcing women's position in the occupation, present and future. A few male copy clerks may have been temporarily dislocated as a result. Generally, though, the absence of a direct threat to male prerogatives in the office removed the potential barrier of male opposition. And the steady march of office modernization after the turn of the century went hand in hand with mechanization. The typewriter was a fundamental aspect of the administrative revolution, as was the telephone. Thus as employers deployed a growing battery of office machines, they did so by hiring more women.

In brief, the ideological underpinnings of female employment in stenography and other typing-related jobs existed prior to the invention of the typewriter. Technological and economic changes merely incorporated them to great advantage. Once typewriting was commonly viewed as a female task, other office machinery was easily placed in the same camp. This was especially apparent when mechanization made great strides during the 1920s, as the *Monetary Times* explains:

> For one reason girls are better than boys when it comes to operating the machines, which today are used in increasing numbers in offices. It is safe to say that the demand for women clerks for these machines will continue to grow, as by the use of machines it is possible to put through a greater volume of work with greater accuracy and clearer records than ever before. Some of the newer systems for the handling of details depend for their success on typing and listing machines of recent invention, and these machines are more satisfactorily operated by girls than men.'[52]

The boom in private business colleges teaching stenography, in addition to commercial courses in secondary schools, equipped most female clerks with typing skills.[53] Stenography, secretarial and typing jobs constituted a variegated labour market. The federal government's monthly *Labour Gazette* appointed the first of its female correspondents in 1913. Their reports trace the undulations of supply and demand in stenography and related fields. As one 1914 report observed, 'the demand for stenographers is an index as to business conditions in general.'[54] Demand certainly fluctuated from city to city. More importantly, however, skill, experience and educational differences internally stratified the market. The conclusion presented by the Report of Ontario's 1916 Commission on Unemployment, that 'a girl can earn a good salary in stenography with a comparatively short period of training

and little experience',[55] was therefore inaccurate. The *Labour Gazette*
usually reported bright prospects for 'better' or 'first class' stenographers.
But those fitting the Royal Commission's image faced difficulties in
finding employment, even during the First World War.[56] Some firms,
such as banks, would only hire 'first class' stenographers in the war.
When demand was strong, 'medium or second class stenographers' could
readily find positions.[57] There was always a subsidiary market for
temporary or substitute stenographers, but these placements typically
went to experienced workers. The pre-war recession carried over well
into 1915, resulting in a 25 per cent unemployment rate for stenographers in
Toronto.[58] Yet even when serious labour shortages developed the next
year, poorly trained and inexperienced young women still had trouble
finding work.

Two unique features of the stenography labour market were the pre-
entry training provided in commercial business schools and the role of
private employment agencies in the job placement process. In 1916,
Toronto had 28 private schools and business colleges teaching stenography.[59] Running two sessions annually, they turned out 2,000
stenographers. But many of the graduates were described as 'half-trained
young girls', suggesting that employers felt these workers lacked a good
general education and, as teenagers, were too inexperienced to enter the
business world.[60] The oversupply of certain kinds of typists and
stenographers, at various times during the 1910s and 1920s, prompted
employment agencies to inject some order into the market. The
typewriter companies had a vested interest in not only marketing
machines, but also the women who could effectively operate them. The
Ontario Commission on Unemployment observed that, 'the employment
agencies maintained by the typewriter companies have standardized this
employment as perhaps no other women's employment has been
standardized.'[61]

Business colleges and employment agencies helped to create a large
female secondary labour market. But closer examination of the skill levels
and changing working conditions of these women reveals interesting
variations. Most offices today have a definite clerical hierarchy, graded
according to pay, status, task content and working conditions. At the
bottom is the lowly file clerk, at the top is the executive secretary.
Historical evidence assembled by Lynne Marks suggests, however, that
actual task responsibilities implied by job titles were often blurred. For
example, in the early part of the century fewer than 20 per cent of women
'stenographers' performed only stenographic work in the Bank of Nova
Scotia.[62] These full-time stenographers were employed in large city
branches and head office. In smaller branches stenographers performed a
range of clerical duties, some fairly routine. Marks also argues that some
of the most desirable positions, such as private secretary, were reserved

for the small body of male stenographers. For these men, stenography offered a launching pad for their business careers, but such was not the case for women. In the Bank of Nova Scotia, fewer than 10 per cent of female stenographers experienced any upward mobility into clerical supervisory positions or higher.[63] We should recognize, though, that even in the boom period of 1911–1921, the typical stenographer worked only six or seven years before withdrawing from the labour force to marry.[64]

The First World War era unleashed some potent rationalizations in the office. One of these directly affecting stenographers was the subdivision and standardization of their jobs. Managers tried to boost clerical productivity in numerous ways. One common method was to eliminate personal dictation by introducing electric dictating machines. Centralized typing pools sprung up, with the result that productivity could be readily monitored, costs cut, and the number of stenographers reduced. Here is how the stenographers in one insurance company reacted to this degradation of their work:

> most stenographers who had seen or heard of transcribing machines were very much prejudiced against them, and the belief was almost generally entertained that the machine would ultimately force all stenographers to abandon their careers in favour of the much lower priced transcribing machine operators. It was, therefore, often impossible to secure first grade stenographers who were willing to spend a part of their time on machine transcription. There was also a natural prejudice on the part of stenographers against working in a Stenographic Department as compared with the more intimate contacts surrounding positions where they were required to take the work of only one or two dictators.[65]

The tempo of office mechanization and rationalization accelerated during the twenties. Standardized salary scales, job classifications and rigid lines of authority became the order of the day for efficiency-conscious office managers. These changes in the work process further entrenched gender divisions. Because women were concentrated almost solely in the rapidly expanding bottom layers of routine administration, they were often the first employees to bear the brunt of rationalization measures. These changes by no means rendered stenography devoid of skill; indeed, the personal secretary and experienced stenographer still hold relatively challenging and advantaged positions, compared with women in typing pools. A sign of the early division of stenographic labour can be found in the Ontario civil service. In 1920, there were three separate classes of secretaries and, just underneath, three for stenographers, all with carefully specified pay and status.[66] But it was

Figure 4.1 Job classification and salary scheme for female employees, Sun Life Insurance Company, 1929
(Reprinted courtesy of Sun Life)

THE FOLLOWING BASIS HAS BEEN ADOPTED FOR THE REMUNERATION OF FEMALE EMPLOYEES:

PROBATIONERS The commencing salary of employees without previous business experience, aged 18 to 20 years, shall be $600 per annum, increasing for satisfactory services at the end of three months to $660 per annum and at the end of six months to $720 per annum.

UPON APPOINTMENT TO THE PERMANENT STAFF, EMPLOYEES SHALL BE CLASSIFIED UNDER ONE OF THE FOLLOWING GRADES:

JUNIOR GRADE The junior grade shall consist of employees who can perform simple mechanical or clerical work requiring little previous training or experience; or who can do routine typewriting. Commencing salary shall be $720 per annum. Increases of $30 or $60 per annum may be granted up to a maximum of $900 per annum for satisfactory services.

LOWER INTERMEDIATE GRADE The lower intermediate grade shall consist of employees who have had experience in operating bookkeeping machines; who can perform varied clerical duties requiring independent judgment; who can take and transcribe routine dictation; or who can supervise simple office routine. Commencing salary shall be $780 per annum. Increases of $30, $60, or $90 per annum may be granted for satisfactory services up to a maximum of $1080 per annum.

UPPER INTERMEDIATE GRADE The upper intermediate grade shall consist of employees who have had considerable experience in operating bookkeeping machines; who are competent to perform more advanced stenographic work; or who can supervise more difficult office routine. Commencing salary shall be $900 per annum. Increases of $30, $60, $90, or $120 per annum may be granted for satisfactory services, up to a maximum of $1320 per annum.

SENIOR GRADE The senior grade shall consist of clerks who can take and transcribe with accuracy difficult dictation; who can perform secretarial or very advanced clerical work; who can handle correspondence without dictation; or who can supervise large groups of employees. Commencing salary shall be $1020 per annum. Increases of $30, $60, $90, or $120 per annum may be granted for satisfactory services, up to a maximum of $1500 per annum.

SPECIAL GRADE The special grade shall consist of experienced clerks who can perform important secretarial work requiring the exercise of independent judgment and a complete knowledge of office procedure; or who by reason of special training can supervise or undertake very advanced work. Commencing salary and future increases shall be in accordance with the qualifications of the individual and the value of the services performed.

MACHINE ALLOWANCES An allowance of $60 per annum shall be paid to competent operators whose work necessitates the use of one of the following machines:
> Graphotype Machine
> Bookkeeping Machine
> Comptometer Machine

An allowance of $30 per annum shall be paid to competent operators in the following sections:
> Multigraph
> Photostat
> Addressograph (Other than Graphotype)
> Switchboard

EXAMINATION ALLOWANCE From July 1st, 1929, for each complete part of the examinations of the Insurance Institute of Toronto passed by an employee, an allowance of $60 per annum shall be granted.

VAULT SERVICE ALLOWANCE For prescribed duties necessitating work in the vault, an allowance of $30 per annum shall be granted.

BONUS For satisfactory service a bonus of $30 or $60 per annum may be granted to an employee who is receiving the maximum salary of her grade. Messengers may also earn a bonus of $30 or $60 per annum for satisfactory services.

In the case of employees whose services may be deemed worthy of special recognition the Management may vary the arrangements set forth herein.

Sun Life, the Montreal-based insurance company, that devised what at the time was perhaps the ultimate system for standardizing typing-based occupations. In July 1929 the company introduced a graded salary and job classification system for female employees only (see figure 4.1). Management proclaimed that 'the salary grading plan has been devised for the purpose of offering better opportunities for progressive employees to earn promotion and receive due recognition for services rendered.'[67] It is questionable whether these lofty objectives could be achieved, given women's high turnover and their concentration in the lowest grades.

Looking at the scheme, one finds that typing is combined with other routine clerical tasks in the junior grade. Both the intermediate grades emphasize skills in operating bookkeeping machines (essential in an insurance firm), in addition to stenographic and some supervisory abilities. In theory, these jobs cannot be described as devoid of skill or responsibility. But in practice, it is difficult to estimate what proportion of a clerk's time would be allocated to different tasks. Finally, the senior grade places considerable emphasis on well-developed secretarial and stenographic skills, in addition to supervision. Those in the special grade, probably few in number, were clearly skilled workers. What is interesting throughout the intermediate and upper grades is how stenographic, advanced clerical and supervisory tasks are integrated into single job descriptions. Those women who functioned as supervisors were not promoted into a separate supervisory or managerial category. Rather, they remained as clerks. What Sun Life created, then, was a highly structured and separate internal labour market for women.

Despite attempts by office managers to bureaucratize and regulate all aspects of clerical work, one area remains relatively unscathed even today. This is the realm of the executive secretary. To be sure, many managers bent on pruning costs and raising efficiency would balk at the idea of giving up their private secretary. Secretaries have been variously described as 'office wives' or 'substitute wives'.[68] These metaphors convey the highly personalistic, non-bureaucratic nature of their employment relations. Kanter accurately refers to the secretary–boss relationship as 'the most striking instance of the retentions of patrimony within bureaucracy.'[69] Instead of being governed by bureaucratic rules, universalistic evaluation criteria, standardized job descriptions, and controlled task sequences as is common for lower ranking clerks, the secretary is subject to the whims of her boss. A secretarial role is often so loosely defined as to include personal services, such as shopping for family presents, picking up cleaning, or fetching coffee. Hence the office wife metaphor. Kanter's study of corporate secretaries suggests that their work has three defining aspects: employment conditions are based on principalled arbitrariness, status is contingent on that of the boss, and personal loyalty to the boss is expected.[70] These criteria are relics from the past, persisting despite massive rationalizations in other parts of the office.

Harry Braverman, surveying the spread of office automation, predicts the eventual demise of secretarial jobs: 'the secretarial function is [being] replaced by an integrated system which aims at centralized management, the breakdown of secretarial jobs into detail operations subdivided among production workers, and the reduction of the number of secretarial workers to one-half, one-quarter, or even smaller fractions of their former number.'[71] The very fact that secretarial work has persisted, largely intact, since the turn of the century challenges Braverman's predictions about the 'end of the social office'. Moreover, secretarial jobs underline the difficulties managerial efficiency campaigns have long confronted in trying to place office work on the same rationalized footing as factory production.

CONCLUSION

To recap, I have examined in this chapter the feminization of clerical work by theoretically linking transformations in the clerical labour market to a new administrative division of labour within offices and, at the societal level, changing ideological currents and female roles. By 1930 the clerical labour market had been Balkanized into male and female compartments. As a result, women competed among themselves for the new, bottom tier of detailed administrative jobs, while men contended for the better positions. The sex-based divisions of power and inequality that came to define the social organization of the office depended on specific jobs acquiring either a male or a female label. Sex-linked characteristics have long determined employment eligibility. Such labels are an integral part of the ideological apparatus of a patriarchical society, justifying the exclusion of women from areas of male privilege and subordinating them in less desirable jobs.

A unifying theme running throughout this chapter is how jobs come to have either male or female labels attached to them. Clerical and other predominantly female occupations form labour market segments in which women mainly compete with each other for a narrow range of jobs with comparatively poor wages and working conditions. Sex labelling is the principal method by which this occurs. Employers manipulate the requirements and rewards of a job so that only women are deemed appropriate. Clerical work graphically illustrates how female labelling took place originally and, moreover, still firmly adheres today.

At issue is why an employer would substitute a female job label for a male one. It is now plainly evident that the increasing availability after 1900 of a cheap, educated, middle-class supply of young women seeking employment was an important prerequisite. So too was the growth of innumerable routine clerical tasks that, in the eyes of employers and junior male clerks alike, provided an inadequate, and penurious, apprenticeship for future businessmen. But the three case studies above have gone much further in exposing the complexities of the labelling phenomenon. In sum, supply and demand characteristics mutually interact in ways which create employment traps for women:

if employers adapt themselves to such a labour supply so that the job in question acquires a 'female only' label, then the demand is not just for cheap labour but for cheap female labour. The job has acquired a traditional sex label, and employers will tend to follow this tradition unless some special problem arises. If, in addition, skills are required, then the employer is probably more firmly committed to the utilization of the labour of one sex. It is hard, for example, for an employer to find a qualified male secretary, even if he should desire one. In addition, several other factors tend to make labour demands sex-specific. If presumed sex-linked characteristics are desired, such as physical strength or manual dexterity, then demand is, of course, sex-specific. If the effects of a sexually mixed work group or of having female supervisors are feared, then employer demand will tend to be sex-specific. If the desire is for a dependable, highly motivated employee who will move anywhere, then employers will tend to prefer males over females.[72]

The effects of sex labelling and job segregation tend to be cumulative. I have argued, for example, that the commercial success of the typewriter and its embodiment of new, relatively sex-neutral skills facilitated women's early access to stenography. Business colleges and commercial courses in high schools began to turn out huge numbers of female typists and stenographers. Hence even before the turn of the century in Canada, Britain and the United States, the occupation could expand only by attracting more women into the labour force. Once commonly recognized as single-sex, a job usually remains that way. In short, custom prevails in hiring practices. Recent efforts to break down the barriers women encounter to the so-called 'non-traditional' blue-collar trades attests to this. Regardless of how skilled they might be, women on construction sites, for example, often face considerable harassment from males who feel that their turf is being invaded.

Yet sex labels are not always permanent. This is now plainly evident with respect to clerical occupations, where the major incentive for employers to keep hiring women was a lower wage bill – not to mention the obvious difficulties of attracting males to these low status, poorly paying jobs. However, defeminization is a possibility under an obverse set of economic and social conditions. Witness the changes occurring in Canada during recent decades in teaching and librarianship: enhanced professional status, marked largely by credentialism, unionization and rising salaries, have attracted an increasing number of men into these jobs.

It therefore is essential to recognize the particular combination of social, economic and organizational factors shaping employers' hiring decisions. At any given historical juncture, an employer has certain options regarding staffing, limited of course by given constraints both within the organization and beyond it in the larger environment. These contextual factors may either facilitate or inhibit feminization. The situation in banking underlines this point. A particular image of the ideal employee defined the social organization of early twentieth-century Canadian banks. This formidable ideological barrier to female employment was eroded by exogenous shocks to the banks' staid hiring patterns. These mainly took the form of First World War male labour shortages and rapid economic growth which, in turn, led to an expansion and reorganization of bank clerical procedures. In contrast, the federal government's Civil Service Commission devised bureaucratic methods to alleviate the perceived disruptive consequences of opening the flood gates to female clerks. By manipulating hiring regulations and job classifications, the commission was able to take advantage of the growing supply of cheap, reliable female clerks, confident that the only route for these women out of the depths of the third division was to return home.

The early development of typing as a woman's vocation presents an entirely different scenario. Crucial was the absence of an existing male labour supply, a combination of job skills which could be deemed as suitably feminine within the confines of late nineteenth-century social values, and the subsequent development of training courses and labour market institutions, such as placement agencies, explicitly geared towards young, single women. There are similar examples to be found outside the realm of clerical work. Research on librarians in the United States is instructive in this respect.[73] Women literally rushed into American libraries during the last quarter of the nineteenth century, unopposed and, indeed, even encouraged by male librarians. The library jobs women performed were entirely consistent with existing social perceptions of them as the transmitters and guardians of culture. But this rapid feminization can only be comprehended against the backdrop of the economic difficulties which libraries faced. Women were cheaper than men, so male librarians in positions of authority were guided by this basic economic motive. The reason was quite simple: as managers of public institutions forced into 'thrifty housekeeping' by their dependence on tax support and charitable donations, and faced with community expectations that budgets should be spent mainly on books, hiring cheaper female employees was a reasonable way out of a fiscal jam.[74] If these examples permit some generalizations about the nature of occupational feminization, surely the most basic one is that aggregate labour force trends indicating shifting sex ratios in job categories mask the dynamic interplay among social, economic, organizational and ideological factors structuring the supply and demand for particular types of workers.

5

The Rationalization of the Office

For many years mechanical production has been carried on as a process in which the individual workman plays an insignificant part, he is a part of the machine which is essential because inventive genius has not been able entirely to eliminate the human element, an element which must judge and direct. With the growth of large corporations during the past years the same tendency in the clerical end of production is more and more making itself felt. Here, too, a great machine has been created. In this machine the human factor is still essential, but the part which the individual plays is less conspicuous, because the method of working the machine is obvious from the design of the machine itself.

The construction of the modern office grows constantly more like the construction of the factory. Work has been standardized, long rows of desks of uniform design and equipment now occupy the offices of our large commercial and financial institutions. With the increasing division of labour each operation becomes more simple. The field in which each member of the staff operates is narrower. As in the case of mechanical production, however, the growth of the machine has meant that the comprehensive plan which somewhere underlies the whole is a new product of modern economic life. Detailed operations may be simplified, but the vision of the organization as a whole must remain.

Monetary Times, (1 October 1920, p.10)

What the above editorial vividly describes is the rationalization process so fundamental to the administrative revolution. I have already outlined how the turn of the century ushered in a new economic era of industrialization for Canada. This economic development depended on, among other things, a massive expansion and reorganization of the office. Rationalization is the common thread in any discussions of modern management strategies and administrative systems. Indeed, Max Weber has argued that rationality is an indispensible factor in capitalist development. According to Weber, 'the factor which produced capitalism is the rational permanent enterprise, rational accounting, rational technology, and rational law.'[1] Complementing these factors was the more general rationalization of economic life. Rationalization basically refers to the hierarchical organization of work, the formalization of work relations, the specialization of tasks, and the standardization of the labour process through predetermined routines and technology. When the office is rationalized, 'management stabilizes the work and brings it under control.'[2] In short, rationalization underpinned the construction of the 'clerical machine' portrayed above by the *Monetary Times*.

The purpose of this chapter is to investigate the organizational reforms implemented by management which gave shape to the modern office. I will explore several of the key themes introduced in chapter 2. It is useful at this point to recall my discussion of the three key factors in the administrative revolution: the creation of a modern industrial economy founded on manufacturing and services; the growing prominence of large corporations and state bureaucracies as work organizations; and the influential role of professional managers intent on profits, productivity and employee compliance. Now I shall elaborate how these forces actually transformed working conditions in major Canadian offices for an ever-expanding group of female clerks. Two kinds of office rationalization were also identified in chapter 2. One was a by-product of a general programme of reform launched by managers throughout the organization. The other, increasingly prevalent after the First World War, was a direct strategy to tackle inefficiencies in the office itself. My evidence below documents both forms of rationalization and, moreover, highlights the diversity of techniques which management used to construct the basic framework for today's office.

THE DRIVE FOR EFFICIENCY AND CONTROL IN THE OFFICE

The basic principles of scientific management were influential in restructuring offices. Faced with explosive clerical growth and the challenge of trying to smoothly process, record and store vast amounts of information, office executives, impressed by efficiency gains in factories, looked there for solutions. Given the general popularity of Taylorism, it is not surprising that by 1910 proponents of scientific office management were finding a receptive audience. We must recognize, though, that during the First World War era the mechanistic rationality of Taylorism became tempered by corporate welfare schemes, personnel administration and, by the 1930s, a whole new approach to management based on 'human relations'.

Nonetheless, managers in major US and Canadian offices began to heed claims by Harry A. Hopf, one of the first experts in office administration. Hopf proclaimed that 'there is no reason why the adoption of scientific management should not be as efficiently applied to the Medical Department of a Life Insurance Company as in the now classic example of the handling of pig iron in the Bethlehem Steel Plant.'[3] His reforms served to emphasize the productivity gains made possible by rationalizing office work. Before the First World War, Hopf set up a facsimile of Taylor's planning department in an insurance company so that managers could directly govern all clerical procedures. Following the lead of factory engineers, Hopf redesigned clerical tasks by carefully analysing the 'one best way' to perform them. He introduced special filing systems for efficient large-scale record-keeping, standardized forms, suggested changes in office layout and building design, and urged improvements in ventilation and illumination.[4] The impact of these innovations for future office work was, in a word, profound.

The first book-length study of office work was published in the United States in 1912.[5] Yet it was not until William Henry Leffingwell's *Scientific Office Management* appeared in 1917 that a systematic 'how-to' guide for office management became available.[6] Leffingwell emerged as the foremost spokesman of scientific office management. He was to the office manager what Taylor was to the factory manager – a purveyor of practical advice on how to boost production, cut costs and regulate employees' work activities. Leffingwell's writings clearly reveal that scientific office management was initially aimed at curbing rising administrative overheads in manufacturing. Gradually a coherent set of office management procedures emerged as the lone bookkeeper was superseded by the huge central office.[7] One very direct managerial response to a rapidly growing clerical staff and mountains of paperwork was to reorganize office procedures. The goal was to cut clerical costs and assert management's control over administrative tasks.

Leffingwell leaves little doubt that effective clerical procedures contribute to overall management control in an organization. If office work was standardized, specialized and performed according to set routines, he claimed managers could rest assured that administration would be conducted like clockwork. Or in Leffingwell's words, 'effective management implies control. The terms are in a sense interchangeable, as management without control is inconceivable, and both terms imply the exercise of a directing influence.'[8] Likewise, managerial control without a reliable clerical staff was, in Leffingwell's mind, equally impossible. Echoing the *Monetary Times* editorial cited above, Leffingwell saw the modern business enterprise as a huge machine with interdependent parts. Embellishing the analogy, he asserted that 'the clerical function may then be correctly regarded as the linking or connecting function, which alone makes possible the efficient performance of hundreds of individual operations involved in the "sub-assembly" cycles and in the cycles of the business machine as a whole.'[9]

Leffingwell articulated the concerns of growing numbers of office managers who recognized clerical work as the Achilles' heel of good administration. Herein lies the rationale for office reorganization. Leffingwell explains: 'If, therefore, coordination be considered as the major function of management, and if this coordination requires clerical mechanisms and cannot function without them, it follows that the problem of management through them constitutes a major function and is unquestionably vital to the conduct of business.'[10] The intent of scientific office management is to ensure that there exists only enough 'clerical links' to connect the various tasks and units which comprise the organization. These clerical functions must then be analysed, in true Taylorist fashion, to determine the 'one best way' of performing them. The resulting system of administration ideally involves a tightly integrated, carefully regulated series of simplified clerical tasks. Office costs are thereby stabilized, inefficiences are banished, and management reigns supreme.

By the end of the First World War a powerful new force was thus being felt in the office:

The entire trend of modern office management is undeniably towards standardization of work – the elimination of chance and uncertainty wherever possible, and the substitution therefore of known and tested methods. This process, as a matter of fact, is the one outstanding proof that office management is becoming a more exact science, for, as we have seen, science itself is but knowledge organized, classified, and standardized for the use of mankind.[11]

Businessmen initially accepted the disproportionate growth of administrative jobs as an unavoidable side-effect of improved factory administration. When a 1905 gathering of Hamilton, Ontario, manufacturers was admonished to eliminate waste and inefficiency through cost accounting, the speaker dismissed any concerns about the resulting office expenses:

Of course it must be understood that to have an accurate Cost System will increase the expense of the office or accounting, though not to a great extent, but with a proper system the results will more than pay the extra expense, while the ways of saving waste, etc., will show up so clearly that the extra clerical expense will be saved again and again in the factory.[12]

But as administrative costs soared, they threatened to undermine the office's role as an administrative control centre. A new conception of managerial control was to crystallize by the First World War. It required the recording, analysis and storage of a growing array of information on costs, worker productivity, market conditions, customer accounts, and so on. The growth of bureaucracy also compounded the problems of administration. Large, multi-departmental office structures were a standard organizational response to the greater complexity and volume of paperwork accompanying industrial expansion.[13] Mounting administrative costs were partly a result of the basic inefficiencies of office bureaucracies. A specialized division of labour was viewed by managers as a vehicle for greater productivity. Yet the resulting lack of co-ordination and integration among the splintered tasks unintentionally generated new difficulties. The managerial response to these problems triggered major office rationalizations. These reforms gained momentum during the twenties, marking a crucial phase in the administrative revolution.

SCIENTIFIC OFFICE MANAGEMENT IN CANADA

The origins of scientific office management in Canada lie in the development of corporate capitalism. Early improvements in office procedures usually involved the adoption of more systematic accounting and record-keeping systems. The first steps in this direction were often small ones, pointing the way for larger future innovations. Especially in manufacturing and resource industries, change was frequently introduced by American multinational firms when they acquired Canadian branches. Such was the case as the Rockefeller empire's Standard Oil expanded into Canada. The Eastern Oil Co. in New Brunswick was bought in 1888 and soon received a modern accounting system, office organization and warehouse controls from its new American parent.[14] Imperial Oil, a much larger firm based in Ontario, adopted American management methods and control systems after it was acquired by Standard Oil in 1898.[15] By 1914 Imperial was run by a team of former Standard Oil of New Jersey executives.[16]

Rationalizations also frequently occurred quite independent of American influence. A good illustration of this is found in the Bank of Nova Scotia, one of the pioneers in the scientific measurement and regulation of office work. Long before William Leffingwell or Harry Hopf entered the scene, the bank implemented its Unit Work System. This sophisticated method for controlling cost, productivity and staffing will be described at length later in the chapter. Around the turn of the century Canadian banks were expanding their operations internationally. Facing management problems similar to those in other large-scale industrial organizations, bankers sought ways of monitoring staff in far-flung branches. It therefore is understandable that head office officials urged branch managers to 'give close study to the systematic management of routine'.[17] This quest for uniform standards, measurement of employee effort and operating costs, simplified methods, and rigid work procedures were part and parcel of the more 'scientific' approach that crept into administration.

Even though many clerical activities defied the precise regimentation possible on a factory assembly line, routines could be established around specialized functions.[18] For example, in 1919 the Canadian Bankers' Association launched a major campaign on behalf of the entire banking industry to standardize banking procedures and reduce clerical details.[19] Similarly, insurance firms around the same time introduced simpler, standardized forms for all types of clerical work. These innovations probably boosted office efficiency, but largely by creating more intensified and monotonous jobs.

Some organizations even went as far as employing American management consultants to rationalize their offices. Just prior to the First World War, for example, the Land and Collection Branch of the Canadian Pacific Railway's Department of Natural Resources, located in Calgary, was handling a larger volume of business than any loan company in Canada. The railway conducted a survey of office methods used in Canadian and American loan companies. The study led to the hiring of 'a thoroughly competent efficiency expert' from the United States to reorganize the branch and simplify its methods.[20]

Public bureaucracies also experienced some rather intractable organizational challenges. For instance, the federal civil service had a long history of inefficiency due largely to rampant patronage. The problem reached crisis proportions with the bloating of civil service ranks during the First World War. 'Efficiency in government' became the rallying cry of the Borden government's attack on the evils of patronage.[21] The result was an elaborate civil service classification and salary scheme developed by a team of American management consultants. And enshrined in the 1918–19 Civil Service Act were the most advanced ideas from progressive US management circles.[22] This monumental reorganization, to which I shall return momentarily, was probably the most extensive in any Canadian organization prior to the post-Second World War period.

E. O. Griffenhagen, the government's major consultant on civil service organization, advocated 'a business-like approach to government'.[23] He modified the entire civil service structure, causing considerable disruption and discontent.[24] To take one example, Griffenhagen applied the heavy artillery of Taylorism to the Department of Public Printing and Stationery – allegedly one of the most lax parts of the bureaucracy. Records and procedures were standardized, staff requirements formalized, plant and office layouts streamlined, and new equipment introduced. And most Draconian of all, 400 'unnecessary' employees were eliminated on the basis of their relatively low efficiency ratings.[25] The results received a hearty approval from the Civil Service Commission, which at the time was recruiting a resident expert in industrial management: 'We are amazed. What was probably as inefficient and unhappy an organization as could very well be found anywhere has been changed into one, we do not hesitate to say, as efficient on the average as any in Canada.'[26]

Provincial governments also inaugurated efficiency reforms. In 1918 Ontario appointed its first Civil Service Commissioner. Like his federal counterpart, the Ontario Commissioner embraced scientific management as a panacea for the maladies of bureaucracy. Empowered by the 1918 Ontario Public Service Act to 'recommend such action as will promote the co-ordination of work in the different departments, and the reduction or reorganization of the staff of any department with a view to greater economy and efficiency in administration',[27] the Commissioner subsequently introduced a merit system, a standardized salary scale, job classifications, and other progressive management methods.[28]

The organizational problems of early twentieth-century industry appear to have been fairly widespread. While the picture is far from complete, available evidence suggests that by the end of the 1920s a broadly defined science of management had found its way into a considerable number of Canadian offices. The Industrial Engineering Department of US-based Arthur Young and Company was separately incorporated in Canada in 1920 as Griffenhagen and Associates. Publicity from its efficiency work in the federal bureaucracy helped land other important contracts. Griffenhagen and Associates was hired by the City of Montreal and the Bank of Montreal to implement organizational reforms and devise employee classification systems, by the Province of Quebec for a budgetary study, as well as by the agricultural equipment producer Massey-Harris, and Canadian Cereal and Flour Mills Ltd.[29] Furthermore, the rapid growth and consolidation in banking during the 1920s led the Royal Bank's staff magazine to call for 'a substantial reduction in clerical labour'.[30] In the spirit of progressive factory management, the bank asserted that 'efficiency has been a much-abused term during recent years, but it has very real significance to the large banking office today.'[31] Other bankers advocated that the logic of the Taylor system should be used to reorganize bank clerical routines.[32] Another indication of the entrenchment of scientific office management during the 1920s was the implementation of 'scientific employment policies'. The goal of these policies was the careful selection and training of employees in order to match them with the job for which they were most suited.[33] This is now a guiding principle in personnel management.

An insurance executive observing these developments provides an apt summary of their significance for office management and, more broadly, for advancing corporate capitalism: 'The office is the base, the centre of control, the repository of the records of the business, the general headquarters of the Company. It is the heart, the brain, the life of the whole machine.'[34] This is the key to understanding the rationalization of the office, a trend closely linked to the growth of subordinate clerical jobs and the parallel drive to recruit females. I now will provide several detailed case studies which amplify my argument about the paramount importance of office rationalizations for the creation of a modern, and largely female, clerical workforce.

MANAGING PUBLIC BUREAUCRACIES SCIENTIFICALLY

By the 1920s employers had smoothed some of the rough edges off the Taylor system. Managers combined science and efficiency with an emphasis on the 'human element' to rationalize personnel administration. The dictates of formal bureaucracy were applied to staff recruitment, classification, promotion and remuneration. These measures were especially useful in organizations with a preponderance of clerical workers. Governments were therefore among the first organizations in many countries to establish rigid job hierarchies and formal entrance requirements.[35] This was certainly true in Canada, as is evident from the following accounts of scientific management in the Ontario and federal civil services.

Ontario civil service reforms

Since the nineteenth-century canal and railway building eras, state institutions have taken an active part in Canada's economic development. This role was expanded as the wheat boom, the rise of corporate capitalism, and the First World War called for greater state involvement in the nation's affairs. More than any other region, Ontario was transformed into an urban, industrial society by the economic surge of the early twentieth century. Yet the provincial government's effectiveness in responding to its changing socio-economic environment was hindered by patronage, high staff turnover, a lack of interdepartmental co-ordination and ineffective personnel management. To remedy the situation, legislators and senior officials standardized employment conditions and streamlined departmental structures.

The impetus for rationalization was provided by the 1918 Ontario Public Service Act. The Act empowered a Civil Service Commissioner to regulate and reorganize the civil service. J. M. McCutcheon, the first Commissioner appointed under the Act, launched a series of reforms inspired by the new science of management.[36] His target was the cumbersome central bureaucracy at Queen's Park, which employed about 900 clerical and other administrative workers. After partly stemming the rising tide of employee discontent over inadequate working conditions by introducing a pension plan, McCutcheon tackled organizational problems. The centrepiece of his reform programme was a detailed job classification system implemented in 1927.

The Commissioner's annual reports express a deep conviction that the most advanced organizational schemes and systems of personnel administration were urgently required in the civil service. The reports clearly enunciate the principle of standardization, a touchstone of modern management. Employment conditions – such as salaries, job descriptions and requirements, methods of recruitment, and promotion procedures – had to be standardized in the interests of equity and efficiency. Merit became the foundation of the new classification plan. This pushed the civil service toward a more formal bureaucratic structure. Moreover, the objective evaluation of an employee's productivity was fundamental to scientific management. Standardized employment conditions allowed departmental supervisors to compare employees on the basis of their performance. McCutcheon explains:

> The merit system is concerned with the selection and the maintenance of an efficient personnel and with the application of sound and scientific employment principles. Its adoption would result in the displacement of the patronage system with all its attendant evils . . . Its uniform application to employment problems would ensure efficiency and economy in the Public Service and eliminate irregularities and anomalies.[37]

Like many managers in private industry, McCutcheon was motivated by a single-minded quest for organizational effectiveness. Asserting that 'classification is an essential preliminary step to efficient organization', McCutcheon argued that bureaucracies required carefully planned systems of integration and co-ordination.[38] During the 1920s government bureaucracies throughout North America were subdivided into functional, hierarchical departments headed by management specialists. This mirrors Chandler's description of the modern business enterprise, suggesting that the forces of organizational rationalization were not confined to the private sector.[39] Yet despite functional organization, government departments were often more cumbersome than similar units in private sector corporations. McCutcheon therefore attempted to streamline individual departments by linking together their diverse and increasingly splintered tasks and work procedures. Using language reminiscent of the Taylorites, McCutcheon urged that: 'Every office of the government should be so organized that all its activities will function smoothly and efficiently – with speed, accuracy, and dependableness. An efficient office controls and co-ordinates activities and conserves time and energy.'[40]

The 1927 job classification system went a considerable distance toward the goal of creating a finely tuned bureaucratic hierarchy. The classification plan outlined the responsibilities and requirements for every position, established a standard salary scale for each job class, specified avenues of promotion, and delineated the lines of authority connecting the top and the bottom of each departmental hierarchy. This formalization of the government's occupational structure was achieved through job analysis, one of the basic tools of scientific management. Jobs were graded, reclassified, and in some cases subdivided. Efficiency ratings for individual employees determined their standing in the new meritocracy. In short, the civil service had grown large, unco-ordinated, and sluggish by the end of the war. 'Scientifically determined standards by which to gauge efficiency' thus became a rallying cry of McCutcheon's reorganization offensive.[41]

Despite earmarks of Taylorism, the rationalization of the Ontario public service was also influenced by the nascent humanistic approach to personnel management. Co-operation and consensus, rather than coercion and discipline, were advocated. In this sense, McCutcheon was one of Canada's early personnel managers. He realized that contented employees – ones who knew that their efforts would be rewarded through the merit system – were more likely to 'conduct the public business with efficiency and economy'.[42] This merging of personnel practices with scientific job analysis and redesign became fairly common among so-called progressive managers in the 1920s.

The spread of bureaucracy, with its more regimented and specialized tasks, had a dramatic impact on clerks' working conditions. Yet there are few signs that clerks or other civil servants resisted the new classification system.[43] The tactic of peaceful lobbying, adopted by the Civil Service Association to push for salary increases after the First World War, apparently was not used to resist organizational reforms. The new pension plan, salary raises and meritocratic criteria for advancement – undoubtedly improvements over the arbitrariness of the old patronage-based system – may have nipped employee discontentment in the bud.

Other provincial and municipal governments also instituted reforms along the lines advocated by McCutcheon. For example, in 1923 the Civil Service Association of Alberta initiated meetings with the provincial Civil Service Commission to discuss the implementation of a merit-based efficiency rating system. The object was 'to define the ability and efficiency of every employee and to award a grading and salary in accordance with the value of the services rendered, the basis of advancement to be merit'.[44] Municipalities were also setting up civil service-type commissions run by professional city managers.[45] Yet these reforms did not approach the massive scale, nor the disruptive consequences, of the rationalization achieved by a team of American scientific management experts in the federal civil service.

Scientific management transforms the federal civil service

The word bureaucracy conjures up images of a quagmire of red tape generated in Kafkaesque government offices run by rule-bound petty officials. This certainly contains a grain of truth. To be sure, the long-standing preoccupation among federal politicians and senior officials with civil service reform underscores the continual tension between rational bureaucratic goals and the realities of organizational life which often fall far short of these.

The first of a series of Royal Commissions on the federal civil service was set up in 1869. This launched a chain of inquiries, some resulting in reforms, which culminated 50 years later with the hiring of American efficiency experts to overhaul the entire job classification system. In an attempt to reduce inequities among staff and to provide more structure for departments, the 1869 Commission classified employees in terms of duties, seniority and salary.[46] Later Commissions in 1880 and 1891 identified the 'baneful influence' of patronage as being the scourge of government, but were unsuccessful in launching changes. When in 1907 Prime Minister Laurier appointed a full Royal Commission to investigate the service 'in the best interests of efficiency', he was setting the agenda for future reform.[47]

Efficiency became the watchword of government managers. How could the state effectively carry out its mandate, it was asked, when low salary scales and uncertain career prospects discouraged bright young male clerks from entering the service? The 1908 Civil Service Amendment Act offered a partial remedy. It invested responsibility for efficient organization and personnel management in a Civil Service Commission. A new Board of Civil Service Examiners was instructed 'to investigate and report upon the organization of the department(s), the conduct and efficiency of its officers, clerks and other employees, and any other matters relative to the department(s) . . .'[48] The original five-tiered departmental hierarchy – deputy minister, principal and chief clerks, first, second, and third class clerks – was replaced by three major divisions each with its own salary scale. I have already noted in chapter 4 that the third division, consisting solely of clerks performing 'copying and routine work', became a female domain.[49] Finally, the Act rationalized recruitment in the Ottawa bureaucracy by establishing competitive entrance exams based on merit.

The 1908 Act did not go far enough, however. The federal

bureaucracy was becoming even more difficult to co-ordinate. Sir George Murray's 1913 report on government administration anticipated the problems faced by all large-scale organizations experiencing rapid expansion: 'The only means by which growth in business of government in amount and complexity can be met is by division of labour and devolution of power. In the absence of some continuous process of this kind the machinery of government must gradually become less efficient and must ultimately break down under the stress imposed upon it.'[50] Murray recommended a pension plan, extension of the recruitment and promotion examinations, uniform accounting methods, and a job classification system. Apparently reform was not politically expedient so these plans were shelved. The First World War only compounded the problems by adding another 16,700 employees.[51] Prime Minister Borden's 1917 union government, in attempting to guide the nation through the war crisis, risked being dragged down by a lumbering bureaucracy. Civil service efficiency became a top priority. The 1918 Civil Service Act extended the powers of the Civil Service Commission, giving it full control over appointments throughout the service. A major shakedown of the bureaucracy had commenced.

The Civil Service Commission concluded that nothing short of broad-ranging reorganization could counteract decades of patronage and inertia. The Commission's secretary, William Foran, was well versed in the latest scientific administrative practices developed in the United States.[52] There is little question that the Commission was strongly influenced by the American management ideas which were gaining converts in Canada by the end of the First World War. The Commission's solution was a sweeping reclassification of all positions, formalizing and standardizing conditions of employment. The leading experts in the field, Arthur Young and Company of Chicago, were contracted to design and implement the reclassification scheme. These consultants applied the most current American scientific management practices to the Canadian government. The goal was to achieve 'the maximum efficiency and economy.'[53]

The Chicago experts clearly understood the interdependence of personnel administration and organizational structure: 'Without an efficient personnel in the public service the most carefully constructed organization and highly perfected methods of procedure will not serve their purpose.'[54] However, the reclassification plan also involved time and motion studies in what constituted a classic Taylorist assault on the work process.[55] Efficiency ratings were taken of each employee, the 'one best way' for performing each task was established, work routines were standardized, and jobs were divided up into their simplest components.

The result presumably was a more efficient organization reminiscent of Max Weber's model of the ideal bureaucracy. The new authority structure incorporated the latest personnel practices. But from the employees' perspective, social relations undoubtedly became impersonal and regimented. A central feature of the new classification was a comprehensive employment plan. Included were systematic methods for recruiting employees, training programmes, efficiency-based merit ratings which determined salary raises and promotions, provisions for weeding out incompetent employees, and benefits schemes to help foster a spirit of staff co-operation.[56] The new classification contained 1729 job groupings. Responsibilities, qualifications, salary levels and lines of promotion were set out for each class. The standardization of tasks and employment conditions was attained by classifying all jobs according to three criteria. For example, 'senior statistical clerk' specified the following: 'clerk' indicated the general nature of the work, 'statistical' the kind of specialization, and 'senior' the rank and responsibility.[57]

The Civil Service Commission heralded parliament's acceptance of the classification plan and accompanying salary scale in 1919 as the dawning of a new era. Its annual report proclaimed:

> Half a century of unscientific methods under a system founded on no definite principle, a happy-go-lucky, hit-or-miss affair, in which political exigencies controlled and merit was a very secondary consideration, could not but develop many startling anomalies and finally evolve a badly balanced and topside structure . . . a tremendous step forward was made when the principles of scientific classification were accepted.[58]

But a chorus of protests arose from the ranks of the civil servants. According to one account, 'the instant the Classification was published the whole service was in an uproar.'[59] Employees appealed against their reclassifications and revised salary scales by the thousands.[60] Arthur Young and Company had introduced major innovations, making the federal bureaucracy a model on which other governments patterned their reorganization plans. Yet the scheme contained serious flaws. A key problem was the linking of salary scales to the pre-First World War cost of living on the mistaken assumption that wartime inflation would subside. The scheme was also criticized for producing an unduly complex and fragmented division of labour. Another source of employee discontent was the guiding principle of the plan, meritocratic promotions. Career mobility had been effectively truncated by escalating educational requirements at each level in the hierarchy. The upshot was the formation of a special Board of Hearing to review the complaints of various civil service associations regarding the classification.

Meanwhile, the Civil Service Commission proceeded with its reorganization work. The Commission's members had learned first-hand about the connection between sound bureaucratic organization and efficiency by observing Arthur Young's rationalization of the Commission's office in 1918.[61] The American experts' next assignment was to restructure the Department of Public Printing and Stationery. A series of scientific management techniques, mentioned above, achieved a 'more economical and efficient' operation. Staff was reduced by 36 per cent and the taxpayers saved $740,000.

In May 1920 the government set up a Council Subcommittee on Reorganization and Efficiency. Griffenhagen and Associates, the newly created branch of Arthur Young and Company specializing in civil service work, was retained as consultants. For almost a year and a half the Griffenhagen team assisted the subcommittee to devise ways of ensuring orderly, business-like government. Four main recommendations were formulated: to incorporate 25 departments and over 50 boards and commissions into 11 departments; to introduce expenditure controls and auditing systems; to further routinize clerical work; and to reorganize the departments of Customs and Revenues and the Post Office.

Despite the $3 million these efficiency measures could have saved, Prime Minister Mackenzie King's government shelved the recommendations when it took office in 1921. Widespread employee unrest over the classification system found expression outside the civil service in the rising tide of anti-Americanism during the early twenties. Reforms which could in any way be associated with US firms such as Arthur Young and Company or Griffenhagen and Associates became a political liability. The Civil Service Commission retreated to safe ground, restricting its activities to administering the classification system and the competitive exams. The 1919 plan left a lasting mark, however, providing the basis of the civil service hierarchy for the next half-century. But because of the fiasco over the 1919 Arthur Young scheme the Commission avoided further organizational reforms until the 1950s.

To summarize, the full impact of rationalization reverberated throughout the Ottawa civil service. Most of the Ottawa inside employees were females in low-level clerical positions. The plan's standardization, specialization and rigid job hierarchies deteriorated clerical working conditions. This seems ironic, given the increasing emphasis on personnel management and 'human relations' emerging in public administration. The American consultants may have recognized the need for a humanistic approach in reorganizing the federal bureaucracy, but in the end Taylorism won out. The dehumanizing aspects of work in a huge, bureaucratic hierarchy were accentuated and, indeed, enshrined in the Civil Service Act.

My accounts of civil service reforms, provincial and federal, show beyond any doubt that modern management practices and the principles of corporate organizational structure had found strong parallels in the public sector. It is thus not surprising to find Ontario's first Civil Service Commissioner embracing the key managerial ideas of efficiency and control:

> Comparatively little has been done in Canada in the matter of keeping efficiency records of employees in the Public Service. But the adoption of the promotional principle necessitates the keeping of such records if promotions are to be made upon a sound basis. The value of recording in a systematic manner, the quantity and the quality of the work of every employee in the government service is unquestioned as a principal factor in obtaining personnel control.[62]

In the federal civil service the influence of American industrial management was even stronger. To quote the historians of the federal Civil Service Commission:

> The passage of the 1918 Civil Service Act and the launching of the Civil Service Commission on its long career in government personnel management came at a time when critical changes were taking place in theories of organizational methods. Scientific management and the classification movement, both American in origin, were decisive influences on Canadian ideas just at that point when they were at their most formative state.[63]

Politicians also became aware of how inefficient bureaucracy could drain the public purse. Even they began to sound like management experts. In 1920 the federal cabinet concluded that 'many millions of dollars can be saved in the Government operations by an application of up-to-date scientific principles of organization and operation.'[64] When applied, it was ideas such as these which transformed government administration. And it was the routine jobs created by this process that provided employment for growing numbers of women.

FUNCTIONAL ORGANIZATION

A standard method for co-ordinating and integrating the diversity of tasks performed in large-scale organizations was to set up a functional departmental structure. Each department performed a specialized activity, such as purchasing, production, marketing or accounting. Non-production departments were typically located within a central bureaucratic office, providing top management more direct control. The functional departmental form, according to Alfred D. Chandler Jr., was the most common structure adopted by the modern business enterprise.

Functional organization was a general rationalization strategy which precipitated changes in administrative methods which, in turn, created less flexible and more intensified work routines for clerks. It signalled a marked departure from the simple organization of the nineteenth-century counting house, making the generalist bookkeeper a relic of the past.

The Bell Telephone Company's introduction of functional organization clearly illustrates how full-scale corporate rationalization resulted in more standardized and specialized clerical procedures. The spread of the telephone after 1900 widened the scope of Bell's operations. The firm encountered difficulties administering its diverse activities and numerous departmental units. Given Bell's close ties with the American Telephone and Telegraph Company, it naturally looked to this corporate giant for innovative solutions.

Bell's early structure was rudimentary, organized by territory. District managers looked after telephone traffic, public relations, installations and maintenance in each area. A superintendent of construction was responsible for erecting telephone wires and poles. Control rested with the president, who was assisted by an advisory staff on technical matters. By 1906 the company's staff had swollen to 4,000, overtaxing its traditional and weakly co-ordinated structure.[65] In 1909 Bell officials visited the United States to study AT&T's latest managerial reform – functional organization. They quickly recognized two chief advantages: a clear delineation of responsibilities and lines of authority made integration and supervision easier; and substantial cost reductions. Yet the scheme did have some drawbacks. In particular, the transition from territorial to functional organization entailed 'a general shake up of the staff'.[66] And because the success of the plan depended on an elaborate new accounting system, with more specialized clerical procedures, administrative costs would rise. Specifically, each regional unit required a minimum of three different clerical functions: statistical, costing and general. Monthly accounts prepared by these clerks outlined all expenditures. This information helped supervisors to reduce costs by providing 'a great incentive to economies even in small units, each district striving to obtain the lowest percentage of costs'.[67]

Four articles written by American telephone executives appeared in the *Telephone Gazette*, Bell's staff magazine, during 1909. Employees were told that they were about to experience a new epoch in telephone administration. Borrowing from contemporary discussions of scientific management, the articles also emphasized the virtues of efficiency, task standardization and cost reduction. However, the over-specialization which had caused co-ordination problems in Taylor's system was carefully avoided. The managerial philosophy underlying the functional plan was summarized in these terms: 'The true purpose of organization or system in business is the production of the most efficient results with the least expenditure of money and labour. Our aim in establishing a system for the handling of our business is to fortify and aid our work of administration by the very best organization that study and thought applied to our particular line of business can devise.'[68] Major telephone companies in the United States and Canada moved to adopt the new structure. The first step was to divide the organization into units, headed up by an 'expert' manager, according to specialized functions. Each functional department then had to achieve internal co-ordination. Finally, all departments had to be horizontally integrated into a cohesive whole. According to one manager, these requirements necessitated a finely tuned bureaucracy in which workers knew their role and obeyed orders.[69]

The architects of the functional blueprint grasped the importance of a line–staff structure. Analogies were drawn between a telephone company and an army. Both must control large numbers of personnel over a wide geographic area; both require centralized administration, line–staff organization and divisional units.[70] A thorough airing of organizational problems characterized discussions of the plan. One prominent issue concerned how many employees a supervisor could effectively control, something administrative theorists did not consider until at least the 1930s.[71] Remarkably, a Bell plant superintendent pinpointed this span of control problem in 1909: 'Recognizing that with the increased size of the department further organization was necessary for the direction, control, and handling of affairs – it was deemed necessary to divide the responsibilities and duties, in order that the affairs might be kept within the scope of those directing the undertaking.'[72]

Bell's first decisive move toward functional organization was in January 1911. Two main functional units were created: the plant department, responsible for construction, maintenance and installation; and the operating department, which looked after customer service, customer accounts and telephone exchanges. Each department was further subdivided geographically. Staff activities such as accounting, engineering, supply and legal departments were also organized according to function. A fully functional organization was achieved in 1917 with the creation of four major departments – plant, commercial, traffic and engineering. Bell by then had installed 270,000 telephones and employed a workforce of 9,000.[73] That task specialization within organizational units increased is evident from the internal subdivision of the three largest departments. For example, the plant department had five divisions and eleven districts. The AT&T plan had at last come to fruition, propelling Bell to the forefront of the rationalization movement in Canadian industry.[74]

The redesigning of organizations on the basis of departments precipitated major changes in the nature of office work. Specialized departments tended to recruit more clerks to perform narrowly focused tasks. This largely was due to rigorous accounting methods which required the collection and analysis of mountains of data. Cost accounting, in particular, was a potent tool for controlling large bureaucracies. Management's growing preoccupation with 'accounting for value' was a major impetus in modernizing the office. Tracing the progress of Bell's reforms clearly documents this point. In 1904, only several small sections of the secretary-treasurer's office were concerned with accounting matters. The first phase of the plan, implemented in 1911, created a separate auditor's department with wider cost control responsibilities. Yet by 1919 there was a complex, internally specialized accounting department. The conception of control inherent in cost accounting filtered into the clerical work of the department.

Bell was not alone in pursuing this course of organizational change. In the Canadian Pacific Railway, for instance, functional organization combined with cost accounting to restructure its offices. The form which had evolved by the 1920s closely resembled the advanced organizational plans developed by the largest American railways. The main features were a line–staff organization, functional departments, geographical divisions and a massive central office. The firm was divided into specialized staff functions, located at head office, and the operating departments which were organized both functionally and geographically. Organizational charts of the head office show that the accounting department occupied a pivotal position. Battalions of clerks in the 13 accounting divisions performed a multitude of routine accounting and administrative tasks. Thus, as in Bell Telephone, the onslaught of major organizational reforms and the growing importance of accounting functions fuelled the growth of subordinate clerical jobs filled by women.

ADMINISTRATIVE CONTROL IN BANKING

An organization's structure is directly influenced by its type of economic activity. Contrary to what some scientific managers believed, there was no 'one best way' to structure an organization, given the need to facilitate a diversity of functions within contrasting environments. Developments in the Bank of Nova Scotia illustrate this point well. With numerous small branches scattered over a vast geographic area, the bank attempted to maintain centralized control by combining a unique cost accounting system with strictly regimented employment conditions.

By the end of the First World War, financial journals were urging banks to achieve greater efficiency through modern managerial methods. In 1919 the *Monetary Times* described how problems associated with tremendous increases in the volume of business forced banks to overhaul their clerical routines.[75] A few years later, the journal argued that 'efficiency has been a much abused term during recent years, but it has a very real significance to the large banking office today.'[76] Bankers were greatly impressed by a paper US efficiency expert Harry A. Hopf presented on scientific personnel management to an Ottawa conference in 1921. Hopf had performed a 'drastic overhauling in the internal organization' of the New York City Federal Reserve Bank.[77] Bankers viewed scientific management as a repertoire of techniques for rationalizing bank routines, allowing clerical tasks to be performed with a minimum of cost and effort.[78] By the 1930s many of these ideas had been put into practice. Bank head offices and the larger branches had evolved to their modern form: standardized procedures, numerous specialized tasks, considerable mechanization and a rigid hierarchy. Yet not all of these changes were products of the 1920s. In fact, the rationalization trend in Canadian banking had its origins in the expansion of branch networks around 1900.

Bank head offices had to control the activities of their far-ranging branch systems. This necessitated a high level of bureaucratic centralization, with the levers of power firmly in the grasp of head office senior management. To this end, Bank of Nova Scotia officials were striving to establish more systematic clerical procedures even before the turn of the century.[79] In 1901 the bank's General Manager, H. C. McLeod, implemented the first cost accounting and efficiency rating system in the Canadian financial sector. The Unit Work System measured employee productivity in each branch. This provided comparative data on branch efficiency, furnished a basis for allocating staff bonuses, and helped the bank set its service charges. Much like Taylor's work measurement plan, the system standardized all clerical tasks into basic 'work units'. A 1905 bank circular elaborates:

> Investigation of the work problem and of the proper distribution of the staff enables us to lay down a general rule by which Managers may judge whether the efficiency of the staff at his office equals or surpasses the standard . . . It is estimated that an average clerk in his seventh year of training should be capable of performing 240,000 units of work per annum, and at the same time enjoy his vacation and have a reasonable time for recreation and improvement.[80]

The Unit Work System was a significant developmental step in modern personnel management. To meet continual changes in branch staffing requirements, the bank relied upon a pool of highly mobile clerical labour controlled from head office. This job mobility requirement was, of course, a major stumbling block to the employment of women. Male clerks regularly received instructions from head office to pack their suitcases and promptly report to another branch miles away. The bank's staff magazine candidly admitted that, 'in the life of a bank clerk, transfers from one branch to another generally come so frequently that he gets used to a somewhat Bohemian existence.'[81] Efficiency ratings were a key piece of information in transfer decisions, for they indicated whether a branch's staff complement should be increased or decreased given its workload.

Co-ordination problems created by high staff mobility were alleviated by a rigid branch hierarchy and strictly enforced regulations governing employee conduct. Descriptions for clerical jobs thus varied little from branch to branch, facilitating the interchangeability of workers. The basic branch hierarchy, from the bottom up, was junior (basically an apprenticeship position for young men), ledger keeper, teller, assistant accountant, accountant, assistant manager and manager. Head office also dictated the branch manager's duties in no uncertain terms. The *1917 Rule Manual* stated that uniform productivity was attainable at every branch 'by the labour saving methods of proper arrangement, distribution and timing of the office routine, and by the prompt despatch [sic] of the Manager's daily duties. A manager who does not give close study to the systematic management of routine, and who is dilatory in attending to his own duties – two defects that generally go together – invariably causes his staff to work overtime or he requires an excessive staff for the performance of regular work within reasonable hours.'[82] Accountants acted as office disciplinarians. They made sure that clerks did not develop 'slovenly habits of working, and that they keep their desks in proper order'.[83]

Bank clerks were subjected to army-like discipline. The *1902 Rule Manual* clearly indicates that, even by this early date, an advanced stage of bureaucratization had been reached. Rules covered all aspects of clerks' work, as well as their personal conduct outside banking hours. Employees had little choice but to obey orders with military precision: 'No departure from or violation of these Rules and Regulations, either through ignorance or neglect, will be overlooked; any wilful violation will be considered sufficient grounds for dismissal from the service.'[84] Management exercised an unprecedented degree of paternalism over employees, insisting that 'unexceptional conduct in private life is required of all its officers by the Bank. Any irregularity, extravagance, or suspicious association must be reported to the General Manager.'[85] While the bank no doubt had good reason to be vigilant about the safety of its customers' money, this vigilance was often excessive. The outstanding case in point was the prohibition against marriage until a male clerk's salary had risen to a level that management considered sufficient to support a family.

Beneath all these rules and regulations lay the principle of managerial control. The bureaucratization of the bank made it easier for management to simplify, standardize and co-ordinate activities in far-flung branches. Whether a clerk worked in Halifax or Vancouver, his or her duties and position in the hierarchy were determined by a single rule book. Near total flexibility in staffing was the goal: 'Every officer [referring to males] must be prepared to service the Bank in such capacity and location as the Board of Directors and the General Manager may consider expedient in the best interests of the Bank.'[86] Head office authority was exercised very decisively through the formal, line–staff style of organization. Organizational charts from the early 1920s indicate a functionally departmentalized structure, with staff departments located at head office and the branch network constituting the line functions. Because most banking operations are clerical in nature, one of the chief results of the Unit Work System and the rule manuals was the routinization of clerical jobs. Paradoxically, the changes in banking designed to help train future executives created the types of menial jobs that male 'juniors' wished to avoid. During the First World War the deep ideological underpinnings of the bank's preference for male clerks were weakened by labour shortages. From then on women were marshalled into these bottom slots.

MANAGING THE CENTRAL OFFICE

Major Canadian life insurance companies have been international corporate powers since the turn of the century. Like the banks, their operations are largely clerical. But unlike the banks, these clerical activities were located mainly under one large, bureaucratic roof. Insurance company head offices resemble a type of white-collar production line. The final product – the customer's insurance policy – is the culmination of a long sequence of clerical operations. And in the jargon of the industry, throughout its 'life', a policy requires regular clerical 'maintenance' – billings, premiums notices, updatings and so forth. Success for any insurance firm thus demands machine-like precision in its clerical systems. Understandably, by the end of the 1920s, many managers in the Montreal and Toronto head offices of these firms were ardent practitioners of scientific office administration.

The boom in insurance sales after 1900 created pressures for streamlined clerical procedures. An early attempt to routinize office activities was the widespread use of card systems.[87] Cards standardized the storage and retrieval of many different types of data pertaining to policies. At the same time, typewriters and adding machines were becoming standard fixtures in insurance offices. According to one observer, by 1911 Sun Life's head office had many 'up-to-date [mechanical] contrivances for the manipulation of the great business that passes through each year'.[88] Typing had been reorganized into a central typing pool with the introduction of Edison phonographs for dictating letters. As I shall explain in chapter 6, mechanization accentuated the division of labour and intensified work rhythms in the office. Another manifestation of this march toward a systematized office was the standardization of forms. The insurance business depends upon a profusion of forms. To impose more orderly procedures, in 1918 Sun Life established a committee to standardize all forms.[89] Along the same line, top management formalized clerical job descriptions in 1920 by providing written instructions to all department heads (still called chief clerks).[90] Sun Life's managers apparently shared William Leffingwell's conviction that established routines are perhaps the most effective way to get office work done.[91]

Cost accounting, I have argued, gave managers greater direct authority over the office by pinpointing sources of clerical inefficiency. A multitude of other rationalization measures were tied to the evolution of accounting: 'The modern Life Insurance Office is constantly seeking such improvements in their methods of accounting as tend to greater efficiency, greater simplicity and reduced cost . . . Card records, loose-leaf ledgers, addressographs, tabulating and calculating machines, etc., have all played an important part in life assurance accounting.'[92] The larger volume of data generated by more sophisticated accounting systems often could be handled without increasing costs, provided clerical work was mechanized and routinized.

Insurance firms were also in the front ranks of the movement toward a comprehensive employee relations strategy at the end of the First World War. Because Canadian financial institutions did not face the same threat of unionization as blue-collar employers, there was little enthusiasm for the industrial councils discussed in chapter 2. Still, there was ample scope for greater diligence and co-operativeness among staff. For this reason, Sun Life appointed E .E. Duckworth as head of personnel in 1920. Duckworth's foremost goals were to 'introduce scientific methods for the selection of the staff, and to promote the competence of its members'.[93]

At bottom, the new personnel manager was interested in obtaining maximum performance from clerical staff. He also recognized the necessity of recruiting and training expert managers. This was a clear reflection of corporate ideology during the 1920s which stressed the role of an elite vanguard of managers. Duckworth's greatest challenge, however, was in the realm of clerical employment. Insurance managers recognized that 'one of the big problems for the Home Office executive in charge of personnel is along the lines of developing a scientific plan of remuneration for clerical workers.'[94] Such salary plans required a more rigorous classification of clerical tasks. Recall in this connection my discussion, in chapter 4, of Duckworth's classification scheme for head office female clerks. This was followed up in the 1930s by a thorough analysis and reclassification of all clerical positions.[95]

A bureaucratic, multi-departmental structure was the organizational framework which Sun Life evolved to impose order on its clerical workforce. This was the guiding principle behind the layout of the firm's new headquarters that opened in 1926. To co-ordinate the activities of up to 1,500 clerks efficiently, the building had been designed 'to make the whole structure an effective workshop'.[96] Sun's functional departments resembled the basic structure of other major corporations of the day. In 1917 Sun had about 19 functional departments, including a stenographic pool and a Hollerith machine division. These units were managed by 37 senior officials and 100 chief clerks.[97] One indication of the efficacy of these managerial reforms is the fact that, 13 years later, the same number of managers presided over a much larger staff spread over 38 departments.[98] The gathering momentum of these and other changes documented above radically altered the simple nineteenth century insurance office. The stark contrast between the old office and the new had a resounding impact on clerical working conditions. As one observer put it:

> In earlier days, when the Head Office staff was small in number, its members, working together in the same room, acquired a comprehensive knowledge of the business in the course of their duties. That is impossible today, however. With the work split up into departments, and each department many times larger than the entire staff of a few years ago, an employee has little opportunity to obtain a broad knowledge of the business.[99]

On a general plane, I have argued that the rise of corporate capitalism was linked to the developments in administration which advanced the frontier of managerial control. Modern business administration evolved through systematic investigations of organizational problems on an industry-wide basis. This co-operative approach was a hallmark of the insurance industry, with the founding of the Life Office Management Association (LOMA) in 1924. LOMA rallied the largest North American life insurance companies in the common pursuit of efficient management techniques. The founding president proclaimed that 'our business is an open book, and we have no secrets.'[100] A co-operative approach to the problem of 'correct organization and administration of . . . clerical activities' would help all firms update their office methods to keep pace with rapid growth.[101]

LOMA's main goals were the development of better head office organization and more efficient ways of administering clerical activities. Canadian companies were actively involved in the association from the start. LOMA was the major conduit through which scientific office management techniques entered Canadian life insurance offices. Managers on both sides of the border agreed that 'efficient handling of such a rapidly growing [clerical] force is . . . a matter of the greatest importance to the welfare of our Companies.'[102] W. H. Leffingwell himself attended some of the association's annual conferences. The influence of management experts such as Leffingwell was obvious. For example, in his presidential address to LOMA a Canadian insurance executive identified seven dominant strands in insurance office management:

1 scientific selection, training, placement and promotion;
2 a scientific basis for remuneration;
3 caring for the physical and social welfare of the worker;
4 supplying adequate supervision over the worker;
5 motivating the worker;
6 mechanizing the work and humanizing work relations; and
7 improving the calibre of management.[103]

This programmatic statement documents how the core ideas of scientific management were to be adapted to the office. It must be recognized, however, that the activities of workers on a factory assembly line are more readily measured and regulated than those of most office workers. This surely is why LOMA went to considerable lengths to achieve efficiency in clerical work. The flow of paper through an office is a rather intangible process compared with the production of physical commodities. The harshest realities of factory life will not be found in the office. Yet the managerial drive to rationalize office work undeniably introduced elements of factory discipline and routine.

CONCLUSION

In summary, the unprecedented growth in clerical employment sparked off by the ascendancy of corporate capitalism and an activist state bureaucracy after 1900 was also accompanied by a sweeping reorganization of the office. That office employment growth and work rationalization went hand in hand is hardly surprising, given similar trends in the factory. To be sure, my evidence meshes with Chandler's explanation of the rise of American big business: 'growth without structural adjustment can lead to economic inefficiency.'[104] This is not to suggest, however, that clerical growth necessarily led to, or was accompanied by, office reorganization. There may have been some large offices which, despite clinging to traditional work methods and structures, did not flounder on the shoals of inefficiency. Indeed, I have explicitly rejected unilinear, deterministic models of change. Thus while I unearthed no evidence contrary to the general pattern of the administrative revolution, this does not mean that some large offices maintain outmoded practices even today or, for that matter, that small offices totally escaped the onslaught of scientific management in the period under investigation.

Furthermore, while the rationalizations discussed above are found mainly in the service sector, both public and private, there is good reason to believe that large manufacturing offices underwent similar changes. My review in chapter 2 of the administrative overhead problem is ample testimony to this. The fact that scientific management, broadly conceived, originated on the factory floor suggests that rationalization principles would have easily filtered into the front office. And given the attention devoted to office administration by *Industrial Canada*, the official publication of the Canadian Manufacturers' Association, the rationalization process was moving into full swing throughout this sector by the 1920s.[105]

I should now like to return to the quotation at the beginning of this chapter from the *Monetary Times*. It portrays the office of the twenties as an immense clerical machine that processes the facts and figures indispensible to modern business and government. However, closer analysis has brought to light a contradictory dynamic between the development of management control strategies, on the one hand, and bureaucratic organizational structure on the other. Specifically, large, hierarchical organizations often evolved specialized departmental units, each with a more simplified and routine division of labour. Departmental activities thus had to be reintegrated into a smoothly functioning whole. This is what underpinned the rationalization of administration. Solutions to the problem of bureaucracy included job classifications with detailed task descriptions, attempts at measuring and regulating clerical productivity, more standardized methods for recording and processing information, increased mechanization, and other schemes all aimed at enhancing office efficiency. Yet a cross-cutting trend surfaced throughout North America in the aftermath of the First World War. The war exacerbated problems of employee turnover and unrest, largely among industrial workers. Managers responded with more comprehensive programmes governing the employment relationship. Hence a convergence of the technical orientation of efficiency management with the more humanistic perspective of welfare schemes and personnel programmes.[106] No better example can be found of this than in the clerical job classification and remuneration schemes outlined above. These reforms cut two ways, routinizing task while at the same time attempting to improve the work environment.

Comparatively speaking, the changes in organizational structure and work processes that catapulted the Canadian office into the modern era mirror developments in the United States. Margery Davies's investigation of scientific management in US offices shows, if anything, a more determined efforted along this line than in Canada.[107] The thrust of office reorganization, Davies notes, was the creation of specialized departments and the attendant fragmentation of clerical jobs.[108] By the turn of the century, major employers tackled the problems of efficiency and discipline not by recruiting more clerks, but by restructuring the office. In some firms, the quantitative measurement of tasks did create factory-like conditions. But it was also the case that other employers, especially smaller ones, were relatively untouched by rationalization. Taylorism in the office was evidently 'a concerted and self-conscious drive by a vanguard among businessmen'.[109] Yet those employers who joined the rationalization bandwagon would have fashioned schemes suited to their particular needs; there was no 'one best way' to harness the full energies of an office. The emphasis did, however, tend to be placed on mechanization and work measurement. Whatever the particulars of a rationalization programme, according to Davies the overall result was a splintering of the clerical division of labour and an erosion of clerks' task control.[110]

Vincent Giuliano has usefully identified three stages in the evolution of American office organization, each defined by a particular management style and hierarchy, performance standards, technology and social relations. Coming between the traditional pre-industrial office and the information age office of today is the industrial office. Emerging in the early twentieth century, the industrial office is typified by a production-line approach to clerical work. As Giuliano explains:

One response to the limitations of preindustrial office organization has been to bring to bear in the office the principles of work simplification, specialization and time-and-motion efficiency articu-lated for factory work some 70 years ago by Frederick W. Taylor. The result is the industrial-stage office, which is essentially a production line . . . There is a need for standardization of jobs, transactions, technologies, and even personal interactions. A frag-mentation of responsibility goes hand in hand with bureaucratic organization and the proliferation of paperwork. Most of the workers have little sense of the overall task to which they are contributing their work, or of how the system as a whole functions.[111]

Admittedly the inefficiencies and limitations in this 'clerical machine' have prompted the computerization of office work in recent decades. Yet the basic strengths of the production line model described by Giuliano are the bedrock of today's information age office.

It is doubtful, however, that rationalization cut as deeply in British offices. David Lockwood's account of office conditions suggests that neither mechanization nor scientific management were very advanced in Britain by the 1950s.[112] Lockwood's analysis of office rationalization revolves around the standardization and specialization of tasks. Organizationally, the post-Second World War British office exhibited a line–staff structure with subdivided departmental functions and small, specialized work groups. Still, in large and small firms alike, Lockwood claims that 'much clerical work is specific, non-repetitive, requiring a modicum of skill and responsibility and individual judgement.'[113] Office conditions, in short, rarely match those of the factory. The nature of production processes, workgroup organization, status differences, disciplinary procedures, and relations with management make this gulf unbridgeable. Even in large offices, remnants of nineteenth-century employer paternalism linger on, partly due to the lack of universalistic and systematic criteria for grading and remunerating work – factors present in Canadian offices even in the 1920s. Lockwood does allow, however, that the work situation in large, post-Second World War bureaucracies was often very routine: 'there have been reproduced impersonal and standardized working relationships comparable with those created by the factory and labour market.'[114] Lockwood attributes the standardization of procedures and task specialization mainly to the expanding size of offices. Scientific management had primarily indirect effects by demanding greater amounts of better quality data, hence feeding the growth of clerical staffs. British managers, on the whole, were less enthusiastic than their North American counterparts in the quest for more scientific techniques to achieve administrative control.[115]

I have alluded to the forceful combination of technology and task reorganization when discussing various office rationalization measures. Certainly many structural reforms in the office were linked to the introduction of mechanization. Some analysts actually define office rationalization in terms of mechanization and standardization.[116] The full impact of such measures was felt in the depths of the office hierarchy, populated increasingly by women. The construction of the clerical machine described so graphically by the *Monetary Times* depended heavily on the introduction of office technology. What the journal's editorial writer took for granted is that the mechanization and rationalization of clerical work was also instrumental in its feminization. It is to the links between office mechanization and the employment of women that I now turn my attention.

6

Mechanization, Feminization and Managerial Control

The focal point of the electronics revolution now overtaking advanced capitalist societies is the automated office. Through the application of silicon chip technology it has been possible to fuse two powerful mediums – computers and telecommunications. This hybrid technology will undoubtedly have a far-reaching impact on all forms of information processing work. Changes will likely be most dramatic in the clerical sector, and much speculation revolves around the office of the future. While the electronic office appears to be a radical departure from earlier phases of automation and mechanization, closer scrutiny reveals basic continuities in the evolution of office technology since the turn of the century. Indeed, the office underwent several mini-revolutions following the introduction of typewriters, calculating machines and Hollerith punch card equipment. Electronic information processing has built upon the changes wrought by these early technologies, but they have received surprisingly little scholarly attention.

This chapter examines the mechanization of the office during the early twentieth century. Mechanization, I shall argue, has had a profound impact on the office especially because of its direct links with the shift to a female labour pool and the development of new managerial control strategies. Viewed in this way, the introduction of office machinery is a defining characteristic of the administrative revolution.

By now there should be little question that changing patterns of clerical employment reflected the growing importance of administration for modern industry. Technology played a central role in the massive restructuring of the means of administration. The turn-of-the-century office differed radically from its predecessor a half-century earlier by its growing reliance on typewriters, telephones, telegraphs, dictation machines, and an assortment of mechanical calculators. Machines were also decisive in changing job requirements and, as a result, the character of the clerical labour force. Earlier chapters documented how the first female to sit behind a desk in many late nineteenth century offices was a stenographer. The typewriter was a gender-neutral piece of new technology when first introduced, but quickly became identified with women. By 1900, four out of every five stenographers and typists were female. The feminine image of typing facilitated the hiring of more women to operate other office machines.

The intensive recruitment of women into the specialized and simplified clerical jobs which proliferated at the bottom of office hierarchies is thus inseparable from mechanization. Equally important in the shaping of the modern office is the interweaving of technological innovations with the application of managerial control strategies. By the 1930s, the interaction of mechanization, feminization and managerial rationalization measures had laid a solid foundation for the automated office of today. It is therefore appropriate to begin by examining how the onslaught of workplace rationalizations, through cost accounting in particular, was a powerful impetus for technological change.

MACHINES AND MANAGERIAL CONTROL

The introduction of cost accounting techniques had a direct impact on office procedures. Basically all accounting schemes involve clerical work. The last quarter of the nineteenth century witnessed a 'costing renaissance' in the industrial world, as businessmen struggled with declining profits, rising costs, keener competition and more expansive operations.[1] Cost accounting was more central to the administrative revolution within large-scale organizations than was general accounting. The latter is based on the principle of double-entry bookkeeping developed by Italian merchants in the fourteenth century. Cost accounting, on the other hand, is a more advanced science directly tied to the rise of corporate capitalism.

American factory engineers made an important contribution to modern management by honing cost accounting into a sharp instrument for eliminating production inefficiencies.[2] Their careful systems for controlling inventory as well as material and labour costs for each job, using job cards and time clocks, laid the basis for Taylorism. In fact, many of the 'new' management schemes around 1900 were accounting systems for monitoring overhead costs.[3] Advances in this area were rapid. By 1905–10 prime cost accounting, which measured materials and direct labour costs, had reached its modern form. In short, cost accounting offered managers a more straightforward solution than Taylorism to rising costs, lagging productivity and inefficient work organizations. By the end of the First World War, sophisticated accounting systems were standard features of corporate administration. Sound management thus came to be equated with cost accounting, as the authors of a 1925 textbook on the subject stressed: 'organization, management and cost accounting are so intimately related that it is almost impossible to consider them separately.'[4]

Canadian businessmen became well aware of the advantages of thorough cost accounting procedures. After 1900, major business publications such as the *Monetary Times* and *Industrial Canada* regularly featured articles on the topic. In one of the first articles to appear, *Industrial Canada's* readers were told how cost accounting facilitated more accurate estimates of production costs, better scrutiny of management techniques and more efficient production methods.[5] It was not long before the connection was made between accounting for costs and greater control over the labour process. A prerequisite for an effective accounting system was a careful record of workers' production, allowing management to keep workers and machinery continually busy.[6] As the practice of cost accounting spread, it was increasingly viewed as a panacea for the most urgent concerns of managers. According to the *Monetary Times*, these included:

1 ascertaining costs in order to set prices and reduce expenses;
2 increasing productivity;
3 promoting organizational efficiency;
4 improving the quality of production;
5 eliminating waste and extravagance;
6 detecting the idleness of men or equipment;
7 distinguishing between productive and unproductive expenditures;
8 promoting economy in capital expenditures.[7]

There was, however, one major unintended consequence of these reforms. By introducing administrative 'systems' throughout a firm, cost accounting demanded a larger clerical staff and eventually created pressures to streamline office operations.

As the accountant became an increasingly important figure, invariably there was a growing body of clerks under his command. 'If your accountant is an unproductive expense,' H. L. C. Hall told Canadian manufacturers in 1907, 'it is time for you to get a new accountant, for this department should be one of the most productive in the plant. Here is where present waste and loss are detected and reported. Here should be the place where any and all details of your operation should be instantly available. And they will be if the department is properly organized.'[8] Hall's last line reverberated throughout the office during the next several decades. He was advocating efficiency in accounting department organization and clerical procedures as a means of ensuring that overall costs were kept in check.

Even though some cost accountants laid claim to a body of expert knowledge quite distinct from the efficiency experts inspired by F. W.

Taylor, both strategies shared a common set of concerns. For example, the Taylorite's preoccupation with efficiency was no less muted in discussions of accounting: 'The secret of efficiency, after all, is costs. A knowledge of what any item in a factory costs to make and to market, the knowledge of costs generally is the cornerstone of a knowledge of business.'[9] The theme of managerial control also dominated. Indeed, a costing system was often the means to achieving this goal. According to the *Monetary Times*: 'cost systems are an essential part of modern scientific business management. For the capital invested in a business proves just as efficient as are the brains employed to handle it; and the best guide for brains is analysis. That is the function of a cost system – to give the manufacturer a detailed knowledge of his business – and to give him this detailed information regularly and automatically.'[10] Thus stated, cost accounting may be seen as a driving force within the schemes found under the umbrella of scientific management which transformed the office into the hub of modern administration.

The interaction between technology and a more professional, 'scientific' approach to office management can be traced back to the First World War period. While the sprawling office bureaucracies of the 1910s and 1920s saddled management with escalating administrative costs, scientific management offered a ready solution. Introduction of machines was high on the list of recommended reforms. W. H. Leffingwell, the prominent office efficiency expert mentioned earlier, informed Canadian and American life insurance managers that, of 15 different office work arrangements, manual clerical tasks had the lowest efficiency rating while office machines had the highest.[11] But Leffingwell emphasized that cost reductions demanded more than just mechanization; office reorganization and task redesign was also necessary to reap the full benefits of machinery.

Office managers attentively listened to claims by efficiency experts that Taylorism could yield cost savings, higher productivity and increased efficiency. During the emergence of the modern office there was an abundance of literature on work rationalization available to the 'progressive' office manager. Lee Galloway, an influential writer on office management, established the organic link between mechanization and managerial concern with efficiency.[12] He stressed the control functions of the office. Galloway argued that accurate information was essential for good management, but so too was a reduction of the office costs incurred by processing this information. Both ends could be achieved, he claimed, by modelling office organization after the factory: 'Much of the routine work of the office employee resembles in one respect that of the factory. The tasks of both frequently entail reproductions of copies from a model. Work of this kind can be done equally well by machines at a great saving in labour and cost.'[13] Galloway attempted to convince managers that this principle was especially applicable to typing work, providing a step-by-step plan for setting up a central stenographic department.[14]

The factory ideal could not, however, be fully achieved. Galloway put his finger on the fundamental difference between office and factory when discussing the problem of measuring clerical work in standardized units: 'There is no more difficult problem in the whole field of office management than the determination of standard units of measurement whereby the output and efficiency of a department may be measured.'[15] Solutions to this problem have subsequently proved to be elusive. According to a 1971 estimate in an office management textbook, the average firm receives only one-half value for clerical salaries because of difficulties in monitoring clerical costs.[16] The authors of the text advocate staff reductions through work measurement, much along the lines initially set down by Taylor. Taylor's definition of scientific management as 'management based on measurement plus control' guides the book's discussion of how to apply time study techniques to the office.[17] Yet even the most precise measures of clerical tasks may be insufficient in face of the abstract nature of office production: 'Inefficiency in the office is not always obvious. Much of the waste and inefficiency in clerical procedures is hidden. It is seldom as perceptible or dramatic as the scrap pile or the shutdown machine.'[18]

What exactly was the impact of cost accounting on clerical work? Clearly the advent of any accounting system induced office growth simply by proliferating information. A prominent Canadian accountant therefore was quick to remind businessman in 1906 that the increase in clerical staff and office expenses resulting from the installation of a costing system would be more than offset through savings in the factory.[19] In practice, however, this often was not the case. By the 1920s cost accounting experts acknowledged that administrative overheads had not been adequately examined, urging that they be computed as a percentage of the cost of each article produced.[20] The problem of administrative inefficiency was particularly acute in white-collar organizations. It is worth stressing, however, that efforts to devise effective general costing systems reaped secondary benefits for management in terms of more rationalized office routines.

The development of sophisticated accounting methods usually went hand in hand with mechanization. These convergent trends were most pronounced in service-sector organizations reliant on enormous volumes of processed statistical data, such as banks, insurance companies, public utilities and some government departments. Accounting methods were of utmost importance to the successful insurance company. 'The modern life insurance office is constantly seeking such improvements in their methods of accounting as tend to greater efficiency, greater simplicity and reduced cost', an annual conference of the Insurance Institute of Toronto was told, 'card records, loose-leaf ledgers, addressographs, tabulating and calculating machines, etc., have all played an important part in life assurance accounting.'[21]

In chapter 5 I described how the core of Bell Telephone's functional organization plan was a cost accounting system which required major advances in clerical mechanization. Leaving little to chance, Bell acquired through its AT&T connection the services of the former auditor of the Iowa Telephone Company to introduce the new accounting system. When Bell created a central accounting department in 1914, at its Montreal head office, it integrated the work previously done by district and division plant offices. The result was a more intensified and simplified form of clerical work. For example, in one section alone, eight women operated key punch machines which recorded maintenance, installation and other expenses compiled by the plant statistical department.[22] Customer accounting was also rationalized. In January 1920, divisional commercial offices introduced 'unit organization' for their accounting departments.[23] In each unit 20,000 accounts were administered by a manager, a chief collection clerk, a chief contract clerk, and their subordinates. This arrangement facilitated closer public contact as well as greater supervision of clerical work. One further example is the introduction of centralized accounting at the Toronto Division in 1926. The growth of the area's business made it more efficient to relocate the accounting clerks from five functional departments in one large office. The new accounting department was divided into six units, each with a supervisor and a chief stenographer to regulate typing and filing work.[24]

Bell's accounting system set the standard for the other Canadian telephone companies. By 1925, it had been fully introduced by four other companies in the industry, and implemented with some modifications by three others.[25] These changes were part of an industry-wide move to establish a uniform accounting system.[26] Underlying this standardization was 'the tendency in public utility accounting over, say the last ten years, . . . toward ever increasing specialization and detail. More and more have managements insisted on fine analysis with the result that the gathering of detailed information has become a considerable task.'[27] C. F. Sise, the president of Bell, echoed this when he claimed that the comparative use of productivity and cost statistics was the best way to judge organizational success.[28] Standardization of accounting and other administrative procedures was all part of the basic philosophy of the Bell network – one system, one policy, universal service. The push toward standardization brought more centralized, routinized and mechanized accounting departments – or in the words of Bell Telephone's comptroller, 'efficient administration'.[29]

The Canadian telephone industry obviously was not alone in extending

managerial control through organizational reforms, clerical mechanization and cost accounting systems. For example, The Consumers' Gas
Company of Toronto found that its traditional system of billing
customers once every four months created alternating periods of slack
and overwork in the accounting department.[30] The problem was
exacerbated by the escalating number of new billing accounts. In
streamlining the accounting system, the firm also restructured the work
of account clerks. Under the new system, accounts were divided into 24
districts of equal size. Changes in office procedures included standardized forms and a higher degree of mechanization. The processing of the
meter-readers' slips – the basis of all billings – involved a number of
specialized clerical tasks, indicating an extensive division of labour.

The systematic handling of accounts posed even greater problems for
companies with more diverse activities. Canadian Pacific Railway
managers, having engaged American scientific management experts on at
least two separate occasions, were cognizant of the inefficiencies
generated by bureaucratic organization. Accounting procedures received
similar attention. The office of the Auditor of Freight and Telegraph
Receipts, in the Montreal headquarters, was only one of 13 accounting
offices by the 1930s. Even so, it was the largest single office in the
company. Employing 213 men and women as audit clerks, statistical
clerks, record-keepers, accountants and machine operators, this office
had advanced light-years beyond the traditional counting room of bygone
eras.[31] Directed by statisticians and accountants, clerks computed the
revenues of the railway's global freight and telegraph operations. Over
3.7 million waybills were processed annually. This Herculean task was
only possible through advanced mechanization. Adding machines were
standard equipment. And a battery of Hollerith machines, located in a
special sound-proofed machine room, processed upwards of 10,000
punch cards hourly.

THE MECHANIZATION OF THE CANADIAN OFFICE

One of the guiding principles in the application of machinery to clerical
work resides in Charles Babbage's conception of the division of labour.[32]
Briefly stated, the capitalist can utilize machine technology to simplify,
standardize, cheapen and regulate the productive process. With respect
to clerical work, mechanization strengthens managerial control by
providing more and better information on which to base decisions,
thereby reducing uncertainty, and, through the closer regulation of
clerical work, is an attempt to cut office overheads. The first process is
amplified in an IBM sales brochure used in the 1930s:

The moment a business grows beyond the point where one man can carry all its essential facts in his head, a need begins for mechanical methods of organizing these facts so that the business can be effectively managed. With each successive increase in the size of a business, the demand for more speed, economy, and precision in dealing with the increasing array of essential facts becomes more insistent.[33]

And once the machine is operating, its regimentation of work activities exerts additional control. The worker's relationship to office machinery is defined largely by rules which the technology embodies. Charles Perrow elaborates:

Any machine is a complex bundle of rules that are built into the machine itself. Machines insure standardized products, thus eliminating rules regarding dimensional characteristics. They insure even output time; they also indicate precisely what kind of material can be fed into them. The larger the machine, presumably the more people it replaces, and this eliminates rules about how workers are to interact and co-operate and co-ordinate their activities.'[34]

In short, mechanization should be seen as a central component of managerial strategies to rationalize information work.

Office mechanization progressed through three distinct stages, each precipitating dramatic changes in the nature of office work.[35] Mechanical innovations were thus cumulative and interconnected, building not only on previous technologies but also modifying the way tasks were organized and regulated. Only through the planned integration of machines and organizational changes could managers come close to achieving factory standards of control and efficiency.

The first stage involved the typewriter and the adding machine. Both had become standard fixtures in most large offices by the First World War, supplementing traditional office methods by helping clerks to perform their tasks with greater speed and accuracy. Clerks were still able to determine the sequence and the pace of the work process. Adding machines augmented the bookkeeper's skills in carrying out computations. Typewriters were largely 'programmed' in their operations by the typist, even if used continuously.

When the single machine was intergrated into a system with other machines a second stage was reached. In the highly rationalized typing pool or accounting office, machines facilitated the mass production of standardized information. By the First World War many adding and computing machines had become multi-purpose, giving rise to full-time machine operator jobs.

The apex of mechanized office technology was achieved with the introduction of punch card equipment. This third stage of mechanization was a watershed in the modernization of the office. Indeed, the origins of the automated office may be traced back to the punch card technology invented by Dr. Herman Hollerith. An integrated series of Hollerith machines recorded, classified and analysed data contained on the punch cards. Hollerith machines interacted with bureaucratization and the rise of scientific approaches to office management during the 1920s. In this context, Hollerith machines 'greatly accelerated the trend toward functional specialization. Many more special-purpose machine-operating jobs evolved, placing women filling these jobs in a relationship to technology similar to the mass-production factory worker. Work in these jobs is repetitive, mechanically paced and minutely sub-divided.'[36] Hollerith operators were few in number, but they nonetheless formed the core of office machine-minders. References to the 'office-as-factory' thus most accurately apply to this group of female operatives. While this epithet is equally appropriate for the typing pool, mechanized information processing reached its height when punch card technology entered the office.

These three stages in office mechanization are prominent manifestations of the administrative revolution. As such, they lie at the centre of the constellation of factors responsible for the movement of women into clerical jobs. In order to bring into sharp relief the links between mechanization and feminization, I now will document the introduction of typewriters, adding and calculating machines, and Hollerith equipment in the Canadian office between the turn of the century and the 1930s.

Typewriters

The typewriter is virtually synonymous with the office. Its impact on the recording and communicating functions of administration has been truly revolutionary. The first typewriter with any commercial potential was patented in the United States and manufactured by E. Remmington & Sons, a firm of New York gunsmiths. The major drawback of the Remmington was that typists could not see their work because of the awkward position of the carriage. This problem was corrected with the introduction of the Underwood upright in 1897. In 1901 over 500 Underwoods were used in Canadian business schools to train the first wave of a new cadre of female office workers.[37] A Canadian advertisement for the Underwood upright in 1905 described the machine as a necessity for modern business.[38] The following year there were over 8,000 Underwoods alone in offices across the country, the railways and the federal government being their largest users.[39] By 1909 Underwood was reporting average daily sales of about 300 typewriters.[40] A general indication of the growing market for typewriters after the First World

War was the large number of advertisements for various models displayed in management publications such as *Industrial Canada* and the *Monetary Times*. Capitalist industrial development and the attendant communications requirements helped to make the typewriter a standard fixture in offices. As a measure of this success, the Underwood Typewriter Company reported net Canadian earnings of $2,130,846 in 1918.[41] Such rapid diffusion of this basic office technology carved a major niche for women in clerical occupations. Indeed, Christopher Latham Sholes, whose version of the machine was first to find a viable commercial market, proclaimed: 'I feel that I have done something for the women who have always had to work so hard.'[42]

New production technologies usually spawn organizational changes to take advantage of the way machines accentuate the division of labour. In this respect, the typewriter contributed to the internal differentiation of the clerical workforce as well as to the rationalization of employment conditions. The impact of the typewriter was especially evident in the specialization and fragmentation of typing activities. In 1920 the Ontario civil service listed three distinct grades for stenographers and an equal number for secretaries.[43] The profusion of job classifications created by the typewriter is well illustrated by the campaign which the National Office Management Association (NOMA) launched after the Second World War. Guided by scientific management, NOMA articulated the type of skill-based job hierarchy which had existed for decades in many large offices:

What the NOMA wants the world to understand is that 'secretary' is a specific job classification. It should not be confused with 'typist', 'junior stenographer' or 'stenographer', for properly speaking, a 'secretary' is more than these. A 'typist' of either sex knows the touch system but not shorthand. A 'junior stenographer' knows shorthand as well as typing and can take and transcribe dictation. A 'stenographer' is proficient in all these skills and also knows letter forms, the various office systems and clerical tasks, like filing, related to the job. Finally, a 'secretary' knows everything a senior stenographer knows and can also relieve the boss of some of his routine work. Above this is the 'private secretary' who works directly with an executive. This is top of the line for a typewriter operator.[44]

In a 1937 study the International Labour Organization identified four main changes in offices which had resulted from mechanization:

1 a high degree of division of labour involving elementary, repetitive and monotonous operations;

2 an increased pace of work;
3 the standardization of work methods;
4 improved methods of work preparation and supervision.[45]

The typewriter had a limited impact in these respects prior to the reorganization of typing work into central pools. The introduction of just one machine into an office furthered the division of labour by creating a new occupation – the typist. Several machines facilitated a finer breakdown of work, allowing each typist to perform one particular kind of task. Hence, in insurance companies we begin to find job titles such as loans typist, policy typist, and renewal typist before the First World War.

The typewriter quickened the pace of work, for new office productivity standards were based on the machine's capabilities. And because machines turned out a uniform product, they facilitated the standardization of forms and recording methods. Furthermore, the operation of a typewriter was easier to regulate by a set of rules and procedures than was the work of the copyist. Yet without a conscious plan to merge typewriter technology with a more streamlined organizational design, management could only reap partial benefits. The full power of the typewriter to rationalize office production was unleashed only with the creation of centralized typing pools.

Typists occupied the lowest rung of the typewriter-based hierarchy mentioned above. These women became the most numerous of the new machine-related workers and, moreover, performed increasingly routine tasks. Given these characteristics, and the associated problems of regulating the work flow of many typists dispersed throughout a large office, managers began to create centralized pools before the First World War. Typing pools resembled paper-generating assembly lines. Fewer typists could produce more, mainly because the flow of work was closely monitored: 'standards will be set, tasks will be assigned and controlled with the same precision and definiteness as in the scientifically managed factory.'[46]

Some of the larger bureaucracies, such as Sun Life, centralized their typing facilities as early as 1911. The most immediate benefit to management was the elimination of costly slack periods, a major problem when each department had its own typists. The introduction of dictating machines around this time meant that the pool supervisor could allot correspondence. When correspondence work slowed, the typists were assigned tasks such as updating mailing lists or typing forms to maintain a steady work flow. An *Industrial Canada* article in 1920 instructed businessmen on how to set up a 'central stenographic bureau'.[47] Stenographic pools, proclaimed the article, will double the efficiency of stenographers and eliminate the need for all but the president and general manager to have private secretaries. A supervisor assigns work to the stenographers, records the quality and quantity of their output, attendance and punctuality – data then used in salary and promotion decisions. Extolling the cost savings and boosted office production thus achieved, the article drew its inspiration from the efficiency drives of factory production engineers. However, in a comment which underscored the hurdles office rationalization has faced right up to the present, the article warned that most managers will be reluctant to give up their own secretary.

Nevertheless, as offices expanded, so did typing pools. Sun Life employed 87 female typists in its stenographic department by the 1930s.[48] In 1935, the Canadian Pacific Railway amalgamated the 20 stenographers and typists from two auditors' departments into a separate office, equipped with dictaphones, under the direction of one supervisor. This reorganization was highly successful, at least from management's perspective:

> In addition to a reduction in the personnel as a result of the increased efficiency obtained by eliminating time occupied in receiving dictation and interruptions, a flexibility is obtained which enables the handling of special work and peak loads which was not possible when operators were located in separate offices. To the dictators there is a greater convenience . . . There is no waiting for a stenographer. The employees displaced have been relocated in positions vacated by clerks pensioned or resigned.[49]

The typewriter, especially in a central pool, introduced a new element of stress into clerical work.[50] Manual typewriters required considerable muscular exertion to operate. Operators frequently suffered from stiff finger joints, sore hand muscles, as well as backache and general muscular fatigue after a day at the keyboard. Furthermore, the perpetual clatter of machines in a busy typing pool caused psychological strain. These negative side-effects of the typewriter suggest that the machine introduced certain similarities with the factory. But the most significant change was the diminished level of control pool typists exercised over their work.

By the end of the First World War, efficiency experts had seized on the typewriter as a vehicle for implementing office production control systems. Because type is more easily measured than handwriting, 'scientific' managers established production quotas and efficiency ratings. For example, W. H. Leffingwell calculated that a square inch of pica type was the equivalent of ten words. By placing a square-inch grid over typed work, a supervisor could determine the quantity of output. This provided a basis for production bonuses and piece rates in the office.

Leffingwell explains how managers used the typewriter to promote greater efficiency in office work:

> In one very large company, having more than 1,000 office employees, the manager is proud of the fact that he has eliminated 21 key-strokes on each letter, and thereby saves 620 strokes of the typewriter operator each day – each operator writes a daily average of 30 letters. This is equal to 10 lines, or 100 words a day. Multiplied by 100 operators, it is a saving of 1,000 lines or 10,000 words a day. Again, multiplied by the working days in a year – 300 – this means a saving of 300,000 lines annually, or 3,000,000 words, with a cash value of perhaps $2,000 a year. An excellent saving to be sure.'[51]

This office was not an aberration in the mind of some over-zealous efficiency expert. While it is uncertain whether any Canadian office managers went to such extremes, Leffingwell's approach embodies an ideal which guided attempts to increase the efficiency of typing operations. Similarly, managers gained tighter regulation over work activities by replacing multi-function stenographers with single-function pool typists. The combination of mechanization and organizational changes I have just outlined set a pattern for future developments. Recent innovations in word processing are essentially logical extensions of the typing pool. C. Wright Mills argued that the 'office-machine age' only develops when 'the machinery and the social organization of the office are fully integrated in terms of maximum efficiency per dollar spent.'[52] The evidence just presented indicates that far from having to wait until computerization occurred, this era was launched around the time of the First World War with the development of central typing pools.

Mechanical accounting and calculating

Unlike the typewriter the adding machine replaced mental, rather than physical, clerical activities. Adding machines assisted clerks in processing the mass of numerical data required by modern business. Machines eliminated tedious calculations, saving time and improving the accuracy of the results. While bookkeeping and accounting clerks no doubt welcomed this assistance, it must be weighed against the reduction of their more challenging and satisfying 'brain work'. To the extent that they embodied many of the skills previously possessed by the bookkeeper, adding and calculating machines contributed to a reduction of skill requirements. The erosion of craft elements in office work was reflected in the rise of a new stratum of female clerks. 'The very word "clerk",' one writer has concluded, 'came to have almost the opposite connotation from that which it had its origin.'[53]

The Burroughs Adding Machine Company was a pioneer in the field of mechanical calculating. William S. Burroughs, an American bank clerk, set out to invent a machine which would expunge the drudgery from his job and provide greater precision in calculations.[54] His adding machine was marketed in the United States in 1883, with subtraction, multiplication and division functions incorporated soon after. Around 1900 advertisements for adding machines began to appear regularly in Canadian business publications. Factory engineers soon claimed that tabulating machines were indispensible in cost accounting, allowing the same set of figures to be analysed in different ways.[55] Organizations which had to process vast quantities of numerical data – the governments, banks, insurance firms and utilities were quick to make extensive use of the machines. Sun Life Insurance Company, for example, purchased its first adding machine in the late 1880s; by the early 1900s it had a whole battery of them in almost constant use.[56] One description of the firm's actuarial department asserted that the machines 'seem capable of thinking'.[57] By the 1920s the basic technology was highly perfected, and Sun Life used many of the machines acquired during these years well into the 1950s.

H. A. Rhee argues that more advanced bookkeeping and accounting machines detracted from the trend toward rationalized offices by accentuating departmentalism.[58] However, my evidence indicates that management usually was able to counter any negative effects by designing mechanized accounting and record-keeping systems with the goals of greater integration and co-ordination foremost in mind. For example, Consumer's Gas Company in Toronto updated its customer billing methods by carefully installing accounting machines within an integrated organzational structure.[59] Sun Life's 1922 mechanization of all bookkeeping records was assisted by Burroughs' experts who designed a set of work procedures which would ensure overall co-ordination.[60] Burroughs also collaborated with American Telephone & Telegraph to develop a mechanized billing system to achieve reduced costs, greater accuracy and better supervision of clerical work. The system was adopted by Bell Telephone's Revenue Accounting Centre in Montreal in 1928, greatly simplifying billing procedures. Eight specially designed billing machines and three statement machines – each only requiring a two week training course for operators – effortlessly handled 240,000 accounts. The machines calculated all charges and credits, as well as the amount payable, printing this information on each customer's bill and three stubs.[61] Adding and calculating machines clearly facilitated a more rationalized form of office organization.

The mechanization of accounting and bookkeeping did, however, produce organizational strains through their tendency to enlarge administrative staffs. As the International Labour Organization noted:

> The number of office employees thus increases with mechanization. The reason is simple enough: office machines make it possible to carry out profitably a whole series of operations which would be too expensive if they had to be done by hand. The growth of large administrative departments and the extension and concentration of undertakings have made it easier to install office machinery on a large scale and to increase supervisory and statistical work to an enormous extent, for the machine reduces the cost of each item to a minute degree.[62]

Somewhat paradoxically, machine-induced clerical growth indirectly helped rationalize the office. In the first place, adding machines created a specialized division of labour in accounting procedures. Fragmented tasks demanded less skill and responsibility over the planning and execution of the work. An example of how the growing number of machine-related jobs was routinized is found in the federal government. A multi-grade classification was implemented for office machine operators. According to the 1930 job description of a Grade Three Office Appliance Operator, the worker was 'to operate, adjust, and maintain in good running condition office appliances requiring a high degree of specialization'.[63] It thus appears that machines afforded management a tighter grip on clerical work, thereby tempering the inefficiencies inherent in larger staffs.

By the 1920s it was rare to find a large office without mechanized systems of accounting and recordkeeping. The most striking changes often occurred in the centralized accounting departments. It was here that rows of routine clerks mechanically transformed mountains of statistics into concise measures of productivity, costs and profits. Yet we must be careful not to idealize the pre-1900 office, where low-ranking male clerks also performed monotonous and unrewarding tasks. Of course, machines created many new 'female' jobs in which low skill requirements, repetition and regimentation were the norm. But the extent of this machine-related work can be too easily inflated. Many adding and calculating machines were simply adapted to existing clerical procedures, used in an auxiliary capacity by clerks. Not until the introduction of Hollerith machines did mechanization trigger fundamental changes in the clerical labour process.

Toward the automated office: Hollerith machines

The first wave of office technology, namely typewriters and adding machines, was essentially single-purpose. Addressographs fell into this category, even though they constituted a more advanced form of machine production. The addressograph clerk merely fed hundreds of name plates – for billings, payrolls, shareholder notices, policy renewals and other purposes – into the machine and let it do the rest. The quest for faster, more efficient methods of machine production sparked the development of complex multi-function machines, signifying a second stage in office technology. Two or more operations were performed continuously and often several machines were linked together. Some of the more common multi-purpose machines found in offices during the 1920s were multi-register bookkeeping machines, combination cheque writing and adding machines, combination cheque sorting, adding, and listing machines (which combined addressing and statistical analysis), and Hollerith punch card equipment. The Hollerith system greatly accelerated the trend towards linking several multi-purpose machines in sequence, bridging the technological gap between mechanization and automation. Punch card machinery thus represented the third and final stage of office mechanization.

One of the early studies of office automation in Canada cogently summarizes the central thrust of Hollerith technology in the office:

> Of all the types of mechanization introduced into the office in the period between the two wars, the most dramatic innovation was the punch card and its accompanying battery of keypunch machines and verifiers, sorters, collators, reproducing punches, and mechanical tabulators. The punch card concept with its advantages of standardization, increased output, and improved quality control over clerical work – especially in accounting-type operations – caught on rapidly and the mechanical accounting or tabulating department is now a familiar feature of most larger Canadian offices. This is the aspect of the modern office that commentators are usually thinking about when they observe that the office is becoming more and more like a factory.[64]

The revolutionary aspect of the Hollerith was its use of a standardized punch card on which a vast assortment of data could be recorded. The card was processed by a series of collating, sorting, tabulating and printing machines. The concept of controlling machines by data cards – a basic principle in computers – was derived from the factory. The relationship between the office worker and a Hollerith machine resembled machine-paced production in, for example, textile factories.[65] While relatively few in number, operators of key punches, tabulators, and other punch card equipment emerged as the machine-minders of the modern office.[66]

Dr Herman Hollerith, a statistician working on the 1880 US census, realized that it would take an army of clerks years to analyse its results. By 1887 he had developed a mechanical means of recording, tabulating and analysing this huge mass of data utilizing standardized punch cards. The machines were soon put to work analysing vital population statistics for several cities, and the US government adopted Hollerith's system for use in the 1890 census. Word of the machine's potential for lightning-fast processing of huge quantities of data opened up a large market. In 1896 Hollerith incorporated the Tabulating Machine Company to manufacture the equipment. A loose alliance with two other small business machine firms created the Computing-Tabulating-Recording Company, which later evolved into the International Business Machine Corporation.[67]

The engineering and marketing capabilities of IBM made Hollerith's name synonymous with electric accounting systems. The company had little difficulty convincing business and government that 'Electric Tabulating Machines prevent the waste of motions, minutes, and material and enable fewer people to do more work in less time.'[68] The basic IBM system used punch cards, a gang punch, a sorter, a verifier, and a tabulating machine. The feature which had the most dramatic repercussions for the clerical work process was the integration of several machines into a semi-automatic data analysis system. The only significant innovation on the basic system was the marketing in 1920 of tabulating machines which printed results. The mechanical printer culminated the progress of pre-computer office technology, eliminating the last remnant of manual clerical labour in mechanical data processing. According to IBM promotional literature:

> Prior to the introduction of [the mechanical printer], the part played by the mechanism in tabulating ended with the appearance of totals on the counters; they had to be transcribed to the record sheets by hand, which of course brought in human fallibility, manifesting itself sometimes in illegible entries and sometimes in outright errors, besides limiting the speed of the operation to the speed attainable in writing down the correct figures in the correct columns. The new device thus carried forward the principle of speed, economy, and precision obtainable only by purely mechanical operation through the final stage of the accounting process.'[69]

Some of the early integrated data processing units were remarkably sophisticated. Hollerith departments in the 1920s used a variety of automatic and semi-automatic machines. Besides the basic components of the punch card system, IBM marketed an array of special purpose equipment: accounting machines which automatically printed reports from tabulating cards at a rate of 75–150 per minute; alphabetic accounting machines which printed names, addresses, descriptions, and so on, eliminating the use of codes; card-counting printers; direct subtraction machines; automatic multiplying punches; automatic checking machines; invoice tabulators; continuous-form bill feed machines; and automatic bill feed tabulators, useful for compiling production statistics and piece work rates.[70] In various combinations, these machines could handle almost any information processing need in business or government.

Hollerith granted a Canadian licence to operate the Canadian Tabulating Machine Company in 1910, supplying the machines at cost in return for 20 per cent of the revenues. The new firm's first order was from the Toronto Library Bureau, and the machines were installed in December 1910. Business took off, and by 1916 there were over 41 customers across the country with annual revenues surpassing $60,000.[71] IBM was incorporated in Canada during 1917. Two years later, the company's Toronto plant was manufacturing punch cards and assembling accounting machines for the Canadian market. That same year sales topped $1 million, and new models were being continually introduced. By 1937 the Canadian factory was producing 16 types of machines for the domestic market.[72]

Figure 6.1 lists the organizations which installed Hollerith systems between 1910 and 1936. Among the 105 customers were some of the largest corporations and government departments. The list probably underestimates the number of installations, as IBM sales records for this period are incomplete. Even so, we must conclude that Hollerith technology precipitated a minor revolution in accounting, bookkeeping, record-keeping, and numerous other clerical procedures in the office.

Over 20 per cent of the firms listed in figure 6.1 are insurance companies. Hollerith methods were especially suited to this industry because of the mountains of uniform statistics required. When Manufacturers Life Insurance Company introduced Holleriths in 1920, an employee observed that the machines 'revolutionized the bookkeeping operations to quite an extent'.[73] Sun Life installed its first Hollerith in 1917, and by 1931 was IBM's largest Canadian customer. The company's extensive use of the machines led to the creation of a centralized Hollerith Service Deparment in 1935. It was reported at the 1924 founding convention of the Life Office Management Association that, despite their high initial costs, Hollerith machines could take over all office record-keeping.[74] Managers were well aware that female Hollerith operators were cheaper to hire and more easily trained than general clerks. A survey by LOMA in 1925 indicated that the use of punch card equipment was sharply accelerating. Of the 80 insurance companies responding, 45 indicated that Holleriths had been introduced with very satisfactory results.[75]

Figure 6.1 Major Canadian organizations purchasing Hollerith equipment from International Business Machines Co. Ltd and its predecessor, the Tabulating Machine Co., 1910–36*

Year	Organization
1910	*Library Bureau of Toronto* *British American Assurance Co.*
1911	*Royal Insurance* *Canadian Government (1911 census)*
1912	*Hollinger Consolidated Mining* *Liverpool, London and Globe Insurance* *Steel Company of Canada* *Toronto Hydro*
1913	*Canadian Pacific Railway* *Canadian Car and Foundry* *Pilkington Bros Glass* *Library Bureau of Montreal*
1914	*Government of Canada, Department of Public Health* *Government of Canada (war registration)*
1915	*Dominion Bureau of Statistics* *Maritime Telephone and Telegraph*
1916	*Ontario Workmen's Compensation Board* *Canada Packers* *Winnipeg Hydro*
1917	*Sun Life Assurance* *Ford Motor Co.* *Patrick Burns*
1918	*Confederation Life Assurance* *Government of Canada (pensions)* *Independent Order of Foresters* *London Life*
1919	*Canadian Kodak* *London Lancashire Insurance* *Norwich Union Fire Insurance*
1920	*Manufacturers Life* *Mutual Life*
1921	*Dominion Steel and Coal Co.* *Canada Life*
1922	*Canadian General Electric* *Great West Life*
1923	*Metropolitan Stores* *Tuckett Tobacco Co.*

Year	Organization
1924	Canadian National Railways General Motors Imperial Life J. E. Clement
1925	Abitibi Power and Paper Co. Canadian Pacific Railway, Department of Natural Resources Canadian Pacific Express Goodyear Rubber
1926	B. F. Goodrich Co. Mercury Mills Mill Owners North American Life Provident Adjustment and Investment Co. Western Assurance
1927	Eaton's Canadian Industries Ltd Dominion Life Eagle Star Insurance Employers Liability Sieberling Rubber
1928	Britannia Canadian Canners Canadian General Electric Dominion of Canada General Insurance Economical Mutual Insurance General Steelwares General Accident Insurance Imperial Tobacco Link Belt RCA Victor
1929	Canadian Car Hudson Bay Mining Wabasso
1930	Canadian Bank of Commerce
1931	Canada Sugar Chrysler Corp. Lake Shore Mines Quebec Power Commission Shawinigan Water and Power Co. Rock City Tobacco
1932	British Columbia Electric The Montreal Gazette Sanford Evans

Year	Organization
1933	Canadian General Rubber
	Government of Canada, Department of Finance
	Quebec Workmen's Compensation Board
	Gutta Percha Rubber Co.
	Government of Canada, Department of National Revenue
1934	Hiram Walkers
	Labatts Brewery
	Toronto Transportation Commission
1935	Bery Moore
	Canadian Cellucotton
	Crown Life Insurance
	City of Montreal (payroll)
	British Columbia, Department of Vital Statistics
	Quebec Department of Health
	Winnipeg Grain Commission
1936	Appleford
	Canadian Wire and Cable
	City of Montreal Association
	City of Toronto Welfare Department
	City of Winnipeg Relief Department
	Industrial Acceptance Corp.
	McIntyre Mines
	Wrigley
	City of Montreal, Department of Relief
	Government of Canada, Department of Trade and Commerce

* This list probably does not represent a complete sales record for the period. IBM's Canadian operation was established in 1917.
Source: Compiled from various sales records, International Business Machines Co. Ltd, Archives, Toronto.

In 1914 the Canadian Pacific Railway also installed the machines in the Calgary office of its department of natural resources as part of a general reorganization of land sale accounting methods by an American efficiency expert. The railway's largest office installed 15 Holleriths in a sound-proofed room in the 1930s.[76] More of the machines were subsequently introduced into two other large departments. Commenting on the Holleriths' 'almost invisible' margin of error, the CPR staff bulletin trumpeted their introduction with these words: 'to say that these machines are "human" in skill and intelligence is grossly to understate the case; they are actually superhuman, performing prodigies of involved arithmetic, sortation and compilation of records.'[77] The Bell Telephone Company had similar Hollerith operations. For example, the plant accounting department employed eight women on key punch machines by the early 1920s.[78] The women recorded plant expense data on cards, which were then sorted and analysed by other machines. But it was the federal government which led the way in merging the new technology with scientific management. The Post Office's money order division introduced a bonus system which tied the wages of key punch operators to their productivity.[79]

Holleriths were responsible for the first automated clerical routines, thereby launching a new era in the office. The machines' greatest impact was on working conditions in the departments where they were located. Computerization would broaden this rationalizing trend to encompass other departments. Still, the impact of punch card equipment should not be underestimated. Information processing became a highly centralized operation in which clerical tasks were carefully paced and planned according to the dictates of the machines. Each mechanical step – coding, key punching, sorting, collating, computing, storing, and so on – became a specialized clerical function.[80] Moreover, sweeping reforms in office administration were facilitated by Hollerith machines. Managers were able to achieve greater control over organizational operations by having precise information at their fingertips. In short, Hollerith machines were 'wizards at producing facts, . . . [and] disclosed to management the value of obtaining essential statistics accurately and on time'.[81] The first computer in Canada was an IBM 650 installed by Manufacturers Life in 1956. This signalled the beginning of the electronic phase of automatic data processing, a development which emerged directly from the solid foundations laid decades earlier by Hollerith machines.

MECHANIZATION AND WORK DEGRADATION

At the forefront of any discussion of technology is its impact on the nature of work. There can be little doubt that certain clerical jobs lost their skill requirements, task variety and worker autonomy as office technology progressed from the typewriter to electronic data processing systems. Nineteenth-century office jobs, I have noted, often possessed craft-like features. The traditional male bookkeeper was an experienced generalist who at any given moment could report to his boss on the state of the business. But with industrial expansion and increasingly complex business dealings, the rise of the large-scale office bureaucracy after 1900 wrought fundamental changes in the division of administrative labour. The mounting volume of routine work induced employers to hire women largely because they could be paid much less than men. As the scope of administration widened, the focus of individual clerical tasks narrowed. By the 1920s the generalist male bookkeeper had disappeared from most large offices, succeeded by teams of female functionaries monotonously processing financial data with the aid of machines.

Observing similar changes, particularly in the United States, a number of analysts have concluded that a revolution had occurred in the areas of technology, organization and management. Elyce Rotella claims, for example, that by 1930 American offices resembled 'factories with specialized labour and continuous work processes. A variety of business machines replaced the pen and ledgerbook.'[82] A contemporary report in the late 1920s reinforces this impression: 'with the last decade mechanical devices have become universal and as essential to almost every detail of office work as it [sic] is in the factory . . . In every corner, human labour is being replaced by devices or is being used to tend machines which seem almost human in their capacities.'[83] From today's vantage point, there can be little doubt that office mechanization was a key ingredient in transforming the United States into an information-based economy. But this was not achieved without certain costs in terms of a deterioration in office working conditions.[84] Mechanical innovations were often complemented by bureaucratized office organizations and management cost-reduction and efficiency programmes. Clerical work thus become more specialized, standardized and constrained. As the International Labour Organization aptly observed, office technology at its most effective level incorporated 'a strictly rationalized system of work organization, without which the machine would be useless'.[85]

Harry Braverman is perhaps the best-known proponent of the thesis that the office has developed a factory-like environment over the course of this century.[86] According to Braverman, technology and Taylorism were the scissor-like cutting edges of work rationalization. Managers in the factory, then the office, applied techniques which fragmented, deskilled and universally degraded labour in order to achieve greater operating efficiency and assert their control over the labour process. This destruction of the craft-basis of the office was a by-product of the rise of corporate capitalism. In Braverman's view, managerial functions related to appropriation and control became discrete labour processes which in turn were delegated to an army of proletarian clerks. The administrative division of labour grew more specialized as tasks were mechanized and reorganized according to scientific management principles. The result of these changes, argues Braverman, is that the office came to resemble a factory with work organized around a paper-processing assembly line.

However compelling Braverman's thesis may at first appear, its bold claims about the homogeneous degradation of clerical work require very careful qualification. As Stephen Wood points out, a 'crude' deskilling thesis which posits workplace rationalization as a sweeping trend within modern capitalism must be replaced by more subtle analysis based on careful empirical documentation.[87] For one thing, it is questionable whether white-collar and blue-collar work can in fact converge. Paper processing is a considerably less tangible activity than manufacturing, often lacking a visible product. The less quantifiable the workers' output, the more difficult it is for management to regulate strictly the labour process. Even a highly automated office cannot be totally equated with a factory. Certainly there remain significant differences in the minds of the clerical workers, who perceive their cleaner jobs, more fashionable work attire and scope (albeit limited) for making work-related decisions as the basis of higher social status.[88] And historical comparisons of white-collar and blue-collar workers show that technology has a less pervasive influence on the former simply because the order and pace of task execution and freedom of worker movement is more difficult to control in the office.[89]

The degradation thesis also implies that the craft ideal was the hallmark of the office around the turn of the century. When C. Wright Mills talked of 'the ideal of craftsmanship', he had in mind workers who are fairly autonomous, can see a job through from beginning to end, and are able to develop their skills further.[90] Yet in reality considerable drudgery was associated with traditional male clerking as was the case, for that matter, with most other nineteenth century crafts. For example, the lowest and largest class of Canadian federal civil service clerks performed tasks every bit as tedious and unrewarding as those executed by today's female functionaries. In the early 1880s, these petty bureaucrats spent their days 'checking, comparing, copying, compiling and transcribing Accounts and Documents. This, so far as we can ascertain, comprises four-fifths of the whole work to be done, and requires for its performance no special attainments beyond what can be acquired in the Common Schools.'[91] In work situations such as this, the introduction of machines may have provided welcome relief from monotonous work. But more to the point, an essential difference between the old and the new office is that clerical positions in the former provided men with a stepping-stone into management or entrepreneurship, whereas the latter gave rise to occupational ghettos which trapped women in menial, dead-end jobs.

With respect to the pervasive effects of work rationalization suggested by Braverman, typing provides good counter-evidence of how mechanization did not necessarily signal a transition to factory-like working conditions. Typing is the oldest of the mechanized office jobs and, as such, one might expect it to be among the most highly rationalized. However, I have documented above striking contrasts within the typing–stenography occupational group. When correspondence and recording work was reorganized into a central typing pool, using numerous typewriters and dictation machines, conditions indeed resembled a paper-generating assembly line. But the pool typists occupied the bottom rung of the machine-based hierarchy. At the top were the private stenographers, a coveted position which offered working women relative economic and social rewards quite similar to the traditional female professions of teaching, nursing and social work.[92] The modern secretary occupies a paradoxical role: despite her use of the most advanced typewriter technology within a bureaucratic organization, her working conditions are shaped by informal, particularistic criteria. This small but privileged group derives status indirectly from their male bosses.[93] Despite being paternalistic and often arbitrary in nature, the interpersonal relations governing much secretarial work may temper the more routinizing aspects of mechanization or bureaucracy.

Recent studies of the impact of automation on female clerks also caution against talking about a uniform downgrading effect. In a recent study, Feldberg and Glenn discovered that office automation had an uneven impact on various segments of the office workforce and, moreover, had different effects at the aggregate, organizational, and work process levels.[94] They found little evidence of an overall trend towards a more degraded and deskilled type of work. Often contradictory forces were present, with some women obtaining access to more rewarding jobs while others experienced negative effects. Likewise, one case study found that while the changeover from copy to video typing had a routinizing, fragmenting and depersonalizing impact, the new word processing equipment provided several benefits for some typists: increased pay and promotion opportunities, greater control over quality and some degree of skill upgrading.[95] Admittedly these findings are challenged by Heather Menzie's Canadian research which, despite being rather speculative, is indicative of the controversy surrounding this particular topic.[96] Nonetheless, one critical point must be borne in mind: it is quite possible that many of the negative aspects of VDT work are not a direct outcome of the new word processing technology *per se*. Rather, they may result from strategic decisions by management to reorganize work around VDT equipment in the interest of higher productivity. Technology thus serves as a tool used by management in their profit-motivated drive to control the labour process.

One final qualification regarding the applicability of the work degradation thesis to the office is required. Most arguments about office work becoming more factory-like rest on the often untested assumption that by 1930, when the foundations of the modern office were in place, most clerks were tied to machines. Our evidence above clearly depicts the sometimes pervasive influence of office machines, especially when integrated into broad managerial strategies to rationalize and regulate the flow of paperwork. However, we must also recognize the tendency in the past to overstate the diffusion and impact of office technology. Grace Coyle, for instance, describes how the American office had evolved up to

1929: 'Within the last decade mechanical devices have become as universal and as essential to almost every detail of office work as it is [sic] in the factory . . . In every corner human labour is being replaced by mechanical devices or is being used to tend machines which seem almost human in their capacities.'[97]

At issue, then, is the extent to which clerks have been tied to typewriters, office machines and computers in the twentieth-century office. It is possible to obtain an accurate picture of the number of clerks whose jobs have been shaped directly by technology. However, the more pervasive indirect use of machines, assisting clerks in performing a wide range of tasks, is difficult to determine. You will recall that the occupational category of 'office machine operator' first appeared in the 1921 census, but there were too few to warrant publication of separate data for this group until 1931.[98] By then, 1503 women – comprising 86.3 per cent of the total employees in this category – operated office machines exclusively in a distinctive female job ghetto. According to the 1981 census, there were 76,340 females classified as office machine operators (see table 3.6) comprising 77.2 per cent of the group and 4.5 per cent of all women in clerical jobs. The situation with stenography and typing occupations is somewhat different. These jobs constitute a much larger share of the total female clerical workforce. In 1981, there were 475,125 female stenographers and typists, accounting for almost 99 per cent of the workers in this group and 28 per cent of all female clerks. Even more than with other office machinery, these jobs are commonly viewed as women's work. The extensive use of the typewriter is evident from the rapid increase in the number of women employed in stenography and typing, from 851 in 1891 to 64,993 by 1931. But as I have already emphasized, full-blown work rationalization only affected that minority of typists organized into central pools.

More generally, office mechanization varied considerably among organizations and industries, depending on the amount and type of paperwork required. For instance, banks, insurance companies and firms with large accounts receivable tended to develop more extensive office operations. But the relative numbers of office equipment operators did not increase with the same velocity as the overall clerical workforce. For example, by 1953 the Bank of Nova Scotia employed a total of 2,275 women clerks, of whom 200 (9 per cent) were office machine operators and 481 (21 per cent) were stenographers and typists.[99]

To shift this analysis to a comparative plane, it is relevant to note that the onslaught of mechanization took a similar path in the United States. Office machine operators first appeared in the US census in 1930, comprising only 1 per cent of all clerks at the time.[100] Certainly the available US evidence, reviewed in earlier chapters, regarding office technology reveals strong parallels with the Canadian case. The same cannot be said, however, for the British office. Again relying on David Lockwood's research, we discover that in the post-Second World War British office technology had registered only a limited impact. Office machines, notes Lockwood, mainly 'reinforce and support' existing clerical functions.[101] It is therefore wrong to argue that the mere presence of machinery 'reduces the status of the clerk to that of a factory operative'.[102] I would not dispute the salience of these points with respect to Canada. The difference between the two countries, however, is more pronounced when it comes to the twin assault of mechanization and work reorganization on the office. In Canada and the United States these forces seemed to have reached a higher pitch, affecting comparatively more clerks than in Britain. Even by the 1950s in Britain, machines organized into a production system – such as the Hollerith equipment described above – were apparently the exception to a more typical pattern of simpler technology used to assist, rather than take over, the activities of clerks.[103]

CONCLUSION

In sum, the empirical evidence presented in this chapter does not totally negate the degradation thesis as it applies to the office; rather, it systematically reveals the limitations of such an argument. Far from denying the existence of factory-like conditions in the emerging modern office, I have sought to bring this image more sharply into focus. Specifically, office machine operators constituted only a fraction of the entire Canadian female clerical labour force. Now conversely, a sizeable proportion of clerks continued to perform their tasks in a more traditional manner, especially in smaller offices. This latter point suggests that office machine operators and pool typists were disproportionately concentrated in the largest corporate and government offices. Such organizations were at the cutting edge of the administrative revolution. It is useful to view the small, traditional office and the huge, modern bureaucracy as polar ends of a continuum along which various technological, organizational and managerial innovations in the realm of administration can be placed temporally. Thus even though the machine-related jobs which gave rise to the most monotonous, oppressive and unrewarding employment conditions were relatively few, a much larger number of clerical jobs were partially affected by the broad thrust of workplace rationalization. Whether it be the intensification of work resulting from the adoption of efficiency measures in the front office of a small manufacturer, or the streamlining of a major financial institution's office routines following the introduction of Hollerith equipment, the rationalizing effects of the administrative revolution often advanced through numerous channels.

Three interrelated themes have guided my analysis: mechanization, feminization and managerial control. Adopting a broad perspective on the trend towards stricter controls over office operations, I have noted that while the more elusive nature of clerical work militated against full-blown rationalization as in the factory, scientific management reforms did influence the development of the modern office. More precisely, it was the combination of technology and modern management, when applied to the growing mountain of facts and figures required by corporate capitalism, that underlay the shift to a female labour supply. In short, mechanization and feminization went hand in hand. By the 1930s women formed a new subordinate class of clerical functionaries relegated to the most routinized and mechanized tasks – a trend which still persists today.

By carefully documenting the complex interplay among machines, managerial strategies and the recruitment of female clerks, I have sketched a picture of the modern office during its emergent stage which differs from that portrayed by Braverman and other advocates of the 'office-as-factory' thesis. My central argument, then, is that the most degraded clerical jobs resulted when machines were organized into rationalized production units according to scientific management principles. Best exemplified by the typing pool and the Hollerith department, only in these corners of the office could one find anything resembling factory-like conditions. This conclusion must be further tempered by the knowledge that pool typists and Hollerith operators comprised a minority of clerical workers. A more substantial proportion of clerks experienced elements of factory-style routinization through the piece-meal diffusion of the administrative revolution.

Having presented a more limited and empirically grounded approach to the deterioration of office working conditions than the degradation thesis, we are left wondering how clerks reacted to the changes which occurred. Did they actively resist new technologies and more restrictive forms of work organization, or did they quietly succumb? This important question deserves separate treatment, which I reserve for the concluding chapter. But to anticipate this discussion, overt resistance, especially in the form of unionization, has been conspicuously absent among Canadian clerks.

7

The Proletarianization of Clerical Work?

One of the most perplexing issues facing students of capitalist development is the impact of economic change on the class structure of a society. Since the late nineteenth century, the advancing capitalist division of labour has created new occupations as quickly as it has discarded old ones. This rise and decline of occupational groups has, in turn, recharted the map of class configurations and cleavages with, of course, major political implications. Marx's vision of a dichotomous class system comprised of workers and capitalists has thus failed to materialize. What has especially confounded Marx's predictions in this regard is the growth of a huge white-collar labour force occupying a middle terrain between the two principal classes. Where to locate the white-collar masses in the class structure has been a persistent source of debate in twentieth-century political and social theory.[1] The focal point of the debate is clerical employees, whose particularly ambiguous socio-economic status would appear to give them a foot in both working and middle classes. The erosion of the clerks' relative wage position, their growing unionization and the factory-like conditions in many offices may signal their descent into the working class. But at the same time, one can point to the clerks' greater mobility prospects, lifestyle differences and generally more favourable working environment than blue-collar workers as indicative of middle classness. In short, the question of whether clerks are the new proletarians or members of a white-collar middle class is far from resolved.

THE PROLETARIANIZATION DEBATE

The proletarianization thesis represents the most concerted attempt to account for the class position of the clerk. Neo-marxists use the concept of proletarianization to describe the deterioration of white-collar working conditions and comparative pay advantages over manual workers.[2] The proletarianization thesis derives its empirical support from historical wage trends and changes in the labour process. Advocates of the thesis posit a direct relationship between the development of rationalized office bureaucracies, a deterioration of clerical wages and working conditions and the movement of clerical workers as a group into the working class. Income is the most widely used measure of the declining class position of the clerk. The general convergence of clerical and manual earnings since the turn of the century in Western capitalist societies is adduced as solid evidence of the destruction of the clerks' once superior socio-economic position.[3] This is usually augmented by a description of the progressive rationalization of administration, such as Braverman's account of the degradation of clerical work mentioned in previous chapters.[4] According to Braverman, as traditional managerial functions became part of the administrative labour process they were delegated to a growing army of routine clerks and rationalized through mechanization and scientific management. The deskilling and regimentation of clerical tasks eliminated previous distinctions between mental and manual work. This loss of the job autonomy and skill typical of the nineteenth-century bookkeeper thus constitute the major criteria for classifying clerks as proletarians.[5]

Essentially the proletarianization thesis infers the class location of an occupational group from its changing market and work situations. It is precisely because of this assumed organic link between workers' class location on the one hand, and job and labour market conditions on the other that the thesis has been criticized.[6] One must thus bear in mind that 'fluctuations in the market and work conditions of particular groups of workers are, of course, a far more common occurrence than any "radical" shifts in their class situation.'[7] An equally fundamental problem with the proletarianization thesis, yet to be explored, is the tendency to overlook how changing labour market and job characteristics of clerical employees are directly tied to the dramatic shift in the sex composition of the office workforce during the early twentieth century. It is difficult to interpret the broader impact of the administrative revolution which transformed clerical work without considering the process of feminization. This lacuna in the proletarianization debate largely reflects the long-standing assumption in stratification theory that the economic and social experiences of males define the class structure.[8] It is thus taken for granted that females, the great majority of whom are married, depend directly on their husbands for their class position. These assumptions are especially problematic in the case of clerical workers.

This blind spot concerning the centrality of gender in the development of modern office work has led to three serious flaws in the clerical proletarianization thesis. In the first place, the tendency to examine wages for all workers in an occupation, rather than disaggregating data by sex, masks how the rapid influx of cheap female labour into the office depressed average salaries.[9] A second flaw stems from not explicitly examining the way in which office expansion and reorganization brought about a shift from a male to a female labour supply. Consequently, a defining feature of the administrative revolution is ignored: that the jobs into which women were increasingly being recruited could not be proletarianized to any great extent because most were mechanized, routinized, and generally unrewarding almost from their inception. Both oversights are evident in Braverman's analysis.[10] While acknowledging that declining wages and the entry of women into the office define the new clerical sector of twentieth-century monopoly capitalism, Braverman failed to explore how these two trends are interconnected. Instead, he treated clerks as an undifferentiated group and presented salary data for males and females combined to document the groups' descent into the working class.

The third flaw, also found in Braverman, results from viewing clerks as a homogeneous group subjected to the all-encompassing onslaught of work rationalization. I have already shown how the administrative revolution wrought fundamental, enduring changes in the labour process, but the trend towards more fragmented, standardized and regulated tasks occurred unevenly. Even within the female clerical sector there are pronounced differences in wages and working conditions across industries, within and among firms, and in occupational subgroups. The proletarianization thesis, in short, does not recognize the importance of gender as a major source of change and variation within the twentieth-century office.

In the light of these weaknesses, the purpose of this chapter is to advance the proletarianization debate by examining the transformation of the clerical labour market and office working conditions from the perspective of the feminization process. I shall argue that the gender segmentation of the office workforce explains many of the characteristics which the proletarianization thesis erroneously interprets as signs of the clerks' declining class position.

The new routine clerical jobs created by the development of the administrative apparatus of corporate capitalism constituted an expanding area of women's work. That many of these jobs were regimented, often mechanized, fragmented, low paying and dead-end suggests the spread of factory-like working conditions. But to conclude further that the incumbents of such jobs were proletarianized in the process is inaccurate. In fact, the shift in the sex composition of office staffs would indicate that neither males nor females were proletarianized in the neo-marxian sense of descending into the working class. On the one hand, male clerks occupied the better clerical positions and many were upwardly mobile as the ranks of management expanded. On the other hand, very few women actually experienced the proletarianization of office working conditions. This is because their recruitment was directly linked to the proliferation of the menial administrative tasks which, as we have seen, became labelled as women's work. Admittedly the onslaught of managerial work rationalization strategies did introduce factory-like conditions into some areas of the office. But evidence presented below shows that the feminization of the office did not entail the creation of a unified mass of unskilled, low-wage tasks. Granted that the basic structure of inequality in the modern office, embodied in the male manager and the female clerk, was forged during the administrative revolution. The experience of women clerks, however, was far from identical considering that the pay and working conditions for some was substantially better than for others.

In sum, the process of work degradation within the office proceeded unevenly across firms and industries, as well as within the clerical occupational structure itself. Braverman's model of the modern office – a paper-processing factory staffed by a uniform administrative underclass – does not bear up under careful empirical investigation. Pronounced inter-industry differences and salary variations in large organizations suggest stratification within the clerical labour market is far more complex than the basic male–female division.

HISTORICAL TRENDS IN CLERICAL EARNINGS

The administrative revolution, by creating a more complex office hierarchy with a greater proportion of simplified tasks, precipitated a decline in clerical earnings. But to what extent did this represent a marked departure from the relative labour market position of the nineteenth-century clerk? Unfortunately, lack of reliable data makes it difficult to estimate any consistent white-collar wage trends for late nineteenth century Canada. Available evidence portrays clerks of this period as a small group of males who came from middle class backgrounds, possessed considerable skills and had good advancement opportunities. A junior clerk hired by the Consumer's Gas Company in Toronto started at $300 annually in 1855, rising to $600 after four years; chief clerks earned over $1,000. In contrast, the company paid the stokers in the gas works $364 and lamplighters received $260 annually.[11] It is difficult, however, to generalize on the basis of a single firm, especially considering that Lockwood's research reveals significant salary variations among British clerks in the latter half of the nineteenth century.[12] He identifies essentially two groups of clerks, both better paid than artisans. Only the select group of financial, civil service, and mercantile clerks could support a middle-class lifestyle, the majority suffering a 'respectable poverty'.[13] Lockwood raises an important point, to which I will return below, regarding the connection between salary and lifestyle. Comparing the earnings of various groups of employees

Table 7.1 Average annual earnings for the total labour force and all clerical workers, by sex, and production workers in manufacturing, Canada, 1901–71*

| | Labour Force | | | Clerical Workers | | | |
| | 1 | 2 | 3 | 4 | 5 | 6 | 7 |
	Total	Male	Female	Total	Male	Female	Production Workers in Manufacturing
1901	$ 384.53	$ 387.16	$ 181.98	$ 446.72	$ 496.49	$ 264.37	$ 375.00[b]
1911	542.17	593.31	305.71	611.91	757.02	449.50	417.00
1921	844.26	1,056.92	572.82	1,056.20	1,248.77	785.10	999.00
1931	847.00	925.00	559.00	1,007.00	1,153.00	830.00	950.00
1941	867.00	993.00	490.00	922.00	1,113.00	731.00	1,220.00
1951[a]	1,860.00	2,131.00	1,220.00	1,771.00	2,166.00	1,546.00	2,434.00
1961	3,170.00	3,660.00	1,993.00	2,743.00	3,381.00	2,339.00	3,762.00
1971	5,391.00	6,574.00	3,199.00	4,139.15	5,868.70	3,402.60	6,695.00

* Data adjusted to 1951 census occupation classification
[a] Median income, columns 1–6.
[b] For the year 1905.

Source: Columns 1–6: 1901 Census of Canada, Census and Statistics Bulletin I, *Wage Earners by Occupations*, table II; 1911 Census of Canada, unpublished working tables for wage earners, Statistics Canada microfilm roll no. 11002; 1931 Census of Canada, volume 5, table 33; Meltz, *Manpower in Canada*, section V, table A1; 1971 Census of Canada, volume III, part 6 (Bulletin 3.67), table 14. Column 7: M. C. Urquhart and K. A. H. Buckley (eds), *Historical Statistics of Canada* (Toronto, Macmillan, 1965), p. 99 [to 1951]; *Manufacturing Industries of Canada*, Section A, Summary for Canada (Ottawa, Dominion Bureau of Statistics, 1961), p. 16 [for 1961]; *1971 Annual Census of Manufacturers*, Summary Statistics, Preliminary (Ottawa, Statistics Canada, July, 973), p. 3 [for 1971].

ascertains their economic positions relative to each other, but says little about the actual standard of living, and therefore lifestyle differences, provided by these earnings.

Beginning with the census of 1901 one can trace wage patterns in Canada with reasonable accuracy. According to table 7.1, the typical clerical employee earned more than the labour force average until 1941, and more than the average wage of blue-collar production workers until 1931. During the depression and Second World War, however, these clerical wage advantages disappeared. In 1941 clerks had an average salary of $922, considerably less than the $1,220 earned by production workers. And in 1951 clerks earned only $1,771 compared with the labour force average of $1,860. Over the following two decades clerks continued to lose economic ground, in the sense that their average earnings increased less rapidly than for production workers and many other groups in the labour force. Table 7.2 furnishes a concise summary: clerical earnings ranged from 13 to 29 per cent above the labour force average from 1901 to 1931, then steadily declined to only 74 per cent of the average wage in 1971.[14]

This precipitous drop in relative clerical earnings may be attributed to a number of factors. The expansion of public education enlarged the supply of suitably trained workers for office jobs. Equally decisive was the reduction of skill and educational requirements as the number of routinized and mechanized clerical tasks shot upward. Gains in blue-collar wages, because of the mounting strength of unions and a dwindling supply of cheap rural labour with the slowing of immigration after 1914, helped to narrow the wage gap with white-collar employees. But the central reason for the decline in clerical earnings was the recruitment of females into the lower ranks of administrative bureaucracies. Two distinct labour markets emerged: one for males in more skilled and highly rewarding jobs, another for women in low-paying routine jobs. Discriminatory hiring and promotion practices became institutionalized as the economic advantages of hiring female clerks eroded the traditional sanctions against employing women in business. In order to assess fully the impact of feminization on clerical wage trends it is essential to examine separately male and female earnings.

There should be little doubt by now that a distinct labour market for female clerical employees has existed since the turn of the century. This is evident from comparing the male and female clerical earnings presented in table 7.1. Female clerks earned 53 per cent of the average male clerical salary in 1901, inching up to 58 per cent by 1971. This persistently lower female wage accounts for the overall decline in clerical earnings, as women comprised a steadily growing proportion of the office workforce. Given that women are Balkanized into subordinate sectors of the labour market, competing amongst themselves for jobs and not with men, it is noteworthy that during the first four decades of this century female clerks earned 49 to 68 per cent more than the average female worker (table 7.2). But this wage superiority diminished after 1941 as thousands of young women who previously would have remained at home acquired sufficient education to meet the minimal requirements for the booming white-collar sector.[15] The growing abundance of qualified female labour interacted with a reduction of skill requirements in many office jobs to depress clerical salaries to within 9 per cent of the female labour force average by 1971.

Table 7.2 Average clerical earnings expressed as a percentage of average labour force earnings, by sex, Canada, 1901–71*

	1901	1911	1921	1931	1941	1951	1961	1971
Total	117	113	127	129	107	95	85	74
Male	116	129	119	126	107	102	92	89
Female	149	154	150	166	168	141	126	109

* Average labour force earnings exclude clerical earnings.
Source: Calculated from table 7.1.

Table 7.3 presents a more finely grained analysis of female clerical earnings during the 1970s. While full-time, full-year female clerks (note that the data in tables 7.1 and 7.2 include part-time and seasonal clerks) earned the female labour force average in 1970, this fell to about 92 per cent in 1980. When compared with four other major female occupations, this relative decline in clerks' wages seems even more pronounced, even though sales clerks, teachers, nurses and waitresses also saw their earnings eroded during the 1970s. Of equal interest is the positioning of clerks between lower-wage retail sales personnel and waitresses, and much better paying – largely due to widespread unionization – teaching and nursing jobs.

But a closer examination of changes in earnings for specific clerical jobs will tell us even more about where the office labour supply has been most cheapened. Scanning the right-hand column in table 7.3, we discover that while female labour force average earnings grew by 188 per cent during the 1970s – a greater increase, by the way, than for the male labour force – clerical earnings rose by a less substantial 162 to 172 per cent. This range of increases is fairly narrow, although it is worth speculating on why two of the mainstays of the female office workforce – stenographers/secretaries and typists/clerk typists – had the lowest and highest rates of increase respectively. Perhaps current applications of

Table 7.3 Female earnings in selected occupations for full-time, full-year workers, Canada 1970–80

	1970		1980		% Change 1970–80
	Average earnings	Average earnings as % of female labour force earnings	Average earnings	Average earnings as % of female labour force earnings	
Male labour force	$8,045	—	$21,441	—	166.5%
Female labour force	4,748	100.0%	13,677	100.0%	188.1
All clerical occupations	4,699	99.0	12,545	91.7	167.0
Bookkeepers and accounting clerks	4,751	100.0	12,616	92.2	165.5
Office machine operators	4,512	95.0	12,012	87.8	166.2
Electronic data-processing equipment operators	4,800	101.1	12,720	93.0	165.0
Stenographers and secretaries	4,884	102.9	12,816	93.7	162.4
Typists and clerk typists	4,327	91.1	11,786	86.2	172.4
Sales clerks (commodities)	3,348	70.5	9,495	69.4	183.6
Elementary and secondary school teachers	7,325	154.3	20,713	151.4	182.8
Graduate nurses	6,351	133.8	18,041	131.9	184.1
Waitresses	2,866	60.4	7,687	56.2	168.2

Source: 1971 Census of Canada, 'Income of Individuals', vol. III, part 6, Catalogue 94–767, table 18; 1981 Census of Canada, 'Population', vol. 1, National series, Catalogue 92–930, table 1.

office automation and attendant reorganizations of the labour process are affecting these typing-based jobs differently. It must be left to future research to clarify this issue. Historically speaking, it nonetheless does seem that despite an overall downward trend, clerical work has ranked right behind the female professions with regard to wages and working conditions throughout this century.

Looking now at male clerks, we note a sharp decline in earnings relative to both production workers and the labour force average. Table 7.2 documents that, comparatively speaking, male clerks began to lose economic ground after 1911, regaining slightly in 1931, then sliding below the labour force average by 1961. Taking production workers in manufacturing industries as the comparison group, table 7.4 indicates that male clerks could claim to be economically better off only up to the 1930s, after which time the situation was reversed. Economic growth and prosperity had, by 1911, created a scarcity of clerical labour which, in turn, was reflected in relatively high wages for clerks of both sexes. But a steady decline then set in and from 1941 to 1971 the average male clerk earned around 10 per cent less than his blue-collar counterpart. This alone is insufficient grounds for concluding that a levelling of class differences had occurred. To be sure, a good number of males recorded as clerks in the censuses were embarking on careers that would elevate them into management. This issue requires further attention, for as I pointed out above little is known about the historical mobility patterns of male clerks in Canada. Scattered evidence raises the possibility that in some early twentieth-century organizations avenues of clerical promotion were actually quite restrictive.

Table 7.4 Average clerical earnings, by sex, expressed as a percentage of average earnings of production workers in manufacturing, Canada, 1901–71

	1901	1911	1921	1931	1941	1951	1961	1971
Male	1.32	1.82	1.25	1.21	.91	.89	.90	.88
Female	.70	1.08	.79	.87	.59	.64	.62	.51

Source: Calculated from table 7.1.

For example, the British-style job hierarchy introduced into the federal civil service in 1882 inhibited promotion opportunities from the lower ranks.[16] Besides facing low starting salaries and meagre annual increments, male junior clerks had little hope of ascending through the ranks. The basic departmental organization was built around one chief clerk, four in the second class, and eight or more in the third and lowest class. The result, according to one observer, was that 'nothing short of the chief clerks being stricken by paralysis every three or four years could create any hope for the scores who are submerged in the lower classes.'[17] Even with regular promotions it would have taken 20 years of steady progress for a male clerk to reach the maximum salary of $1,400.[18] The junior positions became less attractive for aspiring young men, in part resulting in a shift toward a female labour supply. It is difficult to say how widespread this bureaucratic problem was, although I hasten to add that rapid business expansion after 1900 provided mobility opportunities by creating new positions. For example, after examining census data pertaining to the Toronto banking industry in 1911 and 1921, David Coombs estimates that the creation of new management positions during the decade could have provided upward mobility for over one-quarter of the 1911 pool of Toronto-based bank clerks.[19] Whether this reflects conditions in a particular industry or the general economic climate of the war years remains an interesting research question.

Armed with these trends in clerical wages, we now have a stronger foundation for understanding the major transformations in the clerical labour market precipitated by the administrative revolution. The most dramatic change was the creation of non-competing and unequal male and female labour market segments. Females formed an expanding pool of cheap labour for routine office jobs, thereby depressing average clerical earnings. But when each segment is examined separately a more variegated picture emerges. Male clerks experienced an erosion of their relative wage position after 1911 at the same time as mobility prospects were improving. While increases in female clerks' earnings have not kept pace with other groups in the female labour force since the early twentieth century, most office jobs open to women offered above average wages and working conditions.

How representative are these Canadian earnings patterns of the economic situation of clerks in other countries? Pursuing the previous comparisons with Britain and the United States, one indeed discovers striking similarities in this regard. In the case of Britain, most male clerks in the nineteenth century could expect better employment conditions and job security than factory workers. Yet from the 1870s onward, the wage superiority that clerks had over manual workers began to erode.[20] By the First World War earnings of male clerks and skilled manual workers were on a par, remaining that way until 1936. Then clerical salaries declined relative to the skilled manual group; by 1978 semi-skilled males earned more than male clerks.[21]

Britain's earnings profile for female clerks presents an entirely different scenario. From 1913–14, women in clerical jobs could count on better than average remuneration. Whereas female clerks increased their earnings from 56 to 69 per cent of the labour force average between 1913–14 to 1978, the same indicator for male clerks dropped from 122 to

93 per cent.[22] Of course it must be recognized that many young male clerks are at the thresholds of lucrative and challenging careers.[23] And narrowing the focus to just the female labour force, we find a downward slide in full-time female clerical earnings from 103 per cent of the average for all employed women in 1922–4 to 97 per cent by 1960.[24] These data are far from definitive for Britain, nor are they directly comparable with the above Canadian evidence. Still, they help to sketch out some interesting parallels.

As far as American trends go, women clerks earned on average more than other female non-professional workers throughout the 1870 to 1930 period.[25] The gap narrowed, but in 1930 female clerks still commanded higher salaries than women in manufacturing, sales and service jobs. Furthermore, the social status attached to the more skilled clerical positions was equivalent to the lower professions.[26] By expressing the median salaries of female clerks as a percentage of all individual and family income, it is possible to detect a marked decline between 1939 and 1970, from 78.5 per cent to 50 per cent.[27] Against the same base, male clerical earnings fell during the same period from 115.4 to 84.9 per cent. Clerks of both sexes lost ground to manual workers, although managing to retain a slight wage advantage in 1970. A different data series, reporting 1982 weekly earnings for full-time workers in the larger occupational groups, shows both male and female clerks earning less than labour force averages for each sex (93.5 and 97.9 per cent respectively).[28] Within the female labour force clerks are better off than sales persons, manual operatives, labourers and service workers. However, they tend to earn less than female craftworkers and, of course, women in professional and technical jobs.

In short, there is a fairly identifiable uniform trend regarding clerical earnings in North America and Britain. Male clerks have slid down the earnings ladder, losing whatever comparative wage superiority they could have claimed over manual workers in the early twentieth century. And female clerks, while still relatively better off in terms of financial rewards than many other female employees, have nonetheless seen this relative advantage diminish over the decades. Surely these parallel downward wage drifts in the three countries that I have examined reflect, in the main, a cheapening of clerical work due to a changing administrative division of labour.

COMPARISON OF EARNINGS IN A BANK AND AN INSURANCE COMPANY

The clerical labour market is far from homogeneous, even within the major male and female segments. As with most occupational groups, clerical salaries vary regionally, by firm and industry, and by the particular tasks performed. Regional differences, reflecting the specific interplay of supply and demand forces in local labour markets, will not concern us here.[29] My central interest is in salaries paid within individual firms and for specific tasks. This level of analysis, absent in most discussions of clerical proletarianization, is essential for determining how changes in office working conditions affected the clerical labour market.

There have been few attempts to establish earning patterns for individual firms, mainly because these types of historical data are often unobtainable. Fortunately two major Canadian employers of clerical workers, the Bank of Nova Scotia and Manufacturers Life Insurance Company, have maintained salary records from around the turn of the century. Some of these data are presented in table 7.5 for the 1911–31 period, when both organizations initiated major changes in the clerical labour process. Salary data for the bank include the Toronto head office and branches throughout Ontario. In 1911 this encompassed a workforce of 151, of which 38 were in head office; by 1931 this had swelled to 1,102 employees with 219 in head office. The share of clerical positions held by women increased from 8.6 to 30.4 per cent over this period, the majority being concentrated in head office. The Manufacturers Life salary data pertain to Toronto head office, which grew from a staff of 93 in 1911 to 445 by 1931. The proportion of all clerical jobs held by women was high in comparison with the bank, standing at 41.8 and 55.2 per cent in 1911 and 1931 respectively. This alone confirms the uneven impact of the feminization process across firms.

Male clerical earnings in each firm roughly follow the male labour force trend (see table 7.1), except for insurance clerks in 1931. The earnings of these particular bank and insurance clerks were not significantly better than the wages received by production workers in manufacturing during the 1911–31 period. Canadian bank and insurance clerks hardly constituted an 'aristocracy of clerkdom', the term Lockwood applies to similar employees in Britain.[30]

A number of salient observations emerge from a comparison of male salaries in the bank and the insurance company. First, clerks and juniors in insurance appear to have been better off than their counterparts in banking throughout the period. This inter-firm wage spread is even greater in the managerial and professional category. Second, fluctuations in salaries follow a different pattern in each organization, suggesting that they may have been drawing upon different pools of labour. Canadian banks used apprenticeship systems which required young recruits to toil at subsistence wages for several years in order to prove themselves worthy of a banking career. Because low starting salaries failed to attract sufficient numbers of Canadian men with the type of solid middle-class background desired, banks were forced to recruit in England and Scotland before eventually turning towards women as a source of labour.

Life insurance, by contrast, placed greater emphasis on formal education and consequently paid higher salaries. University commerce or mathematics graduates were considered ideal recruits because of the actuarial expertise required in many of the higher positions. Third, part of the salary differential may reflect the fact that the bank's salary data include branches in small towns and rural areas where wage levels were lower than in Toronto.

The two firms were much closer together on female salaries in all clerical categories. Female employees in both organizations, except for new recruits, earned notably more than the average female clerk throughout the period (see table 7.1). In fact, starting salaries in both institutions were close to the average clerical salary for the whole labour force. I should also mention that the gap between male and female clerical salaries was greater in insurance, mainly because of the higher male salaries paid by Manufacturers Life.

The difference between salaries for general clerks and stenographer–typists buttresses my argument that the female clerical labour market is internally stratified. Of all the office jobs available to women, stenography held out the greatest rewards. The special skills and greater responsibilities of stenographers placed them in a distinct labour pool. Stenographers tended to be more career minded, having greater seniority than other female clerks in both firms. Indeed, the early twentieth-century stenographer was the female craft worker of the office. This accounts for the rather anomalous situation in the Bank of Nova Scotia where stenographers were the highest paid clerks of either sex throughout the 1911 to 1926 period.

The accelerating drive for greater office efficiency, however, did fragment and routinize the stenographer's work. Specialized jobs such as clerk typist, dictaphone typist, receptionist, and file clerk were carved out of the stenographer's general domain. Thus while the stenographer remained an administrative accoutrement of the manager in smaller branches, the banks had installed typing pools in their larger urban branches and head offices by the late 1920s. Until the 1920s, the Bank of Nova Scotia hired only stenographers, replacing them with the lower-grade clerk typist as the work became increasingly subdivided and menial. The stenographer, although facing diminishing privileges by 1930, was clearly at the top of the female office hierarchy. This position marked the limit of female advancement within the office, given that women were virtually excluded from managerial and professional jobs.[31]

These two case studies of clerical employers underline the importance of refocusing the analysis away from the entire clerical labour force toward the division of labour within specific firms. This must be supplemented with case studies of other firms located in different industrial sectors before generalizations about the relations between work

Table 7.5 Average annual earnings[a] of male and female employees, selected occupations, Bank of Nova Scotia (Ontario branchdes and head office) and Manufacturers Life Insurance Company (Toronto head office), 1911–31

	1911		1916		1921		1926		1931	
	BNS	MLI	BNS	MLI	BNS	MLI	BNS	MLI	BNS	MLI
Males										
Clerks[b]	$ 529.69	$ 630.62	$ 556.36	$ 985.95	$ 918.29	$1,063.23	$ 907.41	$1,128.10	$1,085.60	$1,328.66
Junior clerks[c]	336.54	369.87	348.11	462.00	507.58	890.37	473.23	757.24	657.14	1,033.53
Stenographers and typists	—	540.00[e]	1,000.00[e]	—	950.00[e]	—	—	1,293.33	—	1,550.00
Junior stenographers and typists[c]	—	540.00[e]	—	—	—	—	—	—	—	—
Managers and professionals[d]	2,601.25	3,850.00	2,211.50	3,687.50	3,008.37	5,056.43	3,153.79	5,537.50	3,458.27	6,431.94

Females

Clerks	$ 603.50	$ 530.63	$ 456.27	$ 587.35	$ 865.43	$ 840.62	$ 917.54	$ 871.81	$ 993.83	$ 923.32
Junior clerks[c]	598.00	412.52	419.70	457.78	900.00[e]	742.73	563.89	729.00	646.00	793.50
Stenographers and typists	610.00	562.36	615.29	660.56	1,001.79	998.53	950.27	915.00	1,023.49	1,403.33
Junior stenographers and typists[c]	560.00	486.00	489.25	520.00	908.57	—	672.11	797.14	730.00	—
Managers and professionals[d]	—	1,400.00[e]	865.00[e]	—	—	—	1,300.00[e]	—	1,550.00	

a Includes average annual salaries, plus bonuses and living allowances, as of 31 December of each year. Earnings of temporary or part-time employees excluded.

b Includes all non-supervisory clerical employees (below the rank of assistant manager in the bank; below the rank of department head in the insurance company) excluding stenographers and typists. The 1951 census definition of clerk was used as a guide for classification.

c The term 'junior' simply denotes those employees with less than one year of service. It provides an approximation of starting salaries. although raises granted to some employees at the end of their probationary period are included.

d For the bank this includes branch managers, assistant managers, accountants, inspectors and general office executives. For the insurance company this includes executives, department heads, cashiers, actuaries, accountants, translators, medical doctors and registered nurses.

e One employee only.

Source: Branch Staff Lists for 1911–31, Bank of Nova Scotia Archives, Toronto; Head Office Salary Books for 1911–31. Manufacturers Life Insurance Company Archives, Toronto.

and market conditions can be offered with any certainty. Nonetheless, it is possible to derive from the above case studies some tentative conclusions about the basic employment patterns of stenographers. From its origins in the late nineteenth century, stenography was labelled as a feminine pursuit, attracting young women with the lure of relatively high salaries and the prestige of an office job. But the explosion of paperwork increased repetitive typing tasks, thereby spawning the position of clerk typist. So widespread was the use of the typewriter that in 1912 the federal civil service began to hire only women with typing skills.[32] The market for stenographers became flooded by the First World War with graduates from commercial courses in high schools and private business college. Yet the potential for high salaries remained good for competent and experienced workers. For example, during the war the 'exceptional stenographer' with 'managing abilities' could command an annual salary in the $1,500 to $2,000 range.[33] This group must have appeared financially privileged in the eyes of women employees in other occupations. Just before the First World War the earnings of female retail clerks fell considerably below those of office workers.[34] Moreover, nurses and teachers commanded salaries roughly on a par with those of female stenographers and bookkeepers. Even in 1921 the female office clerk earned more than 22 other female occupations. Only telegraph operators in Montreal and tailoresses, teachers, as well as telegraph operators in Toronto earned more.[35]

INTERNAL JOB HIERARCHIES

Modern corporations and governments are bureaucratic organizations based on a hierarchical arrangement of specialized tasks. I have already documented the existence of distinct clerical groups in banking and insurance, defined by different functions and remuneration levels. The gradual erosion of employee control over the execution of work because of office rationalizations no doubt exacerbated these trends. The administrative revolution degraded some tasks, but the fact that not all jobs were directly affected contributed to the development of elaborate clerical hierarchies within organizations. In addition, the bureaucratization of corporations employing both white-collar and blue-collar workers tended to magnify the differences between these groups.

From table 7.4 we know that the typical male clerk was economically better off than production workers until 1941. This broad trend, however, does not accurately reflect the experience of many clerks employed in large corporations. Table 7.6 documents that the early twentieth-century male clerk's salary lagged behind other major wage earning groups in the Canadian Pacific Railway. Of six major

Table 7.6 Daily earnings of selected occupations, Canadian Pacific Railway Company, 1907, 1911 and 1916

	1907	1911	1916
General office clerks	$1.83	$2.17	$2.19[a]
Station agents	2.23	2.91	3.32
Telegraph operators and dispatchers	1.84	2.28	N/A
Locomotive engineers	4.03	4.40	4.37[b]
Machinists	2.94	3.76	4.54
Carpenters	2.24	2.76	3.12

[a] Chief clerks earned $4.81 and stenographers and typists earned $2.10.
[b] Includes motormen.
Source: *Annual Report of the Canadian Pacific Railway Company to the Minister of Railways and Canals of Canada*, for the years 1907, 1911, and 1916.

Table 7.7 Average annual salary ranges for various head office clerical jobs, major Canadian and American insurance companies, 1930

	$ $
Keypunch operator	900–1,100
MIB file clerk	900–1,200
Addressograph operator	900–1,200
Typist	900–1,300
Calculating machine operator — routine	1,000–1,300
Policy writer	1,000–1,400
Photostat operator	1,040–1,600
Premium posting clerk	1,040–1,600
Dictaphone operator	1,100–1,500
Telephone operator	1,100–1,600
Hollerith machine operator	1,200–1,500
Stenographer	1,200–1,600
Laboratory technician	1,750–2,500
Secretary to office	1,750–2,500
Clerk on special actuarial computations	1,800–2,600
Legally trained clerk	2,400–3,200
Travelling auditor	2,400–3,600
Lay underwriter — major responsibilities	2,500–4,500
Security analyst	3,000–4,750

Source: Life Office Management Association, *Proceedings* (1932), p. 276.

occupational groups in the railway, general office clerks (mainly males) received the lowest daily wage. And it is unlikely that the clerks' slightly better employment security would significantly alter this disparity on an annual basis. In 1911 clerks earned $2.17 daily compared with $4.40 for engineers and $3.76 for machinists. While these data only cover the 1909–16 period, there is little indication that the situation changed appreciably in later years, considering the general trends for clerical and manual earnings outlined above. It was not that the CPR unduly exploited its clerical employees; the railway clerks' 1911 salary was only slightly below the clerical labour force average. More plausible is that the powerful running trades and craft unions greatly increased the bargaining power of the blue-collar employees. It thus seems that in the CPR, one of the nation's largest employers at the time, it was the colour of the clerk's collar and not their putative economic status which separated them from manual workers. This provides compelling support for my general argument that within-industry market conditions are a more fruitful level of analysis than aggregate labour force trends – especially considering that employees tend to assess their economic standing relative to other groups within their immediate firm or industry.

The second example comes from the insurance industry, specifically the typical head office hierarchy found in Canada and the United States. The white-collar job structure presented in table 7.7 outlines the division of labour after extensive rationalization of the office. The table is largely self-explanatory, but perhaps I should underline the fact that most jobs up to the position of stenographer were performed almost exclusively by women. Interestingly, ten of the 12 are machine-related. Even so, there is a salary range of $900 to $1,200 annually, well above the average female clerical salary of $830 in 1931 (see table 7.1). The jump in the salary scale between stenographer and lab technician, and again between clerk on special actuarial computations and legally trained clerk, demarcate three job clusters: routine female jobs; intermediate-level jobs performed by either sex, but usually by males; and exclusively male jobs at the top level. The income disparity between the first and third groups is wide, as illustrated by comparing the salaries of any of the machine operators with that of security analyst.

A third and final example carries the above analysis a step further, examining the 1929 job classification system for female employees introduced in the head office of the Sun Life Insurance Company. With a Montreal head office staff of over 2,800, the company's personnel experts were always striving to streamline clerical operations through the introduction of the most advanced personnel practices available. The more immediate effect, however, was to accentuate the specialized and standardized character of clerical tasks.

Briefly, the plan classified clerks into five grades of permanent staff and a probationary grade (see figure 4.1). The starting salary of $600 (rising to $720 after six months of good performance) was below that paid to juniors in the bank and insurance company examined above (table 7.5). Senior grade clerks earned a maximum of $1,500 and those in a special grade could earn even more. Salaries were tied to the skill and responsibility requirements of the jobs, as well as to experience. Junior grade clerks performed 'simple mechanical or clerical work requiring little previous training or experience', including routine typing. The middle level of the hierarchy consisted of clerks with 'considerable experience operating bookkeeping machines; who are competent to perform more advanced stenographic work; or who can supervise more difficult office routine'. And the special grade was comprised of 'experienced clerks who can perform secretarial work requiring the exercise of independent judgement and a complete knowledge of office procedures; or who by reason of special training can supervise or undertake very advanced work.' The numbers of staff thinned out as one proceeded up the hierarchy. The top two grades covered supervisory duties that, if performed by males, would bring a higher rank and salary. In short, not all office jobs involving women were routinized and low skilled. That a significant minority demanded considerable expertise and judgement decisively undercuts any general claims about clerical proletarianization.

LIVING CONDITIONS OF THE CANADIAN CLERK

Much of the preceding discussion has revolved around comparisons between various groups of clerks, or between clerks and blue-collar workers. But this type of wage trend analysis remains somewhat abstract unless rooted in the broader context of the minimum standard of living deemed acceptable in a society. It is one thing to trace the historical relationship between manual and clerical earnings, but quite another matter to determine whether the salaries of either group were capable of maintaining a family above the poverty line. The debate on clerical proletarianization has thus far lacked this crucial dimension. As a partial remedy, I shall now provide cost of living data against which earnings of various groups of workers can be measured. This approach is admittedly static in so far as changes in the living standards of individuals during their working lives are not measured. It augments the proletarianization debate, however, by documenting how specific jobs limited the ability of their occupants to achieve anything resembling a middle-class lifestyle. In brief, it is a major step towards evaluating the social significance and individual consequences of earning a particular income.

Table 7.8   Annual Family Budget in 60 Canadian cities, 1900–31*

1900	1910	1916	1921	1926	1931
$487.24	$640.64	$849.16	$1,117.48	$1,116.44	$970.32

* Based on weekly costs of 29 food items, laundry starch, coal, wood, coal oil and rent for the month of December 1900, 1910, and 1921. Data for 1921, 1926, and 1931 cover the entire year. The budget was compiled by the federal Department of Labour and was regularly published in the *Labour Gazette*. It was based on estimates of the weekly consumption of a 'workingman's family of five'. Rental costs were for 'a representative workingman's dwelling of the better class' with 'sanitary conveniences'.

Source: *Canada Year Book, 1921* (Ottawa, King's Printer, 1922), p. 649; *Canada Year Book, 1932* (Ottawa, King's Printer, 1932), p. 692.

Table 7.8 presents the federal Department of Labour's annual budget for a 'workingman's family of five', a fair approximation of a moderate working-class level of existence. Included were the average cost in 60 Canadian cities of 29 basic food items, laundry starch, coal, coal oil, wood and rent. The cost of clothing, medical care, transportation and other necessities were not included. Nor were provisions made for

Figure 7.1   Changes in annual average earnings, labour force, clerical workers and production workers in manufacturing, showing annual family budget, Canada, 1900–31

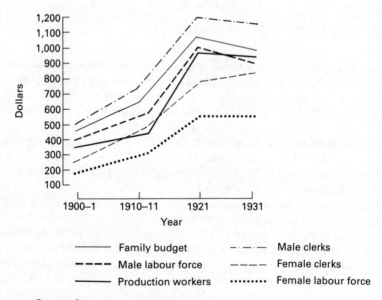

Source: Calculated from tables 7.1 and 7.8.

alcohol, tobacco, entertainment and other 'luxury' items. The budget would have permitted a not altogether uncomfortable working-class lifestyle which would vary, of course, by family size. But a middle-class lifestyle, especially for a family, was simply out of reach on the budget allotted.

The stark economic reality facing the average male worker, according to figure 7.1, was a chronic struggle to support a family at an acceptable subsistence level between 1900 and 1931. Production workers in manufacturing – the industrial proletariat – were even more disadvantaged during all but the end of the period. Only male clerks earned sufficient incomes to boost them above this official definition of a working-class lifestyle. It is likely that some groups of clerks, such as those in insurance, could afford middle-class comforts. Yet for the majority of clerks a middle-class lifestyle probably remained an elusive ideal.

This conclusion is reinforced by contemporary reports of actual living conditions. J. P. Buschlen, a bank clerk turned novelist, gave the following account of the Canadian white-collar workers' lifestyle at the start of the First World War: 'Conditions in the modern business world continue to make it more and more difficult for the "man without means" to live. He may exist – earn enough to pay for clothes, food and other bare necessities of life – but he cannot invest in a home, marry, and build for the future.'[36] Buschlen's reference to marriage was a barb aimed directly at the banks' rule, in force until the late 1940s, forbidding employees earning below a specified salary from marrying. The salary requirement was set at $1,000 in 1911, or about 32 per cent higher than the average male clerk's salary and almost double that earned by the typical male Bank of Nova Scotia clerk. This notorious edict, enforced by threat of dismissal, ostensibly guarded against embezzlement but it indirectly justified low salaries. Even the staid *Monetary Times* saw Draconian overtones in the marriage regulation, proclaiming that it 'smacks of the dark ages' and urging the banks to raise clerical salaries in order to stem growing employee dissatisfaction.[37]

Clerks employed by other industries also confronted economic hardships. When the Civil Service Association petitioned the federal government for higher salaries in 1907, it presented personal expense statements showing individual clerks facing deficits ranging from $9.42 to $31 monthly.[38] The association argued that a male clerk could support himself and his family only 'by the exercise of prudence and, sometimes, rigid self-denial. Under existing conditions, having regard to the continuous increase in the cost of living, he finds the struggle growing harder and harder.'[39] This situation apparently did not improve over the next few decades.[40]

In fact, rampant inflation during the First World War imposed considerable economic hardship on male clerks struggling to support families. Stirrings of collective action can be detected around this issue. For example, the office staff of the British Columbia Electric Railway Co., in Victoria, founded a committee to petition management for better salaries. Their supporting argument reveals much about the declining socio-economic position of the male clerk:

> owing to the rapidly increasing cost of living in the last few years, the office employees have found it correspondingly hard to keep their heads above water . . . Those of the office staff who had money in the bank, saved from happier and more prosperous days, have nearly all completely depleted this, while some have gone deeply into debt through unfortunate circumstances, mainly owing to illness.[41]

The committee calculated that average basic expenditures of married men in the office exceeded their $125 monthly salary by $20.25. Preying on management's concerns about staff performance, the committee underlined 'how absolutely impossible it is for an employee to put his mind wholly to his work when he has the worry constantly with him of trying to make both ends meet'. Whatever slim increases may have been awarded in similar episodes across the country could not reverse the relative decline in clerks' salaries.

As for female clerks, one might discount the fact that their earnings fell well below a subsistence level by arguing that the vast majority were young, single women gaining worldly experience before retreating into domesticity after marriage. The British Columbia Electric Railway Co. staff committee, just mentioned, embraced this assumption and thus excluded women – and even single males – from its purview. Figure 7.1 suggests, however, that unless such employees boarded at home they would have faced economic difficulties. Indeed, the circumstances of widows, women with dependents, and others who were self-supporting were nothing short of tragic.[42] The Ontario Civil Service Association documented that female clerks were just as severely affected as men by the pincer-like squeeze of the First World War era inflation and lagging salaries.[43] The association lobbied the government at the end of the war for a minimum annual salary of $1,000 for female civil servants. Budgets prepared by single, self-supporting women showed that even this substantial increase – about 25 per cent more than the 1921 female clerical average – would leave 'very little for saving' after necessary expenses had been met.[44] The popular contemporary image of the office girl who worked merely for 'pin money' threw up an ideological smoke-screen that masked the economic hardships endured by many female clerks.

CONCLUSION

To summarise this chapter's discussion, I have re-evaluated the clerical proletarianization debate from the historical vantage point of the feminization process launched by the administrative revolution in the office. The model of proletarianization predominant in the literature equates declining relative wages and diminished control over administration with the clerks' descent into the working class. I have challenged the accuracy of this general interpretation of the twentieth-century transformation of clerical occupations by documenting its major weaknesses. First and most crucial is the preoccupation with aggregate clerical wage trends. This has obscured what is perhaps the most remarkable change in the office since 1900, namely the shift from a male to a female workforce. Many advocates of the proletarianization thesis consequently miss the rather obvious point that the increasing recruitment of women as low-priced administrative functionaries largely accounted for declining average clerical salaries.

Second, the degradation of clerical labour alluded to by Braverman and others as evidence of the spread of factory-type conditions requires careful qualification. Admittedly certain office jobs became part of a paper-processing assembly line, their incumbents experiencing the labour process as would some factory operatives. Central typing pools and Hollerith machine rooms quickly spring to mind here. However, concern about this mental–manual division may be somewhat overblown, especially considering that many clerical tasks contain elements of each.[45] Still, for male clerks economic distance from the upper ranks of manual workers was never great during the early twentieth century. The extent and nature of their middle classness thus remains at issue. It seems clear, though, that the line between male blue-collar and white-collar workers held less social and political significance in some societies than in others.[46] The growing importance of management functions within modern bureaucracies certainly offered a sizeable minority of aspiring clerks chances to improve their socio-economic status. My evidence is only tentative with respect to the lifestyles and mobility experiences of the male clerk. But it seems to suggest that despite clerks' declining market position relative to manual workers, their better work environment, job security and greater mobility prospects inhibited the formation of a new white-collar segment of the working class.

Related to this is the fact that males occupy positions of superiority in the modern office. Because women were relegated to the subordinate jobs, it is here that one would expect to encounter signs of proletarianization within the labour process. I have offered an alternative perspective, however, highlighting substantial variation within female clerical occupations. This heterogeneity of work and market conditions actually placed some white-collar women in advantaged positions, even when compared with male clerks. And in relation to other female job ghettos, clerical occupations had obvious social and economic attractions. Furthermore, because the administrative revolution enveloped a constellation of factors related to tasks, managerial controls and working conditions which were registered in the labour market by a swing in recruitment from males to females, it is unlikely that sizeable numbers of clerks of either sex directly experienced the process whereby their working conditions were proletarianized.

The third and final weakness in the proletarianization thesis revolves around the social consequences of a specific wage. Far too little attention has been paid to the actual living standards of manual and white-collar workers. The existence of a clerical middle class is ultimately a matter of lifestyle, broadly defined to include social relations, politics and culture. But as my cost of living analysis revealed, the male clerk would have encountered difficulty supporting himself and a family at a living standard discernably better than the upper reaches of the working class. Whether this economic reality was mirrored in residential and consumption patterns or political attitudes and behaviour is a question demanding further investigation. But the weight of sociological evidence thus far does not point in the direction of this sort of convergence.

These three critical points that I have raised expose the inherent vulnerability of the proletarianization thesis, particularly when confronted by systematic historical evidence of changing task content, working conditions and living standards. Complicating the matter further, discussions of clerical proletarianization are often couched in imprecise language. Perhaps it would be heuristically prudent to wipe the theoretical slate clean of the terminological baggage of proletarianization – at least until we can confidently point to the concept's empirical referents and, moreover, clearly distinguish between the causes and consequences of the proletarianization process. What seems to be lacking, then, is a systematic statement of how changing work arrangements, labour market dynamics and class locations are interconnected at a theoretical level and, at a concrete level, how and why particular combinations of these factors affect the socio-economic situation of people who happen, at a particular time, to be clerks.

A brief excursion into some of the recent literature on clerical proletarianization will underline some of these difficulties. For example, Margery Davies's insightful historical study of the feminization of the US office yields a theoretically ambiguous conclusion when cast into the proletarianization framework. Specifically, Davies concludes that the double thrust of proletarianization and feminization transformed a male clerical labour force 'into female office operatives and members of the working class'.[47] Female operatives perhaps, but it neither follows her overall logic nor her evidence that these women also joined the ranks of the working class.

Wary of using the term proletarianization 'too freely', Abercrombie and Urry nonetheless extract from the white-collar middle class a large group of apparently deskilled jobs, mainly clerical. They proceed to argue that work rationalization, task standardization and fragmentation, and the spread of bureaucratic administration has stripped low-level white-collar jobs of mental labour. Hence, they assert, 'clerks *are* manual workers.'[48] Their general conclusion, then, is that 'the market and work situation of deskilled white-collar workers [is] proletarianized; the class places of these workers are subject to forces similar to those of the working class.'[49] The smattering of secondary evidence adduced by the authors cannot suppport this bold assertion – especially in light of their earlier admission that, 'Unfortunately, little is known about the skills required in white-collar occupations.'[50]

Although firmly grounded on case study evidence from three large office bureaucracies, Crompton and Jones's *White-Collar Proletariat* also becomes mired down conceptually when drawing inferences about the proletarianizaton process. Crompton and Jones draw a clear distinction between occupational places and the people who occupy them. They also recognize that stratification arrangements are fluid and, in particular, that mobility for male clerks is a contingent process dependant upon a high proportion of female clerks with no mobility and a steady turnover of young male clerks. Yet the authors revert to the opaque lexicon of the proletarianization thesis when interpreting their data. For instance, after describing the ghettoization of women at the bottom of the offices studied, they too quickly draw the following theoretical inference: 'In other words, the ranks of the "white-collar proletariat" may be said to be largely filled by women.'[51] Later, we are told that because 90 per cent of these lower-level office jobs give workers no job control – that is, are routine and deskilled – Braverman's thesis regarding clerical proletarianized is therefore correct. According to Crompton and Jones, 'our examination of the non-manual labour process reveals that the vast majority of the positions (or places) generated within this structure are "proletarian".'[52] When considering the people occupying clerical places, the study usefully documents the heterogeneous character of the clerical workforce, especially with respect to gender, age and qualifications. But exactly how these variables mediate the connection between a person's employment in a clerical job, defined as proletarian, and his or her location in the class structure – in particular, under what conditions this probably will be working class – remains ambiguous.

There clearly is an urgent need to rethink our approach to studying the relationship between changing working conditions and class structuration. The sex segregation of the office workforce requires that the experiences of male and female workers be examined separately but within a single theoretical framework which has workplace structures and processes as its starting point. Consequently, one must analyse work histories rather than infer class position from the job an individual holds at one point in time. Thus if an individual's job sequence involves changes in lifestyle, social relationships, as well as socio-political attitudes and behaviour, then movement in the class structure may be taking place. But these are general comments unlikely to attract much disagreement from stratification researchers. Far more contentious is how best to determine the class position of women in clerical jobs. The matter was less complicated during the administrative revolution than it is today. Early twentieth-century female clerks were typically from middle class backgrounds and single, withdrawing from gainful employment upon marriage. Even today, arguments linking occupation and class position are less applicable to the female clerk, largely because lifetime, continuous employment and promotion opportunities are still uncommon for them. An accurate understanding of the social position of such women must necessarily rest on a combination of factors: family background, the type of office job performed, and the links between these characteristics and her later roles of wife and mother. Especially interesting is to what extent a young woman's work situation in a particular office may have influenced marriage opportunities.

This only partially succeeds in clarifying theoretically the relationship between gender, basic issues of social inequality and a woman's location in the class structure. What must be further explored are the links between the gender division of labour within particular workplaces, the family system and women's subordinate position within it, and the persistence of class-based inequalities in the larger society. For as Michael Mann asserts, 'stratification is now gendered and gender is stratified. We can no longer keep them in separate sociological compartments.'[53] But in reality, what does the interweaving of gender and class inequalities mean for the workaday female clerk? The presence in the office of women from solidly working class backgrounds married to blue-collar males may constitute the only true form of proletarianization. But given that a wife's occupation matters in its own rights, perhaps these women should be located separately within the class structure. The fact that they are married to a blue-collar male would be only one of the criteria for establishing this position. This would allow us to distinguish clerks from working class origins – defined on the basis of both parents' economic situation – from their co-workers with middle-class back-grounds and husbands. In any case, we must be careful not to equate people with the type of job they may occupy at a particular moment.[54] Clerical wages and working conditions may deteriorate even further, but without any proletarianizing effect on the class situation of the women who, at a given time, happen to be employed as clerks.

In short, the crux of the issue is how researchers can most accurately identify the class position of women. There are three basic approaches: focus solely on women and their work; use the family as the unit of analysis, examine the economic activities of both spouses; or define women's class location in terms of their fathers or husbands. The extent to which each of these approaches mirrors gender-based inequality is a contentious issue in class theory.[55] Any major advances in our understanding of the class-gender relationship require a creative interplay between theory and data. In this respect the office provides an ideal research laboratory.

Conclusion

Gender divisions in the workplace are a fundamental source of inequality in contemporary societies. Generally, women are poorly rewarded, have few opportunities to pursue interesting and challenging careers and typically work in jobs where they are subordinate to men. The purpose of this study has been to enhance our understanding of how female job ghettos have been created. Once a job is labelled as 'female' the resulting employment patterns become part of labour market structures, reinforced by social ideologies, and consequently resistant to change. By examining clerical work, I have attempted to show in some detail the causes and consequences of an occupation becoming feminized. The dramatic swing from a male to a female labour supply in the early twentieth-century office highlights very clearly the dynamics of female job ghettos. By locating the process of clerical feminization within the administrative revolution which accompanied the rise of big business and big government, I have been able to show that women were recruited in growing numbers as clerks not solely on the basis of being cheap, competent and available labour. Rather, the post-1900 convergence of major social, economic and organizational forces opened the doors of the office to women. Far from displacing the traditional nineteenth-century male clerk, the twentieth-century female office worker was deployed in a subordinate and menial capacity. A multitude of routine tasks prolifer- ated as the administrative division of labour evolved into its modern form. By 1930 women had come to stay; future clerical recruits had to meet gender-based job requirements and expectations. In short, they had to be females who aspired to nothing more than a few years of office employment prior to marriage.

Central to my discussion has been the variations in the timing, pace and pattern of women's entry into the office. The case studies of specific organizations provide an historically grounded explanation of the conditions under which feminization was most likely to have occurred. It is therefore imperative to distinguish between general labour force trends, showing rapid clerical growth through female recruitment after

1900, and the specific factors influencing one employer to change administrative procedures and clerical hiring practices. At this more detailed level of analysis it is the often unique interaction of industrial, organizational, ideological and other contextual factors which shaped the supply of and demand for female clerical labour.

I have also adopted a comparative perspective by sketching out basic contours in emerging clerical labour markets in Britain, the United States and Canada. All experienced explosive growth in clerical jobs and a swing toward a female labour supply in the late nineteenth and early twentieth centuries. But national characteristics – chiefly industrial structure, management practices, technological changes, gender role ideologies and the characteristics of the labour force – render any general theory of feminization highly tenuous. Still, it is possible to propose historically grounded explanations accounting for continuities and discontinuities, be they inter-firm, inter-industry or international, within the overall trend in advanced capitalism to rationalize and feminize clerical jobs. However, a more thorough understanding of the circumstances under which feminization is accelerated or inhibited, and once established, either perpetuated or reversed, must await systematic cross-national comparative research using matched industries and employers as case studies.

The post-Second World War period has witnessed new employment trends. Wives increasingly returned to work after childrearing and young single women first entering the labour force began thinking in terms of careers rather than short-term jobs. Yet clerical work still remains the prototypical female job ghetto. Looking beyond the office, the stark fact remains that gender inequalities are deeply entrenched in the occupational division of labour. As a survey of the economic position of women in OECD nations in the wake of the recession of the early 1980s concluded:

> labour market bias against women persists and this, in combination with the recession, has resulted in greater economic insecurity for them and those who depend wholly or partly on their earnings. Inequality in the education system, in training, in employment and in the tax and social security systems, along with the domestic division of labour have combined to perpetuate occupational segregation and women's greater vulnerability to poverty and dependence.[1]

This begs the question: what can be done to achieve gender equality in labour market opportunities and employment rewards? Legislated affirmative action, comparable worth and other employment equity programmes are widely recognized as necessary steps toward this goal. So too is trade unionism. Determined efforts on the part of female clerks and their unions can pressure employers to make substantial improvements in employment conditions and opportunities. Clerical unionism has been conspicuously absent, however, from the discussion thus far. More than anything, this reflects the scant historical evidence of collective action within the clerical ranks during the administrative revolution in Canada. I am not suggesting for a moment that we should therefore assume that Canadian clerks, especially females, reacted to the tumultuous restructuring of their work world with either indifference or compliance – rather than active resistance. The very nature of the clerks' experiences and the forms of action or inaction they adopted remain highly problematic. I thus feel compelled to devote part of my concluding remarks to the issue of unionism.

CLERICAL UNIONISM

Individuals typically react to their economic circumstances, thereby either reproducing or altering them. How did clerical workers caught up in the administrative revolution respond to the profound changes occurring in their work situation and socio-economic status? Worker responses can be individual or collective, and characterized by either passive adaptation or active resistance. The individualistic strivings of nineteenth-century male clerks, reinforced by small and informal work settings and loyalty to their employer, moulded a pervasive ideology in the office. Trade unionism rarely developed. When women began flooding into offices they inherited this legacy of individualism which had come to define employer–employee relations. But in addition they faced the pressures of gender-based domination and paternalism. Women were subordinate to men in the office and in society. Their employment was defined as only temporary; their self-image was bound up in the roles of wife and mother, not that of clerical worker.

How exactly did work structures, managerial approaches to employee relations, and the job attitudes and behaviour of clerks interact with turn-of-the-century gender ideologies such that the administrative revolution developed unchallenged? This is a tough question to answer empirically. Indeed, throughout this study female clerks have been almost invisible as individuals. The actions and thoughts of male managers, in contrast, figured prominently in my account of the creation of the modern office. The main reason for this imbalance is that organizations maintain detailed records of managerial decisions, whereas personal accounts of the experiences of individual clerks are extremely difficult for researchers today to obtain. An ethnography of the office during the 1920s, based on biographical materials and interviews when possible, may be a promising research strategy. Hopefully other scholars will take up this challenge and document the rise of the modern office through the eyes of female clerks.

For now, however, I will try to piece together what shreds of evidence are available on the responses of clerical employees to changing office conditions. A comparison of clerical unionism in Canada, the United States and Britain is a helpful way of identifying factors which inhibited or encouraged collective responses to management.

The relative absence of unionism among male clerks in all three countries can be traced to several common structural and ideological factors. Foremost was the expectation of career mobility, either into management or one's own business. The rapid expansion of office bureaucracies and the attendant recruitment of women into the least rewarding clerical jobs ultimately benefited male clerks by increasing their career chances. Well into the twentieth century, junior clerkships served as training grounds for higher posts in the business world. A careerist orientation, founded on a belief in individual success, meshed with a white-collar status consciousness thus leading to a rejection of unions as blue-collar, working-class institutions. This occupational consciousness was also fostered by employment in small, scattered workplaces with close employer contact. C. Wright Mills' description of white-collar individualism points out how these employees 'usually remain psychologically the little individual scrambling to get to the top'.[2]

The character of the trade-union movements in advanced capitalist societies has until quite recently been blue-collar and working class. Union recruitment drives historically have by-passed those industries in which white-collar workers are most heavily concentrated. There are some notable exceptions, however. In Britain, the National Union of Clerks was formed in 1890 in London as a kind of industrial union for all clerks.[3] Its success was minor and not until the First World War period did a concerted push for collective representation emerge. Those industries with large, bureaucratic offices, standardized jobs, formal employee–employer relations and few promotion prospects gave rise to early clerks' unions. The inflation during the First World War, a more receptive climate for union activity and an erosion of clerical salaries were equally important precipitating factors. Out of this period grew major white-collar unions in railways, local and national government and banking. These unions were unambiguously male institutions. Women formed a small secondary labour pool in these industries and were seen as having only a temporary stake in employment.

There are some parallels here with developments in Canada. The major difference is that British white-collar unions of the First World War era gained a solid footing from which they were able to expand, while those in Canada were less successful initially. Indeed, union

172 *Conclusion*

activity among Canadian clerks was at best sporadic between 1900 and 1930. Male bank employees launched weak organizing drives before, during and after the First World War, only to be swiftly crushed by management.[4] By 1919 federal and some provincial civil servants had organized staff associations, with only the occasional clamouring for trade-union affiliation. Full-fledged collective bargaining would not be achieved until enabling legislation was instituted in the late 1960s.[5] Railway clerks were apparently the only office workers to embrace unionism roundly in the period under study. For example, Canadian Pacific Railway clerks (mainly men) struck in 1912, shutting down the railway's western lines.[6] Their working proximity to organized blue-collar workers was a determining factor in railway clerks' union militancy. White collar collective protests during the 1900–30 period invariably centred on wage grievances. A major exception was the vigorous opposition of civil service associations to the reorganization of the federal bureaucracy by American efficiency consultants outlined in chapter 5. At the heart of even these protests were the new salary scales which ignored the ravages of wartime inflation.

South of the border, American clerks were even less inclined to abandon their individualistic orientation. Apparently only public employees resorted to sustained collective action. As in Canada, clerks lacked organizational means of countering the effects of the First World War inflation, but despite this were not mobilized the way British clerks were. The sole private sector unions for white-collar workers at the end of the 1920s were the large Brotherhood of Railway Clerks and a small retail clerks' union.[7]

Just as they were marginalized in their employment, so were women largely excluded from attempts at white-collar unionization during the administrative revolution. The anti-union stance of Canadian (and American) employers was a major impediment to any group of employees establishing collective bargaining. But alternatively, one could expect that the poor conditions of work for many women clerks might have sparked agitation for improvements. That this did not occur can be linked to a combination of factors: relatively high earnings compared with other female employees; the virtual absence of white-collar unions in most industries; prevailing gender role images of women as docile and subservient; the male dominance of existing unions and their general disinterest in organizing white-collar workers, especially females; and women workers' individual adaptation to their inferior position in the office. I cannot do justice to the multitude of unique factors found in each national context which impinge upon white-collar unionism in general and among female clerks in particular. Nonetheless some general analytic points do need to be made.

I should point out initially that, while union membership levels are generally lower among women than men, this occurs against a backdrop of substantial cross-national variations in union growth, membership density levels and militancy. Trade-union membership in Britain historically has been well above that in North America. Presently over half of all non-agricultural employees belong to unions in Britain, compared with 39 per cent in Canada and, due to an alarming drop in membership since the late 1970s, less than 19 per cent in the United States.[8] Similarly, white-collar unionism is most widespread in Britain, at 44 per cent in 1979, as is union representation among employed women, at 39.5 per cent in 1979 compared with 24 per cent in Canada and even less in the United States. Remarkably, in all three countries there has been a recent upsurge in unionism among women workers. In other words, women are forming unions at a much brisker rate than men – a development mainly due to ascendant white-collar unionism in the public sector.[9]

Women by no means have a natural aversion to collective action, now or in the past. The issue, it seems, is that the monotonous and unrewarding nature of most female jobs has fostered a type of work orientation and behaviour unconducive to collectivism. This was strongly reinforced, especially among middle-class office workers, well into the post-Second World War period by ideological constraints on women's economic activity. Employment was assumed to be a prelude to marriage. In the decades of the administrative revolution, the vast majority of paid female workers were young and single. During the 1920s in Canada, young women resolved competing demands that they enter the clerical labour force and also marry and raise a family by working until about age 25 then retreating into the matrimonial home.[10] The values supporting this work pattern were articulated by a female bank employee in 1916: 'When the opportunity offers the most successful banking woman amongst us cheerfully retires to her own hearthstone, preferring the love of a husband and little children to thousands a year and a seat in the council of the mighty.'[11] Also constrained by these norms, many employers formally prohibited the employment of married women. I therefore concur with Margery Davies's conclusion that 'the feminization of clerical labour meant a docile workforce and helped to stabilize the power relations between workers and management.'[12]

In addition, the concentration of women's employment in industries with no tradition of unionism has meant that even if females were predisposed to joining a union there was none available. An important exception is the garment industry. This enclave of female manual labour was the key source of female trade unionism in the late nineteenth and early twentieth centuries on both sides of the Atlantic. Such collectivism is now found among some groups of office workers in the public sector, where unionization drives have tallied up high membership gains among women in the past two decades. A complex set of factors lie behind this development. But foremost among them are deteriorating working conditions which made workers more receptive to unionization, the growing influence of feminism, the increasing dependence of many families on two salaries, and in particular, a legal framework that paved the way for union recruitment and minimized employer opposition.

A worker's sex *per se* thus is of little significance in whether he or she joins a union or engages in industrial action. Passivity is not something unique to women workers, nor is militancy a particularly male trait. Rather, it is one's position in an organization coupled with industry-wide traditions of industrial relations which ultimately explain union membership trends. Men and women similarly situated in the same job, workplace and industry typically behave the same way when it comes to unions. In general terms, the gender segregation of the labour market underlies lower levels of female unionization by clustering women into a handful of ghetto-like occupations where conditions reinforce an individualistic approach to solving job problems.[13]

These barriers are now beginning to crumble as the younger generation of women workers challenge the inequities they face. Two Canadian industries historically resistant to unionism, banking and retail department stores, have experienced collective struggles in recent years. These are small yet decisive breakthroughs. In the Second World War period organizing drives among banking, office and retail workers were spearheaded by the Office Employees International Union and the Canadian Congress of Labour's Office and Professional Organizing Committee. Failure of the two most vigorous campaigns – among Quebec and Ontario bank employees in the early 1940s and in Eaton's Toronto department store between 1948 to 1952 – did not bode well for the future. All this changed dramatically in the 1970s and early 1980s, as unions scored several important victories in these previously impenetrable industries.[14] It may not be overly optimistic to suggested that unions have now established a beachhead, with several thousand female members in bank branches, bank data processing centres and several major department stores.

Whether or not this trend will be sustained depends on many factors beyond the control of clerks themselves. Chief among these is labour legislation, which can be decisive in helping workers achieve union recognition and negotiate a first contract, the escalation of American-style anti-union tactics by employers, and more bold initiatives by unions to organize white-collar female workers in the private sector.

Historical evidence indicates that skilled manual workers often registered their discontent over their employer's drives to rationalize the labour process by striking.[15] Similarly, there is some suggestion that the current wave of office automation may have precipitated union organization in protest against deskilling and routinization. One must therefore investigate possible connections between the impact of technology on jobs and worker resistance to such changes. British research has found a link between office automation and a rising tide of unionism in banks and insurance companies.[16] Moreover, American studies suggest that automation leads to more collective forms of work organization which foster nascent impulses for greater workplace democracy, potentially through unions.[17] Yet in the case of the early office technologies – and, indeed, the present onslaught of micro-technology in Canada – these questions remain unanswered. Of central importance is the form resistance may take among clerks. I have speculated that overt signs of collective action were hard to detect during the early twentieth-century administrative revolution. Future research may uncover informal modes of resistance among those most affected by the march of office rationalization. As we stand on the threshold of a late twentieth-century revolution in the office, one thing seems certain: whether automation develops in ways which enhance or diminish the quality of working life depends largely on female clerks having a voice in how it is applied.

Let me now leave the issue of clerical unionism aside and endeavour to tie together the main strands of my analysis of the feminization process. In the interests of highlighting the generalizations flowing from this study, I have organized my concluding comments around four prominent theoretical themes: gender and labour markets; gender and the labour process; gender and class; and finally, how the administrative revolution casts light on the question of human agency.

GENDER AND LABOUR MARKETS

Guiding this study has been the question of how gender inequalities became structured into labour markets and, more specifically, individual organizations. There is little doubt that the creation of a female clerical labour market was a direct result of the growth and rationalization of the administrative labour process. Labour supply factors, such as the rise of public education, more tolerant social attitudes to women's paid employment, and rising work aspirations among young middle-class women, must not be overlooked. But given the availability of female labour, the processes by which certain clerical jobs became labelled as female are only intelligible by focusing on the demand side of the equation. If any general claim can be made from my evidence in this respect, it is that the task content, the product or service, the employer ideology and the established practices of labour utilization in a firm are determinate. We need go no further than the above case studies of banks, insurance firms and government bureaucracies to see the impact of these economic and organizational characteristics on when and how women were employed as clerks.

Studies by other researchers permit further generalizations. In particular, Ruth Milkman's analysis of the US auto and electrical industries, while focusing on female manual workers, nonetheless draws identical conclusions regarding feminization.[18] My research dovetails with Milkman's on the decisive role played by gender ideologies in the workplace. Once sex-typing has occurred, whether it be attaching a female label to light assembly line work in electrical goods factories or to routine clerical tasks in a government office, a structural inertia sets in. Job hierarchies have been built around the assumption that men will occupy superior positions, while a stream of women will flow through subordinate jobs, always temporary and ultimately moving on to the higher callings of marriage and motherhood. Employers are guided in future hiring decisions by gender labels. And the very conditions of most female jobs lead to adaptive responses on the part of women – low job commitment, few career ambitions, high turnover, seeking alternative rewards in social relations – which fortify the image of women as suitable for only lower-level jobs. In the long run, a particular sexual division of tasks gets taken for granted as a necessary and natural feature of a firm's labour process.

The same logic applies to management's initial resistance to hiring women. In both banking and the auto industry, the feminization of routine jobs proceeded less rapidly than in comparable industries. This is explicable by looking at what Milkman calls 'the supremacy of gender ideology . . . over short-term profitability considerations'.[19] In banks and auto factories, social stereotypes of male and female characteristics were mobilized to justify the exclusion of women. Another powerful influence was the notion of the family wage, espoused by male workers and employers.[20] This assumed that the male breadwinner earned enough to support a family. While the cost-of-living data in chapter 7 show widespread impoverishment, the fact remains that this ideology under-pinned occupational sex segregation and lower female wages. The underlying reasons for this exclusion had to do with how each industry's labour process evolved. Different products or services, technologies, and male recruitment and placement practices distinguished auto firms and banks from their nearest comparisons, electrical goods and insurance. Paradoxically these latter firms drew on the same vocabulary of gender traits, only using an inverse logic, to justify hiring large numbers of women. By mobilizing popular conceptions of male and female attributes to define sex-specific traits as job characteristics, employers could either include or exclude women. Ideologies of gender, in short, are fundamental to the creation and perpetuation of labour market inequalities in both internal and external labour markets. Future research should give top priority to examining how gender ideologies perpetuate the allocation of men and women to particular jobs within organizations.[21]

GENDER AND THE LABOUR PROCESS

Another theoretical focus concerns whether clerical work has been degraded and deskilled, thereby making clerks the new twentieth-century proletarians. Earlier I rejected the teleological determinism of a Bravermanesque work degradation thesis in favour of an empirically grounded approach sensitive to historical contingencies. Discussions of proletarianization have not gone far enough in distinguishing changes in clerical jobs from the changing personal characteristics of those individuals employed as clerks. I therefore have linked the expansion, rationalization and fragmentation of clerical work triggered by the administrative revolution to a shift in recruitment patterns. The overall trend in office work was undeniably toward routinized tasks performed in large bureaucracies. But given that women were hired to perform these new jobs, and that men typically occupied positions defined by a higher degree of authority, responsibility and mobility prospects, few clerks of either sex were personally proletarianized.

But what of the general decline in task complexity and employee control over his or her work process – two criteria on which the work degradation argument hinges? The deskilling debate often falters because of the inherent difficulties in measuring changing skill levels over time. Skill changes can involve different things: the shifting occupational composition of the labour force; the escalation of job requirements so that more highly trained workers take over an occupation; changing social definitions of what 'skilled work' entails and which individuals possess skills; or redesigning a job in accordance with scientific management principles so as to diminish worker control. In addition, common measures of skill often assumed to be highly correlated by researchers – such as wage levels and the degree of discretion required on the job – need not change in tandem. Contemporary research is equivocal on clerical skill levels. Recall that Crompton and Jones's study of three British offices found that the vast majority of non-supervisory jobs required employees of either sex to exercise no control. On the other hand, information on the US labour force suggests that clerks have considerably more task discretion and self-pacing than most manual workers.[22]

The recent onslaught of office automation complicates the issue, and much debate surrounds the possible upgrading and downgrading effects. Mechanization and job rationalization were, I have argued, major forces reshaping offices in the early part of the century. No doubt the emerging gender division of labour which shunted massive numbers of women into routine jobs buffered the impact of internal changes in the office on males.[23] Women entered the office in subordinate positions and were stuck there. But the range of skill requirements and job content that I have documented, the education required to conduct even the most routine clerical work, and the inherent problems of removing the discretionary elements from information work suggest that clerical jobs were not as 'degraded and deskilled' as other analysts have claimed. Equally misleading is the tendency, exemplified in the work of Abercrombie and Urry, to equate routine clerical jobs with manual work – and then to accept this as solid evidence of proletarianization. The concept of a job ghetto surely involves more than just task content. The relative economic and social rewards, general working conditions and opportunities for advancement are also important in this respect.

GENDER AND CLASS

The impact of the administrative revolution on the class structure of advanced capitalist societies is an even thornier problem. A satisfactory resolution to the theoretical imbroglio surrounding gender and class has yet to be formulated. There are some promising developments in this direction, however. To begin to understand the class position of the early twentieth-century female clerk, one would require three essential pieces of information: her family's socio-economic status, her eventual marital status and her employment history. All are interconnected, and, at the very least, will allow us to chart changing class configurations among clerical employees.

The mutual interdependence of occupational experiences, marriage and class position for both men and women is a starting-point for any new theoretical perspective. Moreover, men and women must be examined individually and as members of a family unit – the relationship between these two levels of analysis constituting a key theoretical problem. Work and marriage quite obviously have very different meanings and consequences depending on one's gender. At a more societal level, we can usefully distinguish men's and women's occupations – given the high degree of occupational sex segregation in the labour market – in terms of their different stratification consequences. Looking at the clustering of women's jobs, Michael Mann concludes that on this basis alone they form a number of quasi-class fractions. As such, women in routine clerical and sales jobs form a 'buffer zone' between manual and non-manual male workers. This idea requires critical exploration; for now I would accept Mann's more general point that: 'Gender is no longer segregated from the rest of stratification: its segregating mechanisms have become a central mechanism of economic stratification.'[24]

The implications of employment in a female job ghetto for future life chances remain unclear. Marriage is obviously important here. Ken Prandy's empirical analysis of recent British survey data on the social class of husbands and wives shows, for example, that only 28 per cent of marriages are made up of people from the same (occupationally defined) class.[25] Female clerks in banks and the civil service are three to four times more likely to have husbands in professional or managerial occupations than in semi- or unskilled manual jobs. Curiously, the reverse was true for wages clerks, cashiers and routine clerks. These findings underscore the importance of occupational position for male–female social interaction. They also point out the folly of applying the same occupationally based class model to all workers regardless of gender.

THE QUESTION OF HUMAN AGENCY

The dialectal nature of social life is an endless source of puzzlement and fascination. Marx's famous dictum that people make their own history, but not under circumstance of their own choosing, neatly captures this. Yet the degree to which individuals and their groups are free to choose from alternative courses of action, or are tightly constrained by given social institutions, is a core problem in social theory. Transposing these issues into the emergent modern office raises several interesting considerations.

Critics of the labour process literature are quick to identify its overly determinate nature, which leaves little room for humans – be they managers or workers – to exercise any discretion or respond to economic events in ways that may redirect their outcome. The concept of control has come under heavy fire for this reason. Michael Buraway, for instance, claims that the concept of control has been applied to organizations in an ahistorical and mystifying way.[26] Why is control in capitalist organizations necessary? Who actually does the controlling, and who are the objects of this control? These are highly pertinent questions and ones for which we have offered some tentative answers, at least with regard to the office.

Admittedly my discussion of the administrative revolution and the resulting gender divisions in clerical work leans towards a structural interpretation. But I have been careful to show that there was no hidden, inexorable drive to modernize administrative systems. The variable pace of this enormous change and its diverse manifestations in specific organizations attest to this. Even more crucial, however, is my argument that the source of administrative change can be located in decisions made by the new professional cadre of managers. Such decisions are necessarily contingent on particular historical and contextual factors. To be sure, all managerial decisions are influenced by the societal, industrial and organizational contexts in which they are made. Also important is the social background, education, training and past behaviour of the managers themselves. Moreover, apparently clear-cut goals are sometimes subverted by the unintended consequences of certain management policies. Recruiting greater numbers of clerks solved immediate workload strains, for instance, but created future problems around how to co-ordinate larger clerical staffs. Nor is it necessary to assume office managers were propelled by some innate need to exert their authority, or that they were merely pawns swept along by the grander logic of the administrative revolution. By hiring clerks to process the mountains of paper required by expanding economic frontiers, managers exercised control through the office. These systems of administrative controls themselves became rigid, slow and costly. Most managers, but certainly not all, responded by instituting more careful regulations of the quantity, quality and costs of clerical activities.

In sum, administrative control resulted when managers attempted to regulate and monitor the internal operations and external environment of an organization. Not to move in this direction could have spelled potential disaster in terms of uncompetitiveness, mounting costs, and generally, the hazards of an unpredictable environment. But administrative systems, regardless of the industry, required some fine-tuning of their own to be fully effective. In this way, the administrative revolution imposed greater controls on clerical work through bureaucratic structure and regulations, mechanization and direct supervision. And, to return finally to the feminization theme, these dynamic forces reshaping the means of administration had a lasting impact on the working lives of generations of women. Whether the work patterns and conditions which now divide men and women in the office will be thrown into a state of flux due the new automation-induced revolution in administration will no doubt take on unprecedented scholarly and practical significance as we approach the twenty-first century.

Notes

ABBREVIATIONS

IC   *Industrial Canada*
JCBA   *Journal of the Canadian Bankers' Association*
LG   *Labour Gazette*
LOMA *Proceedings*   Life Office Management Association, *Proceedings* of the
                     Annual Conference
MT   *Monetary Times*
RCSCO   *Report of the Civil Service Commissioner for Ontario*
ROCU   *Report of the Ontario Commission on Unemployment*
TG   *Telephone Gazette*

INTRODUCTION

1. Based on a forecasting scenario developed in 1983 by Informetrica Ltd that includes all non-supervisory occupations in Canada. The two leading occupations in terms of their contributions to overall employment growth between 1983 and 1992 are secretaries/stenographers, and bookkeepers. Government of Canada, *Consultation Paper – Training* (Ottawa, Supply and Services, December 1984), p. 29.
2. Michel Crozier, *The World of the Office Worker* (Chicago, University of Chicago Press, 1971), p. 9.
3. C. Wright Mills, *White Collar: The American Middle Classes* (New York, Oxford University Press, 1956), p. 206.
4. See especially Gregory Anderson, *Victorian Clerks* (Manchester, University of Manchester Press, 1976) and David Lockwood, *The Blackcoated Worker: A Study in Class Consciousness* (London, George Allen and Unwin, 1958). The available evidence on living and working conditions among nineteenth-century male clerks has prompted Rosemary Crompton and Gareth Jones to conclude that there was no 'golden age' when clerical employment was synonymous with good earnings, career prospects and job security. See their *White-Collar Proletariat: Deskilling and Gender in Clerical Work* (London, Macmillan, 1984), p. 34.
5. Anderson, *Victorian Clerks*, p. 9.

6. Alfred D. Chandler Jr., *The Visible Hand: The Managerial Revolution in American Business* (Cambridge, Mass., Harvard University Press, 1977), p. 37.

7. See Margery W. Davies, *Women's Place is at the Typewriter: Office Work and Office Workers, 1870–1930* (Philadelphia, Temple University Press, 1982), chapter 2.

8. Philip Abrams, *Historical Sociology* (West Compton House, Somerset, Open Books, 1982), p. 314.

9. Anthony Giddens asserts that: 'There simply are no logical or even methodological distinctions between the social sciences and history – appropriately conceived.' *Central Problems in Social Theory: Action, Structure and Contradiction in Social Analysis* (London, Macmillan, 1979), p. 230. The argument is expanded by Abrams as a main theme in *Historical Sociology*.

10. The best outlet for the new working-class history in Canada is the journal *Labour/Le Travail*. For Canadian social history more generally see *Histoire sociale/Social History*. A very useful bibliography on the Canadian working class has been compiled by Craig Heron and Greg Kealey, 'Labour conflict and working-class organization', in Daniel Drache and Wallace Clement (eds), *The New Practical Guide to Canadian Political Economy* (Toronto, James Lorimer, 1984).

11. The sociology of work, organizations and industry has traditionally ignored the work experiences of women. For critiques see Richard Brown, 'Women as employees: comments on research in industrial sociology', in Diana L. Barker and Sheila Allen (eds), *Dependence and Exploitation in Work and Marriage* (New York, Longman, 1976); Roslyn L. Feldberg and Evelyn Nakano Glenn, 'Male and female: job versus gender models in the sociology of work', *Social Problems*, 26 (1979), pp. 524–38; Jeff Hearn and P. Wendy Parkin, 'Gender and organizations: a selective review and a critique of a neglected area', *Organization Studies*, 4 (1983), pp. 219–42.

12. Theda Skocpol, 'Sociology's historical imagination', in Theda Skocpol (ed.), *Vision and Method in Historical Sociology* (Cambridge, Cambridge University Press, 1984), p. 1. Another useful discussion of how sociologists can examine historically large-scale social change is Charles Tilly's *Big Structures, Large Processes, Huge Comparisons* (New York, Russel Sage Foundation, 1984).

13. Cited in Abrams, *Historical Sociology*, p. 314. Sociology is probably at its worst when applying deterministic, stage-type models to social and economic change. Gareth Steadman Jones is especially critical of the primitive ahistoricism which creeps into sociological theory in his incisive article, 'From historical sociology to theoretical history', *British Journal of Sociology*, 27 (1976), pp. 295–305.

CHAPTER 1 THEORETICAL PERSPECTIVES ON CLERICAL FEMINIZATION

1. This point is made by L. Murgatroyd in 'Gender and occupational stratification', *Sociological Review*, 30 (1982), p. 580. For a cogent discussion of the importance of gender to the study of social stratification,

see Elizabeth Garnsey, 'Women's work and theories of class stratification', *Sociology*, 12 (1978), pp. 223–43.

2. See Paul Ryan, 'Segmentation, duality and the internal labour market', in Frank Wilkinson (ed.), *The Dynamics of Labour Market Segmentation* (London, Academic Press, 1981), pp. 3–4, for a definition of segmentation as both process and result.

3. Rosabeth Moss Kanter, *Men and Women of the Corporation* (New York, Basic Books, 1977), p. 18.

4. A seminal source for the concept of a dual labour market is P. B. Doeringer and M. J. Piore, *Internal Labor Markets and Manpower Analysis* (Lexington, Mass., DC Heath, 1971). Also useful is David M. Gordon, *Theories of Poverty and Underemployment: Orthodox, Radical, and Dual Labor Market Perspectives* (Lexington, Mass., DC Heath, 1972). The 'radical' labour market segmentation perspective is best represented in the following: Richard C. Edwards, Michael Reich and David M. Gordon (eds), *Labor Market Segmentation* (Lexington, Mass., DC Heath, 1975); Richard C. Edwards, *Contested Terrain: The Transformation of the Workplace in the Twentieth Century* (New York, Basic Books, 1979); David M. Gordon, Richard C. Edwards and Michael Reich, *Segmented Work, Divided Workers* (New York, Cambridge University Press, 1982). There is a huge sociological literature on segmented, or dual, labour markets. For overviews see: Eric Hirsch, 'Dual labour market theory: a sociological critique', *Sociological Inquiry*, 50 (1980), pp. 133–46; Aage B. Sorensen, 'Sociological research on the labour market: conceptual and methodological issues', *Work and Occupations*, 10 (1983), pp. 261–87; Don Clairmont, Richard Apostle and Reinhard Kreckel, 'The segmentation perspective as a middle range conceptualization in sociology', *Canadian Journal of Sociology*, 8 (1983), pp. 245–71.

5. This description is based on Hirsch, 'Dual labour market theory'.

6. See the various citations of work by Gordon, Edwards, Reich in note 4 above.

7. Gordon, *Theories of Poverty*, p. 71.

8. Edwards, *Contested Terrain*, proposes three market segments, one secondary sector and a two-tiered primary sector, each defined in terms of a different form of job control found in the workplace. In other words, differences among jobs explain differences among workers.

9. See note 4 above for full citations.

10. Edwards, *Contested Terrain*, p. 195.

11. Ibid., pp. 194–9.

12. See Christine Craig, Elizabeth Garnsey and Jill Rubery, 'Labour market segmentation and women's employment: a case-study from the United Kingdom', *International Labour Review*, 124 (1985), pp. 267–80; and Elizabeth Garnsey, Jill Rubery and Frank Wilkinson, 'Labour market structure and work-force divisions', in Rosemary Deem and Graeme Salaman (eds), *Work, Culture and Society* (Milton Keynes, Open University Press, 1985).

13. Craig, Garnsey and Rubery, 'Labour market segmentation', p. 277.

14. The researchers (ibid., p. 279) found that in the firms they studied,

unionization was the major explanation of better wage levels and working conditions among women.

15. Garnsey, Rubery and Wilkinson, 'Labour market structure', pp. 47–9.
16. The marxist–feminist view of patriarchy is articulated by Heidi Hartmann in 'Capitalism, patriarchy, and job segregation by sex', *Signs*, 1 (1976), pp. 137–70 and 'The family as the locus of gender, class and political struggle', *Signs*, 6 (1981), pp. 366–94, as well as by Veronica Beechey in 'On patriarchy', *Feminist Review*, 3 (1979), pp. 66–82.
17. Veronica Beechey, 'Some notes on female wage labour in capitalist production', *Capital and Class*, 3 (1977), p. 47.
18. Paul Thompson, *The Nature of Work: An Introduction to Debates on the Labour Process* (London, Macmillan, 1983), pp.196–7.
19. Kanter, *Men and Women*, p. 25. A recent study in the United States shows how prevailing stereotypes of women infuse the control strategies that management use for female clerks. These stereotypes involve assumptions such as women being more oriented towards pleasing others, more sensitive to their surroundings, more honest and less mercenary than men. Many women internalize these beliefs. See Roslyn L. Feldberg and Evelyn Nakano Glenn, 'Technology and work degradation: effects of office automation on women clerical workers', in Joan Rothschild (ed.), *Machina Ex Dea: Feminist Perspectives on Technology* (New York, Pergamon, 1983), pp. 59–78.
20. Fiona McNally, *Women for Hire: A Study of the Female Office Worker* (London, Macmillan, 1979).
21. Ibid., p. 123.
22. A number of authors have criticized labour market segmentation theory for failing to explain adequately the nature of women's employment. See, for example, William P. Bridges, 'The sexual segregation of occupations; theories of labour stratification in industry', *American Journal of Sociology*, 88 (1982), pp. 270–95; Craig, Garnsey and Rubery, 'Labour market segmentation'; Veronica Beechey, 'Women and production: a critical analysis of some sociological theories of women's work', in A. Kuhn and A. M. Wolpe (eds), *Feminism and Materialism: Women and Modes of Production* (London, Routledge and Kegan Paul, 1978); Shirley Dex, *The Sexual Division of Labour: Conceptual Revolutions in the Social Sciences* (Brighton, Wheatsheaf Books, 1985), pp. 130–41; Pat Armstrong, *Labour Pains: Women's Work in Crisis* (Toronto, Women's Press, 1984), pp. 28–32; Martha MacDonald 'Economics and feminism: the dismal science', *Studies in Political Economy*, 15 (1984), pp. 166–70.
23. Valerie K. Oppenheimer, *The Female Labor Force in the United States* (Berkeley, Institute of International Studies, University of California, 1970), p. 115.
24. Janice Fanning Madden, *The Economics of Sex Discrimination* (Lexington, Mass., Lexington Books, 1973), p. 78.
25. Francis D. Klingender, *The Condition of Clerical Labour in Britain* (New York, International Publishers, 1935); Mills, *White Collar*; Lockwood, *Blackcoated Worker*; Crozier, *World of the Office Worker*; R. M. Blackburn, *Union Character and Social Class* (London, B. T. Batsford, 1967).

26. A. Stewart, K. Prandy and R. M. Blackburn, *Social Stratification and Occupations* (London, Macmillan, 1980); K. Prandy, A. Stewart and R. M. Blackburn, *White-Collar Work* (London, Macmillan, 1982) and *White-Collar Unionism* (London, Macmillan, 1983).
27. Crompton and Jones, *White-Collar Proletariat*.
28. Anderson, *Victorian Clerks*, p. 56.
29. Much of this account is drawn from Rosalie Silverstone, 'Office work for women: an historical review', *Business History*, 18 (1976), p. 98–110.
30. Ibid., p. 102.
31. Ibid.
32. Ibid.
33. Samuel Ross Cohn, 'Clerical labour intensity and the feminization of clerical labour in Great Britain, 1857–1937', *Social Forces*, 63 (1985), pp. 1060–8.
34. Ibid, p. 1061.
35. Lockwood, *Blackcoated Worker*, p. 122.
36. Ibid.
37. Ibid.
38. This discussion of US clerical feminization draws on Margery W. Davies, *Women's Place*, and Cindy S. Aron, '"To barter their souls for gold": female clerks in federal government offices, 1862–1890', *The Journal of American History*, 67 (1981), pp. 835–53. For an analysis of the feminization process during a later period see Mark McColloch, *White Collar Workers in Transition: The Boom Years, 1940–1970* (Westport, Conn., Greenwood Press, 1983).
39. Grace L. Coyle, 'Women in the clerical occupations', *Annals of the American Academy of Political and Social Science*, 143 (1929), p. 180.
40. Leslie Woodcock Tentler, *Wage–Earning Women: Industrial Work and Family Life in the United States, 1900–1930* (New York, Oxford University Press, 1979), pp. 5, 96. Davies, in *Women's Place*, pp. 64–5, observes that even before 1900 working class daughters aspired to clerical jobs because of their relatively high pay – second only to professional work.
41. Davies, *Women's Place*, chapter 5.
42. Coyle, 'Women in the clerical occupations', p. 138. Tentler, in *Wage Earning Women*, p. 143, comments more generally about the tight restrictions on married women's employment during this era.
43. Coyle, 'Women in the clerical occupations', p. 183.
44. Davies, *Women's Place*, pp. 174–5.
45. See ibid., chapter 6, for an insightful analysis of scientific office management.
46. Ibid, p. 170.
47. Elyce J. Rotella, *From Home to Office: US Women at Work, 1870–1930* (Ann Arbor, Mich., UMI Research Press, 1981).
48. Ibid., p. 65. The 1910–20 decade experienced the most dramatic growth in clerical jobs of the entire 1870 to 1930 period: one-quarter of all additional workers became clerks and 69 per cent of the change in the female non-agricultural labour force in these ten years was due to increases in clerical employment.
49. Ibid., p. 102.

50. Ibid., pp. 164–8. The seminal work on human capital theory is Gary Becker, *Human Capital* (New York, Columbia University Press, 1964).
51. Rotella, *From Home to Office*, p. 166.

CHAPTER 2 CORPORATE CAPITALISM AND THE ADMINISTRATIVE REVOLUTION

1. D. W. Birchall and V. J. Hammond, *Tomorrow's Office: Managing Technological Change* (London, Business Books, 1981), p. 15.
2. Mills, *White Collar*, p. 189.
3. What sparked this debate was Harry Braverman's *Labor and Monopoly Capital: The Degradation of Work in the Twentieth Century* (New York: Monthly Review Press, 1974). John Storey, 'The means of management control', *Sociology*, 19 (1985), p. 194. Other cogent theoretical critiques of the labour process literature are provided by C. R. Littler and G. Salaman, 'Bravermania and beyond: recent theories of the labour processes', *Sociology*, 16 (1982), pp. 251–69; Thompson, *Nature of Work*. Case studies amply documenting the manifold managerial control tactics and labour process forms, influenced by occupational, industrial and national factors, are presented in the following: Andrew Zimbalist (ed.), *Case Studies on the Labor Process* (New York, Monthly Review Press, 1979); Stephen Wood (ed.), *The Degradation of Work? Skill, Deskilling and the Labour Process* (London, Hutchinson, 1982); Craig Heron and Robert Storey (eds), *On the Job: Confronting the Labour Process in Canada* (Montreal, McGill–Queen's University Press, 1986).
4. Allan A. Murdoch and J. Rodney Dale, *The Clerical Function* (London, Sir Isaac Pitman, 1961), p. 2.
5. Lockwood, *Blackcoated Worker*, p. 36.
6. There is an extensive literature examining the impact of staples production on Canadian economic development. Perhaps the best summary of the staple thesis is found in Harold Innis, *The Fur Trade in Canada* (Toronto, University of Toronto Press, 1970), pp. 383–402. For general overviews of Canadian economic development from a staple perspective see Richard E. Caves and Richard H. Holton, *The Canadian Economy: Prospect and Retrospect* (Cambridge, Mass., Harvard University Press, 1961); W. T. Easterbrook and Hugh G. J. Aitken, *Canadian Economic History* (Toronto, Macmillan, 1956). The new political economy, synthesizing Innis and Marx, is outlined in Mel Watkins, 'The staple theory revisited', *Journal of Canadian Studies*, 12 (1977), pp. 83–95; Daniel Drache, 'Harold Innis and Canadian capitalist development', *Canadian Journal of Political and Social Theory*, 6 (1982), pp. 35–60. However, the staple theory is increasingly under dispute. For recent interpretations see William L. Marr and Donald G. Paterson, *Canada: An Economic History* (Toronto, Macmillan, 1980). Richard Pomfret, *The Economic Development of Canada* (Toronto, Methuen, 1980) offers a well-documented rejection of the staples model.
7. For an excellent discussion of Canada as a late industrializing nation, see Gordon Laxer, 'Foreign ownership and myths about Canadian develop-

ment', *Canadian Review of Sociology and Anthropology*, 22 (1985), pp. 311–45.

8. O. J. Firestone, 'Canada's economic development, 1867–1952', paper prepared for the Third Conference of the International Association for Research in Income and Wealth, Castelgandolfo, Italy, September 1953, p. 178.

9. For useful discussions of this point see Laxer, 'Foreign ownership', and Glen Williams, *Not For Export: Toward a Political Economy of Canada's Arrested Industrialization* (Toronto, McClelland and Stewart, 1983).

10. Hugh G. J. Aitken, 'The changing structure of the Canadian economy', in Hugh G. J. Aitken et al. (eds), *The American Economic Impact on Canada* (Durham, NC, Duke University Press, 1959), p. 7.

11. O. J. Firestone, 'Development of Canada's economy, 1850–1900', in *Trends in the American Economy in the Nineteenth Century* (Princeton University, Studies in Income and Wealth no. 24, 1960), pp. 218, 219, 230.

12. M. C. Urquhart, 'New estimates of gross national product, Canada, 1870 to 1926: some implications for Canadian economic development', (Kingston, Queen's University, Institute for Economic Research, Discussion Paper no. 586, 1984), p. 95. Economic historians typically have portrayed the period from 1896 to 1914 as one of successful industrialization. See G. W. Bertram, 'Economic growth in Canadian industry, 1870–1915: the staple model', in W. T. Easterbrook and M. H. Watkins (eds), *Approaches to Canadian Economic History* (Toronto, McClelland and Stewart, 1967), p. 78; Kenneth Buckley, *Capital Formation in Canada, 1896–1930* (Toronto, McClelland and Stewart, 1974); Pomfret, *Economic Development*, chapter 6. For a dissenting view see Laxer, 'Foreign ownership'.

13. Pomfret, *Economic Development*, pp. 56–8.

14. Ibid., p. 146. Pig iron output leaped from 104,882 tons in 1896–8 to 1,937,144 tons in 1901–11.

15. Robert Craig Brown and Ramsay Cook, *Canada 1896–1921: A Nation Transformed* (Toronto, McClelland and Stewart, 1976) pp. 83–4. For an analysis of the political economy of wheat see Vernon C. Fowke, *The National Policy and the Wheat Economy* (Toronto, University of Toronto Press, 1957).

16. Firestone, 'Canada's economic development', p. 152.

17. Gideon Rosenbluth, *Concentration in Canadian Manufacturing Industries*, National Bureau of Economic Research, no. 61, General Series (Princeton, NJ, Princeton University Press, 1957), p. 9; Firestone, 'Canada's economic development', p. 156. Investment in manufacturing achieved a peak in 1929 not to be surpassed until the 1950s (ibid.).

18. H. F. Marshall, F. Southard and K. Taylor, *Canadian–American Industry*, (Toronto, McClelland and Stewart, 1976), p. 18.

19. In 1922, the value of US direct investment surpassed that of British indirect, or portfolio, investment. See Mira Wilkins, *The Maturing of Multinational Enterprise* (Cambridge, Mass., Harvard University Press, 1974), p. 155.

20. Mira Wilkins, *The Emergence of Multinational Enterprise* (Cambridge, Mass., Harvard University Press, 1970), pp. 136, 141–2. The list includes Johns-

Manville, International Nickle Co., International Paper, Westinghouse, Standard Oil, Goodyear, US Rubber, du Pont, and International Harvester.

21. Arguments about the role of commercial capitalists in suppressing indigenous forces of industrialization are outlined in Wallace Clement, *The Canadian Corporate Elite* (Toronto, McClelland and Stewart, 1975); R. T. Naylor, *The History of Canadian Business, 1867–1914* (2 vols, Toronto, Lorimer, 1975); L. R. Macdonald, 'Merchants against industry: an idea and its origins', *Canadian Historial Review*, 56 (1975), pp. 263–81; William K. Carroll, 'The Canadian corporate elite: financiers or finance capitalists?', *Studies in Political Economy*, 8 (1982), pp. 89–114; Jorge Niosi, 'The Canadian bourgeoisie: towards a synthetical approach', *Canadian Journal of Political and Social Theory*, 7 (1983), pp. 128–49.

22. Firestone, 'Development of Canada's economy', p. 226.

23. David A. Worton, 'The service industries in Canada', in Victor R. Fuchs (ed.), *Production and Productivity in the Service Industries* (New York, Columbia University Press, 1969), p. 238. This refers to the percentage of the labour force employed in the service sector.

24. W. A. Mackintosh, *The Economic Background of Dominion–Provincial Relations* (Toronto, McClelland and Stewart, 1964), p. 56. Also see Brown and Cook, *Canada*, chapters 11 and 12, for discussions of how World War I affected Canadian economic and social structures.

25. Firestone, 'Canada's economic development', p. 155; Brown and Cook, *Canada*, p. 234.

26. Donald V. Smiley (ed.), *The Rowell–Sirois Report, Book I* (Toronto, McClelland and Stewart, 1963), pp. 108–37.

27. Ibid., p. 120.

28. Chapter 4 gives details of female recruitment into offices during the First World War. For more general documentation see Enid M. Price, 'Changes in the Industrial Occupations of Women in the Environment of Montreal during the Period of War, 1914–1918', unpublished MA thesis, McGill University, 1919.

29. Brown and Cook, Canada, p. 241, n. 60.

30. Firestone, 'Development of Canada's economy', p. 230.

31. 'Personnel File No. 2', Sun Life Archives, Montreal.

32. *Imperial Oil Review*, August 1922, p. 9.

33. See Alfred D. Chandler Jr. and Herman Daems (eds), *Managerial Hierarchies: Corporate Perspectives on the Rise of the Modern Industrial Enterprise* (Cambridge, Mass., Harvard University Press, 1980), for comparative perspectives on the development of the modern firm in the US and Western Europe (Canada is not covered in the volume), p. 3.

34. Naylor, *Canadian Business*, vol. I, p. 211.

35. P. A. Linteau, R. Durocher and J. C. Robert, *Quebec: A History, 1867–1929* (Toronto, Lorimer, 1983), p. 335. On the Canadian merger movement see J. C. Weldon, 'Consolidation in Canadian industry, 1900–1948', in L. A. Skoech (ed.), *Restrictive Trade Practices in Canada* (Toronto, McClelland and Stewart, 1966); Pomfret, *Economic Development*, pp. 136–8.

36. A Canada–US comparison of firm size in 14 leading industries for 1923–4

shows that, while the United States had a higher proportion of firms employing over 500 workers, Canada had proportionately more in the 100 to 500 employee category. V. W. Bladen, 'The size of establishment in Canadian and American industry', *Contributions to Canadian Economics*, 1 (1928), pp. 56–68.

37. See Adolf A. Berle and Gardiner C. Means, *The Modern Corporation and Private Property*, revised edn (New York, Macmillan, 1968).
38. John S. Ewing, *The History of Imperial Oil Limited*, unpublished MS prepared for the Business History Foundation, Inc., Harvard Business School, 1951 (mimeographed copy in IOL's Business Library, Toronto), vol. 4, chapter XIX, p. 1.
39. O. J. McDiarmid, 'Some aspects of the Canadian automobile industry', *Canadian Journal of Economics and Political Science*, 6 (1940), p. 258.
40. E. P. Neufeld, *The Financial System of Canada* (Toronto, Macmillan, 1972), p. 97.
41. Meredith G. Rowntree, *The Railway Worker* (Toronto, Oxford University Press, 1936), p. 12.
42. Bank of Montreal, *The Service Industries*, study no. 17, Royal Commission on Canada's Economic Prospects (March 1956), p. 128.
43. As of 31 December. 'Personnel File No. 2', Sun Life Archives, Montreal. Neufeld (*Financial System*, p. 257) describes Sun Life's expansion up to 1930 as 'The most remarkable of any financial intermediary in Canada's history'.
44. *Sunshine* (Sun Life's employee magazine), January, 1905, p. 12.
45. Emil Lederer, *The Problem of the Modern Salaried Employee*, tr. E. E. Warburg (New York, State Department of ·Social Welfare and the Department of Social Science, Columbia University, 1937), pp. 11–14, 18.
46. Reinhard Bendix, *Work and Authority in Industry* (Berkeley, University of California Press, 1974), pp. 223, 254–5. Bendix claims that the best index of internal bureaucratization of an organization is the proportion of salaried employees in its labour force. Also see Fritz Croner, 'Salaried employees in modern society', *International Labour Review*, 69 (1954), pp. 97–110, who emphasizes the importance of the delegation of management responsibilities for clerical growth.
47. Mills, *White Collar*, p. 66. David Lockwood, commenting on Britain, denotes two processes in the transformation of administration: the rising A/P ratio in manufacturing, and the proliferation of non-production functions in commerce, finance, distribution and government. See *Black-coated Worker*, p. 36.
48. International Labour Organization, 'The use of office machinery and its influence on conditions of work for staff', *International Labour Review*, 36 (1937), p. 513. The Canadian A/P ratio in manufacturing rose steadily from 9.2 in 1910 to 16 in 1930 and 30.7 in 1959. See M. C. Urquhart and K. A. H. Buckley (eds), *Historical Statistics of Canada* (Toronto, Macmillan 1965), p. 463. Also, Donald W. Wood documents that salaries accounted for 17 per cent of the total manufacturing payroll in 1917, rising to 38 per cent by 1958. See his 'The changing environment in the office: retrospect and prospect', *Canadian Personnel and Industrial Relations Journal*, 7 (1960), p. 21.

49. Seymour Melman, 'The rise of administrative overhead in the manufacturing industries of the United States, 1899–1947', *Oxford Economic Papers*, new series 3 (1951), p. 92.

50. Joseph A. Litterer, 'Systematic management: design for organizational recoupling in American manufacturing firms', *Business History Review*, 37 (1963), p. 374.

51. See Sidney Pollard, *The Genesis of Modern Management* (Harmondsworth, Penguin, 1968), p. 245; Chandler, *Visible Hand* p. 273.

52. David S. Landes, *The Unbound Prometheus: Technological Change and Industrial Development in Western Europe from 1750 to the Present* (Cambridge, Cambridge University Press, 1969), p. 322.

53. Harry Braverman, *Labor and Monopoly Capital*, p. 125.

54. Life Office Management Association, *Proceedings* of the 1927 Annual Conference (hereafter LOMA, *Proceedings*, followed by conference year), p. 188.

55. Chandler, *Visible Hand*, p. 8.

56. See Daniel Nelson, *Managers and Workers: Origins of the New Factory System in the United States, 1880-1920* (Madison, University of Wisconsin Press, 1975), chapter 1.

57. Pollard, *Genesis of Modern Management*, p. 78.

58. Bryan Palmer refers to this eclectic reform programme as the 'broad thrust for efficiency'. See his 'Class, conception and conflict: the thrust for efficiency, managerial views of labour and the working class rebellion', *Review of Radical Political Economics*, 7 (1975), p. 32. Leland H. Jenks views the works management movement in the United States and Britain as spawning professional managers through a two-stage process. During the first stage, firms in various industries communicated their managerial experiences to one another. This forged a consensus regarding which problems should be subjected to systematic managerial inquiry. Standards for effective solutions were collectively established. As these ideas spread, a second phase was entered, in which the movement became institutionalized in newly formed professional management associations. Jenks's concept of consensus and institutionalization guides my discussion of the evolution of modern management in Canada. See his 'Early phases of the management movement', *Administrative Science Quarterly*, 5 (1960), pp. 421–47.

59. Nelson, *Managers and Workers*, pp. 48–9.

60. Litterer, 'Systematic management', pp. 376–7.

61. Jenks, 'Early phases', p. 428.

62. Judith A. Merkle, *Management and Ideology: The Legacy of the International Scientific Management Movement* (Berkeley, University of California Press, 1980), pp. 1–2. Also see Daniel Nelson, *Fredrick W. Taylor and the Rise of Scientific Management* (Madison, University of Wisconsin Press, 1980). Taylor first presented his system in a paper read before the American Society of Mechanical Engineers (ASME) in 1895. It was entitled 'A piece-rate system, being a step toward partial solution of the labour problem', *ASME Transactions*, 16 (1895), pp. 860–1. It discussed wage incentives, a topic of some concern to US businessmen who faced rising costs and increasingly competitive international markets. Cost accounting already had

provided a partial remedy. But Taylor's innovation was to advocate objectively determined times for the performance of all tasks. If workers completed a task within the specified time, they received a good piece rate. If they failed to achieve this, their pay was so low that they eventually would be forced to quit. This carrot-and-stick approach appealed to manufacturers, mainly because of its double-pronged effect of eliminating lazy workers, thus alleviating the 'labour problem', and encouraged worker–management co-operation in the interests of higher productivity. Also see Taylor's *Shop Management* (New York, Harper Bros., 1919).

63. Samuel Haber, *Efficiency and Uplift: Scientific Management in the Progressive Era, 1890–1920* (Chicago, University of Chicago Press, 1964). Reg Whitaker examines the ideological underpinnings of scientific management in 'Scientific management theory as political ideology', *Studies in Political Economy*, 2 (1979), pp. 75–108.

64. Nelson, *Fredrick W. Taylor*, p.149. Only 69 of the documented cases were successful.

65. Merkle, *Management and Ideology*, p. 3. She does, however, note that the impact was muted in Britain because the traditional attitudes of management tended to restrict innovation to technology (p. 240). Members of the French technocratic elite were rapid converts to Taylorism, but employers and workers resisted its application (p. 15).

66. John E. Kelly, *Scientific Management, Job Redesign and Work Performance* (London, Academic Press, 1982), p. 25. See chapter 1 for an overview of the development of scientific management.

67. Paul Craven *'An Impartial Umpire': Industrial Relations and the Canadian State* (Toronto, University of Toronto Press, 1980), p. 94. Documentation of the application of scientific management in Canada is limited. See Bryan D. Palmer, *A Culture in Conflict: Skilled Workers and Industrial Capitalism in Hamilton, Ontario, 1860–1914* (Montreal, McGill-Queen's University Press, 1979), pp. 216–22; Craig Heron and Bryan D. Palmer, 'Through the prism of the strike: industrial conflict in southern Ontario, 1901–14', *Canadian Historical Review*, 58 (1977), pp. 423–58.

68. S. D. Clark, *The Canadian Manufacturers' Association* (Toronto, University of Toronto Press, 1939), p. 42.

69. *Labour Gazette* (hereafter *LG*), August 1922, p. 846. In the same year the Trades and Labour Congress also endorsed the joint council scheme (*LG*, September 1922, p. 972).

70. LOMA, *Proceedings*, 1928, p. 66.

71. *Monetary Times* (hereafter *MT*), 24 September 1920, p. 10.

72. *MT*, 19 December 1908, p. 1010.

73. *LG*, January 1920, p. 3.

74. In 1907 *Industrial Canada* (hereafter *IC*) ran a series of three articles by H. L. C. Hall, a Fellow of the International Accountant's Society, on the 'model factory'.

75. *IC*, February 1907, p. 586.

76. Ibid, p. 588.

77. *IC*, May 1911, p. 1073.

78. Nelson, *Frederick W. Taylor*, p. 149.

79. *Railway and Marine World*, January 1912, pp. 1–3.
80. H. L. Gantt, 'The straight line to profit', *IC*, March 1911, p. 837.
81. *IC*, April 1913, pp. 124–5. Also see F. W. Taylor, 'Principles of scientific management', *IC*, March 1913, pp. 1105–6; 'How scientific management works', *IC*, May 1913, pp. 1349–50.
82. See e.g. 'A tight check on piece work', *IC*, January 1916, p. 693.
83. *LG*, August 1921, pp. 1019–25.
84. *IC*, 1 May 1902, p. 337.
85. IBM Canadian Sales Record, 10 February 1921 (IBM Archives, Toronto). Such an advertisement appeared in *IC*, September 1921, p. 81. The advertisement computed that if an office staff of 40 loses 15 minutes each day, then the annual loss to the company would be $1,500.
86. *MT*, September 1919, p. 30.
87. *MT*, 6 October 1916, p. 9.
88. John P. Jordon and Gould I. Harris, *Cost Accounting: Principles and Practice*, 2nd edn (New York, Ronald Press, 1925), p. 19.
89. *IC*, August 1903, p. 26.
90. *MT*, 26 September 1919, p. 30; also see 5 December 1919, p. 23.
91. See *LG*, April 1925, pp. 358–69. There has been little research on welfare work in Canada. The most thorough treatment is in Robert Storey, 'Unionization versus corporate welfare: the "Dofasco Way" ', *Labour/Le Travailleur*, 12 (1983), pp. 7–42. For the United States see Nelson, *Managers and Workers*, chapter 6.
92. LOMA, *Proceedings*, 1927, p. 75.
93. National Cash Register Co. in Dayton, Ohio, pioneered welfare work in the late 1890s under the direction of John H. Patterson, its president. The modern personnel department dates from the 1901 NCR strike (Nelson, *Managers and Workers*, p. 148). Also see Samuel Crowther, *John H. Patterson: Pioneer in Industrial Welfare* (Garden City, NJ, Doubleday, 1924). The National Association of Employment Managers was launched in the United States in 1919 and the following year began publishing the journal *Personnel*.
94. *IC*, 2 June 1902, p. 432.
95. *IC*, January 1907, p. 506.
96. For discussions of the Williams, Green and Rome scheme see *LG*, February 1907, pp. 892–4; *IC*, February 1910, pp. 693–6; *IC*, March 1910, pp. 786–7.
97. *IC*, March 1910, p. 787; *LG*, April 1911, pp. 1138–9.
98. An editorial on personnel policies in *MT* (4 March 1921, p. 10), noted that Canadian financial institutions were following the lead of large US firms in implementing welfare schemes.
99. *LG*, February 1930, p. 154.
100. *LG*, October 1928, pp. 1108–10.
101. See Bendix, *Work and Authority*, chapter 5.
102. Canada, Department of Labour, *Report of a Conference on Industrial Relations*, Bulletin no. 2, Industrial Relations Series, published as a supplement to *LG*, March 1921, p. 3. See the *LG* for detailed coverage of these developments beginning in 1919. Seventeen large corporations

introduced full-fledged industrial councils right after the First World War, with others to follow during the 1920s.

103. See Henry Ferns and Bernard Ostry, *The Age of Mackenzie King* (Toronto, Lorimer, 1976), and Craven '*Impartial Umpire*'. King's major legislative achievements were the 1907 Industrial Disputes Investigation Act and the 1910 Combines Investigation Act.

104. Nelson, *Managers and Workers*, p. 51.

105. Murdoch and Dale, *Clerical Function*, p. 2.

106. United States Congress, Senate Committee on Education and Labor, Systems of Shop Management, Report no. 930, 17 July (Washington, GPO, 1912), p. 12 [cited in Merkle, *Management and Ideology*, p. 32].

107. William Henry Leffingwell, *Scientific Office Management* (Chicago, A. W. Shaw, 1917), p. 5.

108. *Telephone Gazette* (hereinafter *TG*) May 1909, p. 2.

109. LOMA, *Proceedings*, 1924, p. 8.

CHAPTER 3 THE GROWTH OF CLERICAL OCCUPATIONS

1. Labour Canada, *Women in the Labour Force: Part 1 – Participation* (Ottawa, Labour Canada Women's Bureau, 1983), p. 33. For a general overview of historical labour force trends see Warren E. Kalbach and Wayne W. McVey, *The Demographic Basis of Canadian Society*, 2nd edn (Toronto, McGraw-Hill Ryerson, 1979), chapter 11.

2. M. S. Devereaux and E. Rechnitzer, *Higher Education – Hired? Sex Differences in Employment Characteristics of 1976 Post Secondary Graduates* (Ottawa, Statistics Canada, 1981), p. 5.

3. Toronto *Globe and Mail*, 2 June 1984, p. 13. According to the 1981 census, only 6.35 per cent of general managers and administrative officials in the private sector were women. There was, however, increasing recruitment of women into lower-level managerial and administrative posts between 1971–81. The proportion of women in managerial, administrative and related occupations rose from 15.7 per cent in 1971 to 24.8 per cent in 1981, although I should note that over the same period women became even more highly concentrated in clerical occupations. See: Canada, *Women in the Work World* (Ottawa, Statistics Canada, 1984), chart 10b.

4. Canada, *1871 Census*, volume II, table XIII; and Canada, *1881 Census*, volume II, table XIV.

5. I adopted the methodology developed by Noah M. Meltz in *Manpower in Canada, 1931 to 1961* (Ottawa, Queen's Printer, 1965), pp. 5–7 and Appendix, pp. 31–56. The 1951 census definition of clerical worker provides a base for reclassifying data on clerical occupations. All census data from 1891 to 1971 pertaining to clerical labour force and earnings trends reported in this book use this reclassified series. (The exceptions to this are the 1971 and 1981 census date reported in tables 3.6 and 7.3, which use the classification systems for these respective census years.) In developing these time series data, I am grateful to Amy Kempster and her staff at the Economics Characteristics Branch of Statistics Canada for providing me

with unpublished working tables for the 1901, 1911 and 1921 censuses.

6. R. Marvin McInnis, 'Long-run changes in the industrial structure of the Canadian work force', *Canadian Journal of Economics*, 4 (1971), pp. 353–61. McInnis attributes this shift to technological changes.

7. For American librarians and teachers see Dee Garrison, 'The tender technicians: the feminization of public librarianship, 1876–1905', *Journal of Social History*, 6 (1972/73), pp. 131–59; John G. Richardson and Brenda Wooden Hatcher, 'The feminization of public school teaching, 1870–1920', *Work and Occupations*, 10 (1983), pp.81–99; and Oppenheimer, *The Female Labor Force in the United States*, pp. 77–96. For Canadian teachers see Alison Prentice, 'The feminization of teaching in British North America and Canada, 1845–1875', *Histoire sociale/Social History*, 8 (1975), pp. 5–20. For nursing see E. Gamarnikow. 'Sexual division of labour: the case of nursing', in Kuhn and Wolpe (eds), *Feminism and Materialism*.

8. Few comprehensive studies of the impact of office automation in Canada have been published to date. Rather bleak tentative scenarios are, however, set out by Heather Menzies in *Women and the Chip* (Montreal, Institute for Research on Public Policy, 1981), and in the report of the Labour Canada Task Force on Micro-Electronics and Employment (*In the Chips: Opportunities, People, Partnerships* (Ottawa, Labour Canada, 1982). For more general discussions of possible downgrading effects on female clerks and a reduced demand for office workers see: J. Gregory and K. Nussbaum, 'Race against time: an analysis of the trends in office automation and the impact on the office workforce', *Office: Technology and People*, 1 (1982), pp. 197–236; and Dennis R. Eckart, 'Microprocessors, women, and future employment opportunities', *International Journal of Women's Studies*, 5 (1982), pp. 47–57; Wassily Leontif and Faye Duchin, *The Future Impact of Automation on Workers* (New York, Oxford University Press, 1986), chapter 3; and Paul Osterman, 'The impact of computers on the employment of managers and clerks', *Industrial and Labor Relations Review*, 39 (1986), pp.175–86.

9. Braverman, *Labor and Monopoly Capital*, chapter 15.

10. Canada, *Standard Occupational Classification* (Ottawa, Statistics Canada, 1981).

11. Mills, *White Collar*, p. 206.

12. Kanter, *Men and Women of the Corporation*, chapter 4.

13. Catherine Hakim, 'Job segregation: trends in the 1970s', *Employment Gazette*, December 1981, p. 521.

14. Pat Armstrong and Hugh Armstrong, *The Double Ghetto: Canadian Women and their Segregated Work*, revised edn (Toronto, McClelland and Stewart, 1984), p. 33.

15. For an overview of the impact of micro-electronics on women's work in Canada, see Armstrong, *Labour Pains*, chapter 7. For an interesting case study of office automation see Feldberg and Glenn, 'Technology and work degradation'.

16. The precise figures for clerks as a proportion of the total labour force are: Canada (1982), 16.1 per cent; United States (1981), 17.8 per cent; West Germany (1980), 19.4 per cent; Australia (1982), 16.1. I should also note

that comparable figures for Japan (1980) and Sweden (1981) are somewhat lower, at 9.1 per cent and 12.1 per cent respectively. (International Labour Office, *Year Book of Labour Statistics, 1982* (Geneva, ILO, 1983), table 2, pp. 94–128). There are no comparable data for Britain, although the 1984 Labour Force Survey indicates that 16 per cent of people in employment are clerks (Office of Population Censuses and Surveys (OPCS), *Monitor*, 17 December 1985, p. 10).

17. For the same years as cited in note 16 above, women comprised the following proportion of all clerks: Canada, 78.9 per cent; United States, 80.6 per cent; West Germany, 57.9 per cent; Australia, 70.7 per cent (ILO, *Year Book, 1982*, table 2, pp. 94–128).
18. Crompton and Jones, *White-Collar Proletariat*, p.18.
19. Silverstone, 'Office work for women', p. 101.
20. Ibid., pp.107–9.
21. OPCS, *Monitor*, 17 December 1985, p.9.
22. Susan Vinnicombe, Secretaries, Management and Organizations *(London, Heinemann, 1980), p. 7.*
23. Davies, *Woman's Place*, pp. 51–2.
24. Janice Weiss, 'Educating for clerical work: the nineteenth century private commercial school', *Journal of Social History*, 14 (1981), p. 407.
25. Ibid., p. 413.
26. Davies, *Woman's Place*, pp. 52–3.
27. Elyce J. Rotella, 'The transformation of the American office: changes in employment and technology', *Journal of Economic History*, 41 (1981), p. 57.
28. ILO, *Year Book, 1982*, table 2, pp. 94–128.

CHAPTER 4 CLERICAL FEMINIZATION IN BANKS

1. Jean Thomson Scott, 'The conditions of female labour in Ontario', in W. J. Ashley (ed.), *University of Toronto Studies in Political Science*, series III (1889), p. 24.
2. Ibid., p. 24.
3. *Sunshine*, June 1902, p. 83. Also see, 'Personnel File No. 2', Sun Life Archives. Perhaps one of the reasons insurance companies were more receptive to female clerical employment was their recognition of the potential market for life insurance among working women. A *Sunshine* editorial (February 1896, p. 24) advised that, 'there is no better way in which a wage-earning woman can provide for her old age than by carrying a good endowment policy' (i.e., one of Sun's).
4. Ceta Ramkhalawansingh, 'Women during the Great War', in Janice Acton et al., (eds), *Women at Work: Ontario 1850–1930* (Toronto, Canadian Women's Educational Press, 1974), p. 261. For a discussion of women's economic roles during the Second World War, see Ruth Pierson, 'Women's emancipation and the recruitment of women into the labour force in World War II', in Susan Mann Trofimenkoff and Alison Prentice (eds), *The Neglected Majority* (Toronto, McClelland and Stewart, 1977), pp. 125–45.
5. The war decade witnessed a tremendous expansion of clerical occupations, from 103,543 in 1911 to 216,691 by 1921. The segmentation of the labour

market received a great boost; clerical jobs increased their share of the total female work force from 9.1 per cent in 1911 to 18.5 per cent in 1921. Fully 50.2 per cent of the growth in office occupations over the decade was accounted for by women flooding into offices. This compares with 45.5 per cent a decade earlier. While the figure for the 1921–31 decade increases to 61.5 per cent, numerically the growth in clerical occupations is considerably less than in the war decade. In fact, 69,165 more clerical jobs were created during the 1911–21 decade than during the twenties. This works out to approximately four times more jobs, and therefore about four times more women entering the office.

6. Price, 'Changes in the Industrial Occupations of Women in The Environment of Montreal', p. 26.
7. Ibid., p. 60.
8. *Journal of the Canadian Bankers' Association* (hereafter *JCBA*), July 1916, p. 316.
9. Ibid., p. 316.
10. *MT*, 11 May 1907, pp. 1764–5.
11. *MT*, 4 May 1907, p. 1734. The author of the article on women in banking, Mrs E. B. B. Ressor, was manager of the Crown Bank of Canada's Women's Department. The bank employed only 100 men and 17 women, yet seems remarkably advanced in institutionalizing the employment of women. Mrs Ressor advised that to do well in banking, women must be brainy, have keen intuition, good executive ability and excellent judgement. But, alas, such were fleeting attributes for, 'a women's heart generally rules her head' (p. 1734). In the 1920s, US banks apparently did not undergo the same retrenchment due to failures and mergers. Women therefore had greater opportunities for employment and, according to one report, upward mobility (*MT*, 15 June 1923, p. 12).
12. *JCBA*, July 1916, pp. 294–5.
13. The occupational census of Canadian forces overseas on 31 December 1916 records a total of 285,562. By far the largest occupational grouping is manual workers (178,670), followed by a much smaller clerical group (40,765), then farmers (38,045). Canadian Pacific Railway, Shaughnessy Letterbooks, Col. J. Dennis to President, memo, 8 February 1917 (# 107621), CPR Archives, Montreal.
14. *JCBA*, July 1916, pp. 314–15.
15. 'Circular No. 1,699 from the General Manager, 6 April 1916', Bank of Nova Scotia Archives, Toronto.
16. Ibid.
17. *MT*, 29 March 1918, p. 22. The appeals were made to the tribunal set up under the Military Service Act.
18. *JCBA*, July 1917, pp. 316–317. A year earlier, this official organ had already recognized the inevitability of a permanent corps of female bank clerks, tempered with the caveat that women have 'centuries of prejudice to overcome' (*JCBA*, July 1916, p. 318).
19. *MT*, 8 August 1919, p. 10.
20. Ibid.
21. *MT*, 15 June 1923, p. 12.

22. *MT*, 20 May 1927, p. 11.
23. Ibid.
24. *JCBA*, January 1911, p. 11.
25. Scott, 'Conditions of female labour', p. 25.
26. Scott's observation applies equally to working-class as well as middle-class women. Bettina Bradbury's research on female work in mid-nineteenth-century Montreal suggests that, between 1861 and 1881, less than 5 per cent of married women reported wage work to census-takers. The typical working-class wife of the time contributed to the family economy through household, not wage, labour. See 'Women and wage labour in a period of transition: Montreal, 1861–1881', *Histoire sociale/Social History*, 17 (1984), pp. 115–31. Well into the twentieth century the employment of married women in white-collar positions was prohibited. There is evidence of such rules in the federal civil service, and at least one insurance company, Manufacturers Life, refused to grant women pregnancy leave as late as 1959. Instead, they had to resign and then reapply for a job with no guarantee that they would be hired back. In the 1920s it seems that the ban on employing married women was fairly common. For example, the standard teacher's contract in Ontario in the early 1920s forbade the marriage of women teachers (John Crispo, *The Canadian Industrial Relations System* (Toronto, McGraw-Hill Ryerson, 1978), pp. 112–13).
27. Mary Vipond, 'The image of women in mass circulation magazines in the 1920s', in Trofimenkoff and Prentice (eds), *Neglected Majority*, p. 117.
28. *Bluebell* (Bell Telephone Company of Canada staff magazine), August 1930, p. 8.
29. W. Elliot Brownlee and Mary M. Brownlee, *Women in the American Economy* (New Haven, Yale University Press, 1976), p. 18.
30. *JCBA*, July 1917, p. 318.
31. Vipond, 'Image of women', p. 120.
32. Kathleen Archibald, *Sex and the Public Service* (Ottawa, Queen's Printer, 1970), p. 16.
33. J. E. Hodgetts, W. McCloskey, R. Whitaker and V. S. Wilson, *The Biography of an Institution: The Civil Service Commission of Canada, 1908–1967* (Montreal, McGill-Queen's University Press, 1972), p. 483.
34. Robert M. Dawson, *The Civil Service of Canada* (London, Oxford University Press, 1929), p. 190.
35. Ibid., p. 190.
36. Canada, *First Report of the Civil Service Commission*, Sessional Paper no. 113, 1881, p. 26.
37. J. L. Payne, 'The civil servant', *The University Magazine*, 6 (December 1907), p. 511.
38. Dawson, *Civil Service*, p. 191.
39. Hodgetts et al., *Biography*, p. 483.
40. Payne, 'Civil servant', p. 511. Many of these women were hired on a temporary basis.
41. Canada, Civil Service Commission, *First Annual Report*, Sessional Paper no. 31, 1910, p. 17.
42. Archibald, *Public Service*, p. 14.

43. Ibid., p. 16.
44. Ibid., p. 16. Hodgetts et al., *Biography*, pp. 486–7, document that, in 1938, an investigation in the civil service uncovered at least 189 married women working under their maiden names to circumvent rules designed to exclude them.
45. Hodgetts et al., *Biography* , p. 487.
46. Archibald, *Public Service*, p. 19.
47. *The Montreal Daily Witness*, 4 January 1879.
48. 'The office, yesterday and today', manuscript, November 1974, IBM Archives, Toronto.
49. 'Notes', p. 7, L. A. Winter, Former Secretary Treasurer, Manufacturers Life Insurance Co. Archives, Toronto.
50. Lynne Marks, 'New opportunities within the separate sphere: a preliminary exploration of certain neglected questions related to female clerical work, focusing on stenography in Canada, 1890–1930', (unpublished research paper, Department of History, York University), p. 25.
51. William Henry Leffingwell, *Office Management, Principles and Practice* (Chicago, A. W. Shaw, 1925), p. 621.
52. *MT*, 8 January 1926, p. 29.
53. See Marks, 'New opportunities', for a discussion of the influence these business colleges had on the development of stenography.
54. *LG*, August 1914, p. 118.
55. *Report of the Ontario Commission on Unemployment* (hereafter, *ROCU*), (Toronto, A. T. Wilgress, 1916), p. 183. The report suggested that more than typing skills were required: 'The appearance of the stenographer is in her favour . . . and this is not without a good effect on the character of her work' (ibid.).
56. See, e.g. *LG*, February 1915, p. 924; December 1915, p. 696.
57. *LG*, May 1916, p. 1184.
58. *LG*, February 1915, p. 924.
59. *ROCU*, p. 182.
60. Ibid.
61. Ibid.
62. Marks, 'New opportunities', p. 30.
63. Ibid., pp. 28–9.
64. *ROCU*, p. 183.
65. LOMA, *Proceedings*, 1926, p. 82.
66. Ontario Civil Service Association, statement presented to the Government of Ontario, 1920 (pamphlet, Ontario Provincial Archives).
67. 'Announcement to Women Employees Regarding Salary Grading', from E. E. Duckworth, 1 July 1929, Montreal Head Office, Sun Life Archives.
68. See Kanter, *Men and Women*, chapter 4; Mary Kathleen Benet, *Secretary; Enquiry into the Female Ghetto* (London, Sidgwick and Jackson, 1972), chapter 3.
69. Kanter, *Men and Women*, p. 73.
70. Ibid., chapter 3.
71. Braverman, *Labor and Monopoly Capital*, p. 346–7.
72. Oppenheimer, *Female Labor Force*, p. 120.

73. Garrison, 'Tender technicians'. By 1910, 78.5 per cent of US library workers were female (p. 131).
74. Ibid., p. 132.

CHAPTER 5 THE RATIONALIZATION OF THE OFFICE

1. Max Weber, *General Economic History* (New York, Collier Books, 1967), p. 260.
2. Leffingwell, *Office Management, Principles and Practice*, p. 53.
3. This refers to F. W. Taylor's well-known reorganization of pig iron production at Bethlehem Steel. Hopf is cited in Homer J. Hagedorn, 'The management consultant as transmitter of business techniques', *Explorations in Entrepreneurial History*, 7 (1955), p. 157.
4. Ibid., p. 167.
5. Hagedorn, in 'The management consultant', p. 166, cites J. William Schulze's *The American Office* in this connection.
6. In addition to the book cited in note 2, above, see Leffingwell's *Scientific Office Management*; 'The Office, through a microscope', *National Efficiency Quarterly*, 1 (August 1918), pp. 85–111; 'The present state of the art of office management', LOMA, *Proceedings*, 1926, pp. 21–37; *A Textbook of Office Management*, 1st edn (New York, McGraw-Hill, 1932).
7. Leffingwell, *Scientific Office Management*, p. 17.
8. Ibid., p. 35.
9. Ibid., p. 111.
10. Ibid., p. 109.
11. Ibid., p. 175.
12. *IC*, July 1905, p. 843.
13. Chandler, *Visible Hand*, documents how a standard organizational response to problems of industrial management, adopted by most major US corporations by the 1920s, was a centralized bureaucracy divided into functional departments.
14. Ewing, *History of Imperial Oil*, vol. I, part II, chapter IV, pp. 14–15.
15. Ibid., vol. II, chapter VI, p. 369.
16. Ibid., vol. II, chapter VIII, pp. 7–9.
17. *Rules and Regulations of the Bank of Nova Scotia*, Revision of 1917, p. 37. Bank of Nova Scotia Archives, Toronto.
18. Leffingwell, in works cited in note 6, above, emphasized the importance of simplified, predetermined clerical routines as the key to office efficiency.
19. *MT*, 5 December 1919, p. 24.
20. 'President to Mr. Dennis, 30 January 1914', Shaughnessy Letterbook 105, p. 653, Canadian Pacific Railway Archives, Montreal.
21. Hodgetts et al., *Biography*, pp. 45–46.
22. Ibid., pp. 59–65.
23. Ibid., p. 76.
24. Ibid., pp. 71–75.
25. Canada, Civil Service Commission, *10th Annual Report*, Sessional Paper no. 32, 1919, p. 17.

26. Canada, Civil Service Commission, *12th Annual Report*, Sessional Paper no. 32, 1921, p. 9.
27. Ontario, Public Service Act, 1918, section 4f.
28. See Canada, Civil Service Commission, *Annual Reports*, 1918–30.
29. Hodgetts et al., *Biography*, p. 87, n. 54.
30. *MT*, 7 July 1922, p. 12.
31. Ibid.
32. *MT*, 3 April 1925, p. 14.
33. *MT*, 1 May 1925, pp. 12–13; *MT*, 18 September 1925, p. 12.
34. *MT*, 26 November 1926, p. 14.
35. International Labour Office, 'Effects of mechanization and automation in offices: II', *International Labour Review*, 81 (1960), p. 260.
36. McCutcheon was born in Listowell, Ontario, and graduated from Queen's University in arts and pedagogy. He pursued a career as an educationalist before being appointed as Secretary of the Workmen's Compensation Board in 1914 (Ontario, *Public Service Bulletin*, August 1918, p. 316).
37. Ontario, *Second Annual Report of the Civil Service Commissioner for Ontario* (hereafter *RCSCO*). (Toronto, A. T. Wilgress, 1920), p. 12.
38. Ontario, *Third Annual RCSCO* (Toronto, King's Printer, 1921), p. 9.
39. Chandler, *Visible Hand*, pp. 1–3.
40. Ontario, *Third Annual RCSCO*, p. 13.
41. Ontario, *Fifth Annual RCSCO* (Toronto, Clarkson W. James, 1923), p.11.
42. Ontario, *Sixth Annual RCSCO*, Sessional Paper no. 66, 1924, p. 5.
43. McCutcheon claimed that the classification and salary plan created stability and efficiency in the public service because employees were more contented. The absence of overt employee protests seems to confirm this. Ontario, *Eleventh Annual RCSCO*, Sessional Paper no. 48, 1929, p. 2.
44. *LG*, November 1923, p. 1184.
45. *MT*, 30 October 1925, pp. 22–23.
46. See Canada, *First Annual Report of the Civil Service Commission*, Sessional Paper no. 19, 1869.
47. Dawson, *Civil Service*, p. 74.
48. Hodgetts et al., *Biography*, p. 27.
49. Ibid., p. 27.
50. Canada, *Report on the Organization of the Public Service of Canada*, by Sir George Murray (Ottawa, King's Printer, 1912), p. 8. Also contained in Sessional Paper no. 57A, 1913.
51. Hodgetts et al., *Biography*, p. 10.
52. Ibid., p. 60.
53. Canada, *Report of Transmission to Accompany the Classification of the Civil Service of Canada*, by Arthur Young and Company (Ottawa, King's Printer, 1919), p. 3.
54. Ibid., p. 3.
55. Hodgetts et al., *Biography*, p. 81.
56. Canada, *Report of Transmission*, pp. 36–38.
57. Ibid., p. 9.
58. Canada, Civil Service Commission, *Tenth Annual Report*, Sessional Paper no. 32, 1920, pp. 10–11.

59. Dawson, *Civil Service*, p. 95.
60. See Canada, House of Commons, Special Committee on the Civil Service, *Proceedings*, 1923, p. ix.
61. Hodgetts et al., *Biography*, p. 76. The data in this paragraph come from this source, especially chapter 4.
62. Ontario, *Fifth Annual RCSCO*, p. 11.
63. Hodgetts et al., *Biography*, p. 65.
64. Ibid., p. 77.
65. 'Functional Organization', File, Telephone Historical Collection, Bell Telephone Company, Montreal.
66. 'L. B. McFarlane and J. A. Baylis to C. F. Sise, 7 November 1909', President's Letterbooks, letter no. 1151, Telephone Historical Collection. There was frequent correspondence on the matter between Bell and AT&T in 1909.
67. Ibid.
68. *TG*, May 1909, p. 2.
69. *TG*, May 1909, p. 3.
70. *TG*, June 1909, p. 6.
71. See Luther Gulick 'Notes on the theory of organization', in L. Gulick and L. Urwick (eds), *Papers on the Science of Administration* (New York, Institute of Public Administration, 1937), pp. 7–9.
72. *TG*, July 1909, p. 2.
73. 'Functional Organization', File, Telephone Historical Collection.
74. A further organizational innovation was introduced in 1930. The territory was divided into two areas, east and west, each with an operating department under a general manager, a separate headquarters, and separate accounting facilities. It is worth noting that Bell was not alone; Aldred D. Chandler Jr. claims that The International Nickle Co. of Canada had a functional organization when it set up in 1916. See his *Strategy and Structure: Chapters in the History of the Industrial Enterprise* (New York, Anchor Books, 1966), p. 408.
75. *MT*, 5 December 1919, p. 24.
76. *MT*, 7 July 1922, p. 12.
77. *JCBA*, October 1921, p. 7.
78. *MT*, 18 September 1925, p. 12.
79. *Nova Scotian* (Bank of Nova Scotia staff magazine), November 1907, p. 4.
80. 'Circular no. 964', 4 February 1905. Bank of Nova Scotia Archives.
81. *Nova Scotian*, November 1907, p. 24.
82. *Rules and Regulations*, 1917 edn, p. 37, Bank of Nova Scotia Archives.
83. Ibid., 1902 edn, p. 13.
84. Ibid., 1902 edn, Introduction.
85. Ibid., 1917 edn, p. 10.
86. Ibid:, 1927 edn, rule #11.
87. *MT*, 21 October 1904, pp. 522–6.
88. *Sunshine*, November 1911, p. 142.
89. 'Officer's Advisory Committee Minutes', File, Sun Life Archives.
90. 'Officers' Advisory Committee Minute Books', 5 February 1920, Sun Life Archives.

91, W. H. Leffingwell and Edwin M. Robinson define a clerical routine as 'a series of steps in the performance of work, each step in the series being performed in the same order and in the same way every time'. See their *Textbook of Office Management* 2nd edn (New York, McGraw-Hill, 1943), p. 59. The diminished quality of working life resulting from such routines is obvious.

92. Insurance Institute of Toronto, *Annual Proceedings*, 1922–3, p. 84.

93. George H. Harris, *The President's Book: The Story of the Sun Life Assurance Company of Canada* (Montreal, Sun Life, 1928), p. 252.

94. LOMA, *Home Office Salary Scale and Personnel Data*, Special Report no. 5, 1926, p. 13.

95. 'Assistant Comptroller to Officers and Department Heads', memo of 11 August 1939, Personnel file no. 14, Sun Life Archives.

96. Harris, *President's Book*, p. 340.

97. 'T. B. Macaulay Letterbook', no. 12, letter no. 249, 24 May 1917, Sun Life Archives.

98. 'Officers and Chief Clerks', Personnel file no. 1, Sun Life Archives.

99. *Sunshine*, 20 November 1929, p. 2.

100. LOMA, *Proceedings*, 1924, p. 70.

101. Ibid., p. 8.

102. Ibid., 1927, p. 7.

103. Ibid., p. 6. Canadians played a prominent role in LOMA. For example, an official of Imperial Life was the association's vice-president in 1925, and the general manager of London Life was elected LOMA president in 1927.

104. Chandler, *Strategy and Structure*, p. 19.

105. *IC* began publishing a regular feature on office management, called 'Office and Finance', in the early 1920s. Also, articles from prominent US management publications were reprinted. One from *Industrial Management* argued for 'the intelligent revision of office methods' through better measurement and regulation of the work flow' (*IC*, August 1923; pp. 91–4).

106. See Nelson, *Scientific Management*, p. 200 for the United States. Evidence of a similar trend in Canada is found in the pages of *IC*. An editorial in April 1919 (p. 47) observed a growing employer interest in personnel matters.

107. See Davies, *Women's Place*, chapter 6.

108. Ibid., p. 26.

109. Ibid., p. 107.

110. For further evidence see Rotella, *From Home to Office*; and Coyle, 'Women in the clerical occupations'.

111. Vincent E. Giuliano, 'The mechanization of office work', *Scientific American*, 247 (1982), p. 160.

112. Lockwood, *Blackcoated Worker*, pp. 95–6.

113. Ibid., p. 78.

114. Ibid., p. 207.

115. Merkle, *Management and Ideology*, p. 240.

116. Carl Dreyfuss, *Occupation and Ideology of the Salaried Employee*, vol. I, tr. E. Abramovitch (New York, Works Progress Administration and Department of Social Sciences, Columbia University, 1938), p. 55.

CHAPTER 6 MECHANIZATION, FEMINIZATION AND MANAGERIAL
CONTROL

1. Robert H. Parker, *Management Accounting: An Historical Perspective*
(London, Macmillan, 1969), pp. 19–20.
2. Nelson, *Scientific Management*, p. 13.
3. Paul Craven, *Impartial Umpire*, p. 96, argues that scientific management
was primarily concerned with cost accounting techniques.
4. Jordan and Harris, *Cost Accounting*, p. 19.
5. Kenneth Falconer, 'Practical value of cost accounting', *IC*, August 1903, p.
26.
6. H. L. C. Hall, 'Economy in manufacturing', *IC*, February 1906, pp.
430–1.
7. *MT*, 16 February 1923, p. 6.
8. *IC*, February 1907, p. 588.
9. *MT*, 6 October 1916, p. 9.
10. *MT*, 26 September 1919, p. 30.
11. W. H. Leffingwell, 'The present state of the art of office management',
LOMA *Proceedings*, (1926), p. 27.
12. See Lee Galloway, *Office Management: Its Principles and Practice* (New
York, Ronald Press, 1918); *Organizing the Stenographic Department* (New
York, Ronald Press, 1924). The latter is essentially a reprint of part IV of
the 1918 book.
13. Galloway, *Office Management*, p. 75.
14. Galloway, *Stenographic Department*.
15. Galloway, *Office Management*, p. 50.
16. Harold W. Nance and Robert E. Nolan, *Office Work Measurement* (New
York, McGraw-Hill, 1971), p. 1.
17. Ibid., p. 16.
18. Ibid., p. 3.
19. Hall, 'Economy in manufacturing'.
20. E. W. King, 'Administrative expense', *MT*, 1 January 1926, p. 31.
21. W. G. Reburn, 'Life assurance bookkeeping', *Proceedings*, 1922–3 Annual
Conference of the Insurance Institute of Toronto, p. 84.
22. *Blue Bell*, March 1923, pp. 8–9.
23. Ibid., December 1921, p. 4.
24. Ibid., February 1928, p. 10.
25. Telephone Association of Canada, *Proceedings*, Fifth Annual Convention,
1929, p. 14.
26. By the late 1920s, the Telephone Association of Canada was holding
sessions on functional organization at its annual meetings, evidence that
other phone companies were following Bell's lead. (*Proceedings*, 1929,
1930, 1931). A number of companies had already instituted a uniform
accounting system derived from the AT&T functional organizational plan.
27. Ibid., *Proceedings*, Eighth Annual Convention, 1928, p. 39.
28. Ibid., *Proceedings*, Fifth Annual Convention, 1925, p. 32.
29. E. Palm, 'Uniform system of accounting for Canada', *Proceedings*, Second
Canadian Telephone Convention, 1922, pp. 50–68.

204 Notes to Chapter 6

30. See John J. Armstrong, 'Consumer's accounting and recording system', *Intercolonial Gas Journal of Canada*, 1 November 1912, p. 416.
31. *Canadian Pacific Staff Bulletin*, 1 April 1936, p. 3.
32. Braverman, *Labor and Monopoly Capital*, pp. 79–82. According to Braverman, Babbage translated Adam Smith's famous example of pin making into a basic axiom of modern business: by fragmenting the labour process, and thereby downgrading skill requirements, labour costs can be reduced.
33. IBM Corp., *Machine Methods of Accounting* (New York, 1936), p. 1. Pamphlet in IBM Archives, Toronto.
34. Charles Perrow, *Complex Organizations: A Critical Essay*, 2nd edn (Glenview, Ill., Scott Foresman, 1979), p. 23.
35. This typology is derived from the four-stage model used by Jon. M. Shepard, *Automation and Alienation: A Study of Office and Factory Workers* (Cambridge, Mass., MIT Press, 1971), p 63
36. Ibid., p. 63.
37. *MT*, 20 September 1901, p. 376.
38. *MT*, 18 August 1905, p. 204.
39. *IC*, October 1906, p. 329.
40. *IC*, December 1909, p. 530.
41. *MT*, 21 February 1919, p. 50.
42. Cited by Bruce Bliven Jr., *The Wonderful Writing Machine* (New York, Random House, 1954), p. 15.
43. 'Statement presented to the Government of Ontario, 1920', by the Ontario Civil Service Association. Ontario Provincial Archives.
44. Cited in Bliven, *Writing Machine*, p. 3.
45. International Labour Office, 'Use of office machinery', p. 491.
46. Leffingwell and Robinson, *Textbook of Office Management*, p. 25.
47. *IC*, September 1920, pp. 119–20.
48. 'Personnel Files, number 2, data for 1 December 1939', Sun Life Archives.
49. *Canadian Pacific Staff Bulletin*, 1 December 1935, p. 5.
50. For details see International Labour Office, 'The effects of mechanization and automation on offices: III', *International Labour Review*, 81 (1960), pp. 350–69.
51. Leffingwell, 'The office, through a microscope', p. 91.
52. Mills, *White Collar*, p. 195.
53. H. A. Rhee, *Office Automation in Social Perspective* (Oxford, Basil Blackwell, 1968), p. 44. See ibid., pp. 44–7, for a good summary of the development of adding and calculating machines.
54. Burroughs Adding Machine Co., *A Better Day's Work* (Detroit, 1908), chapter VI.
55. Parker, *Management Accounting*, p. 24.
56. 'T. B. Macaulay to Mr Tate', n.d., letterbook no. 31, letter no. 1437. Sun Life Archives.
57. *Montreal Standard*, 14 October 1911.
58. Rhee, *Office Automation*, p. 47.
59. *Intercolonial Gas Journal of Canada*, 1 November 1912, pp. 416–7.
60. *Sun Dial*, August 1927, p. 16.

61. *Blue Bell*, November 1928, pp. 25–6.
62. International Labour Office, 'Office machinery', p. 515.
63. Gilbert Jackson, *The Civil Service of Canada in 1930: Position, Salary Scales and Number of Appointments for Each Department*, vol. 3, prepared for the Royal Commission on Technical and Professional Service, 1929–1930 (mimeo, n.d.), p. 90.
64. John C. McDonald, *Impact and Implications of Office Automation* (Ottawa, Queen's Printer, 1964), pp. 3–4.
65. According to one report, 'the speed at which [office machines such as Holleriths] function imposes a rapid work rhythm comparable to assembly-line production.' International Labour Office, 'Effects of mechanization and automation, III', p. 351. A more accurate comparison would be with the type of worker-machine relationship found in machine production, such as in the textile industry. See Robert Blauner, *Alienation and Freedom* (Chicago, University of Chicago Press, 1964), chapter 4.
66. Ida R. Hoos, *Automation in the Office* (Washington, Public Affairs Press, 1961), p. 67.
67. This brief historical sketch is based largely on the following: IBM Corp., *Machine Methods of Accounting* (New York, 1936). Pamphlet in IBM Archives.
68. 'Antique machines file', 1916 sales brochure. IBM Archives.
69. IBM Corp., *Modern Methods for Modern Business Needs* (New York and Toronto, 1932), p. 8. Pamphlet in IBM Archives.
70. Ibid.
71. 'Canadian chronology file', 'Personal observations and comments concerning history and development of IBM, as customer, salesman and executive', by Walter D. Jones (August 1944), p. 25. IBM Archives.
72. These included six types of key punches, two verifiers, three tabulators, and sorting, reproducing, collating, interpreting, and bank proof machines.
73. Transcript of interview with G. L. Holmes by N. T. Sheppard, 19 January 1977. Manufacturers Life Insurance Co. Archives.
74. LOMA, *Proceedings* (1924), p. 22. In 1931 LOMA held a conference on the use of punch cards in insurance head offices. See LOMA, Special Conferences, *Proceedings*, pp. 115–296.
75. LOMA, 'Use of tabulating punch cards in connection with home office operations', Questionnaire Summary, Special Report no. 5 October p. 1.
76. *Canadian Pacific Staff Bulletin*, 1 April 1936, p. 3. Six card punches, three sorters, one non-printing tabulator, and two summary printers hooked up to two tabulators processed 710,000 punch cards daily.
77. Ibid., p. 3.
78. *Blue Bell*, March 1933, p. 8.
79. Canada, *16th Annual Report of the Civil Service Commission*, Sessional Paper no. 24 (1925), p. vi.
80. Rhee, *Office Automation*, p. 49.
81. I. O. Royse et. al., *Significant Developments in Office Management*, American Management Association, Office Management Series no. 78 (New York, AMA, 1937), p. 31.
82. Rotella, 'Transformation of the American office', p. 53.

83. Coyle, 'Women in the clerical occupations', p. 182.
84. Giuliano, 'Mechanization of office work', p. 134.
85. International Labour Office, 'Effects of mechanization and automation in offices: I', *International Labour Review*, 81 (1960), p. 161. For an up-date of this argument see Mike Cooley, 'Computerization – Taylor's latest disguise', *Economic and Industrial Democracy*, 1 (1980), pp. 523–39.
86. See *Labor and Monopoly Capital*, especially chapter 15 on clerical workers. Ibid, p. 301.
87. Stephen Wood, 'Introduction', in Wood, *Degradation of Work?*, p. 18.
88. Benet, *Secretary*, pp. 140–1.
89. Jurgen Kocka, *White Collar Workers in America 1890–1940* (Beverly Hills, Sage, 1980), p. 12.
90. Mills, *White Collar*, p. 220.
91. Canada, First Report of the Civil Service Commission, Sessional Paper no. 113 (1881), p. 20.
92. During the 1910s and 1920s stenographers could command salaries at least on a par with nurses and teachers. See chapter 7 below for details.
93. See Kanter's excellent analysis of the secretarial role in chapter 4 of *Men and Women*. Also see Davies, *Women's Place*, chapter 7.
94. Feldberg and Glenn, 'Technology and work degradation'.
95. David A. Buchannan and David Boddy, 'Advanced technology and the quality of working life: the effects of word processing technology on video typists', *Journal of Occupational Psychology*, 55 (1982), pp. 1–11.
96. Menzies, *Women and the Chip*.
97. Coyle, 'Women in the clerical occupations', p. 182.
98. For the specific occupational titles within the clerical category, see Canada, *Classified Index of Occupations*, 1921 census.
99. *The Nova Scotian* (employee magazine published by the bank), Spring–Summer 1953, p. 2.
100. Rotella, *From Home to Office*, p. 144. This clerical group had a slightly higher concentration of women (86 per cent) than in Canada.
101. Lockwood, *Blackcoated Worker*, p. 88.
102. Ibid., p. 87.
103. Ibid., p. 94.

CHAPTER 7 THE PROLETARIANIZATION OF CLERICAL WORK?

1. For overviews of the pertinent literature, see Adam Przeworski, 'Proletariat into a class: the process of class transformation from Karl Kautsky's The Class Struggle to recent controversies', *Politics and Society*, 7 (1977), pp. 343–401: M. P. Kelly, *White-Collar Proletariat: The Industrial Behaviour of British Civil Servants* (London, Routledge and Kegan Paul, 1980), pp. 6–24; Stewart, Prandy and Blackburn, *Social Stratification and Occupations*, pp. 91–113; Richard Hyman and Robert Price (eds), *The New Working Class? White-Collar Workers and Their Organizations* (London, Macmillan, 1983), especially part I; Nicholas Abercrombie and John Urry, *Capital, Labour and the Middle Classes* (London, George Allen and Unwin, 1983), especially

chapters 3–5; Crompton and Jones, *White-Collar Proletariat*, chapters 1 and 6.

2. Marx originally used the concept of proletarianization to explain the incorporation of the independent *petit bourgeoisie* into the expanding capitalist wage labour market. But because this process has now largely run its course, given that the vast majority of individuals are propertyless employees, it is the neo-marxist version of the concept which predominates. Concise definitions of the term 'proletarianization' are found in Przeworski, 'Proletariat into a class', pp. 353–67; and Giorgio Gagliani, 'How many working classes?', *American Journal of Sociology*, 87 (1981), p. 261.

3. This reflects the general reduction of the income gap between white-collar and blue-collar workers in capitalist societies as documented by Colin Clark, *The Conditions of Economic Progress* (London, Macmillan, 1940). For more detailed data pertaining to Britain and the United States see respectively, Lockwood, *Blackcoated Worker* and R. K. Burns, 'The comparative economic position of manual and white-collar employees', *Journal of Business*, 27 (1954), pp. 257–67.

4. Braverman, *Labor and Monopoly Capital*, pp. 293–358.

5. This line of argument is found in neo-marxist class theory. See especially E. O. Wright, 'Class boundaries in advanced capitalist societies', *New Left Review*, 98 (1976), pp. 3–41 and G. Carchedi, *On the Economic Identification of Social Classes* (London, Routledge and Kegan Paul, 1977). A similar but theoretically less rigorous argument is contained in Glenn and Feldberg's definition of clerical proletarianization as resulting from 'changes in the organization of work designed to increase managers' control of the work process' (p. 62). See Evelyn Nakano Glenn and Roslyn L. Feldberg, 'Degraded and deskilled: the proletarianization of clerical work', *Social Problems*, 25 (1977), pp. 52–64.

6. There are some knotty theoretical problems, falling beyond the scope of this book, involved in determining an individual's class position on the basis of present market situation and job characteristics. As David Lockwood reminds us in *The Blackcoated Worker*, despite the economic decline of once high-status British insurance clerks, their jobs continued to offer better security, promotion opportunities, work environment and benefits thereby socially differentiating them from manual workers. The argument that movement across class boundaries involves considerably more than changing income was first articulated in the British affluent worker studies. See John H. Goldthorpe and David Lockwood, 'Affluence and the British class structure', *Sociological Review*, 11 (1963), pp. 133–63. A forceful elaboration of the basic point is presented by Stewart, Prandy and Blackburn, *Social Stratification and Occupations*, pp. 91–113, as the foundation of their critique of the clerical proletarianization thesis.

7. John H. Goldthorpe, 'Class mobility in modern Britain: a reply to Crompton', *Sociology*, 14 (1980), p. 122.

8. For critical discussions of the effects of this male bias see Joan Acker, 'Women and social stratification: a case of intellectual sexism', *American Journal of Sociology*, 78 (1973), pp. 932–45; Garnsey, 'Women's work and theories of class stratification'; Rosemary Crompton and Michael Mann

(eds), *Gender and Stratification* (Cambridge, Polity Press, 1986); Eva
Gamarnikow, David Morgan, Jane Purvis and Daphne Taylorson (eds),
Gender, Class and Work (London, Heinemann, 1983).

9. This point is not a new one – although it seems to have been lost sight of in
the proletarianization debate – having first been enunciated by Richard
Hamilton in 'The income differences between skilled and white-collar
workers', *British Journal of Sociology*, 14 (1963), pp. 363–73.
10. Braverman, *Labor and Monopoly Capital*, pp. 296–8.
11. David Coombs, 'The Emergence of a White-Collar Work Force in Toronto,
1895–1911', unpublished Ph.D. thesis, York University, 1978, p. 114.
12. Lockwood, *Blackcoated Worker*, p. 22.
13. Ibid., p. 24.
14. It should be noted that in computing table 7.2 clerical earnings were
excluded from the labour force totals to ensure that average labour force
trends are not confounded by changes occurring in clerical occupations.
15. Noah M. Meltz, *Changes in the Occupational Composition of the Canadian
Labour Force, 1931–1961* (Ottawa, Queen's Printer, 1965), p. 66.
16. Dawson, *Civil Service of Canada*; Payne, 'The civil servant'.
17. Payne, 'The civil servant', pp. 508–9.
18. Ibid., p. 508.
19. Coombs, 'Emergence of a White-Collar Work Force', p. 166.
20. Anderson, *Victorian Clerks*, p. 129.
21. Crompton and Jones, *White-Collar Proletariat*, p. 27.
22. Richard Hyman, 'White-collar workers and theories of class', in Hyman
and Price (eds), *New Working Class?*, p. 8.
23. See Stewart, Prandy and Blackburn, *Social Stratification and Occupations*, p.
172 for a solid empirical documentation of this point.
24. J. Westergaard and J. Resler, *Class in a Capitalist Society* (London,
Heinemann, 1975), p. 100.
25. Rotella, *From Home to Office*, pp. 158–9. Davies, in *Woman's Place is at the
Typewriter*, p. 64–5, points out that in Boston during the 1883–1910 period
clerical jobs were second only to professional occupations in annual net
income for women. This, coupled with higher status and better working
conditions, made many working class girls aspire to clerical work.
26. Coyle, 'Women in the clerical occupations', p. 181.
27. United States Department of Commerce, Bureau of the Census, *Historical
Statistics of the United States, Colonial Times to 1970*, part I (Washington,
US Government Printing Office, 1975), pp. 303–4.
28. Earl F. Mellor, 'Investigating the differences in weekly earnings of women
and men', *Monthly Labor Review*, 107 (June 1984), pp. 20–3.
29. In 1921, for example, weekly wages of male clerks in Canada's seven largest
cities varied from $22.93 in Quebec to $28.23 in Vancouver; and for female
clerks from $12.60 in Quebec to $19.02 in Winnipeg. See *Canada Year
Book* (Ottawa, King's Printer, 1928), pp. 778–9.
30. Lockwood, *Blackcoated Worker*, p. 67.
31. The exceptions included a woman manager in the Bank of Nova Scotia
stationery department, a non-banking service unit, and a nurse and a
translator in Manufacturers Life (see table 7.5).

32. Civil Service Commission of Canada, *Fourth Annual Report*, House of Commons Sessional Paper, no. 31 (1913), p. xi. Also see *ROCU* (Toronto, A. T. Wilgress, 1916), pp. 181–4.
33. *ROCU*, p. 184.
34. *LG*, April 1913, pp. 1078–9.
35. *Canada Year Book* (1928), p. 799.
36. J. P. Buschlen, *Behind the Wicket* (Toronto, William Briggs, 1914), p. 256.
37. *MT*, 20 May 1911, p. 2021.
38. *Report of the Royal Commission on the Civil Service*, House of Commons Sessional Papers no. 29A (1907–8), p. 805.
39. Ibid, p. 1339.
40. Dawson, *Civil Service*, p. 189.
41. 'Staff Committee to A. T. Goward, BC Electric Railway Co., Victoria, 16 April 1920', ADD.MSS 4, vol. 288/F49, British Columbia Provincial Archives.
42. In June 1931 there were 256 married women employed in eleven major departments of the over 10,000 strong Ontario Public Service, of whom one was divorced, 46 were separated, and others were undoubtedly supporting disabled husbands or young children. See Ontario Provincial Archives, RG25, Administrative Service Branch, Statistical Files, 1919–68, 'Report on Married Women in the Public Service as of June 1931'.
43. Ontario Civil Service Association, 'Statement Presented to the Government of Ontario', (Toronto 1919), p. 8, Ontario Provincial Archives. In 1918 the Ontario government established a Civil Service Commission in a move to rationalize the expanding bureaucracy in the interests of efficiency. J. M. McCutcheon, the first Commissioner, pressed for a standardized job classification system based on merit, recognizing that low salaries undermine morale and efficiency. His second annual report documented the problem facing most white-collar workers as a result of the war: 'As a general rule, the compensation of salaried workers responds tardily to changing conditions in the cost of living, a fact which makes such employees in a peculiar measure the victims of the present rule of high prices. This is true of employees in the Public Service whose salaries have not kept pace with the high cost of living.' *Second Annual RCSCO* (Toronto, King's Printer, 1920), p. 10. Arguing in his next report that the state should be a model employer, McCutcheon asserts the principle that 'salaries should be adequate, fair and equitable . . . at least sufficient to enable the employee to maintain a proper standard of living.' *Third Annual RCSCO* (Toronto 1921), p. 10.
44. Ontario Civil Service Association, 'Statement', p. 8.
45. See Hyman, 'White-collar workers and theories of class', on this point.
46. Kocka, *White Collar Workers in America*, p. 75, claims that the white-collar demarcation was far more rigid in Germany than the United States between 1890 and 1940, which in part explains German clerks' political reactions to their fear of proletarianization.
47. Davies, *Woman's Place*, p. 5.
48. Abercrombie and Urry, *Capital, Labour and the Middle Classes*, p. 118
49. Ibid.

50. Ibid., p. 112.
51. Crompton and Jones, *White-Collar Proletariat*, p. 161.
52. Ibid., p. 210.
53. Michael Mann, 'A crisis in stratification theory', in Crompton and Mann (eds), *Gender and Stratification*, p. 56.
54. Stewart, Prandy and Blackburn, *Social Stratification and Occupations*, p. 112.
55. See e.g. Acker, 'Women and social stratification'; Garnsey, 'Women's work and theories of class stratification'; Max Haller, 'Marriage, women and social stratification: a theoretical critique', *American Journal of Sociology*, 86 (1981), pp. 766–95; Heidi Hartmann, 'The family as the locus of gender, class and political struggle: the example of housework', *Signs*, 6 (1981), pp. 366–94; Nancy Halstrom, 'Women's work, the family and capitalism', *Science and Society*, 45 (1981), pp. 186–211; Nickey Britten and Anthony Heath, 'Women, men and social class', in Gamarnikow et al. (eds), *Gender Class and Work*; and, in particular, the essays in Crompton and Mann (eds), *Gender and Stratification*.

CONCLUSION

1. Organization for Economic Cooperation and Development, *The Integration of Women into the Economy* (Paris, OECD, 1985), p. 11.
2. Mills, *White Collar*, p. 309.
3. See Anderson, *Victorian Clerks*, chapter 7, on trade unionism in the nineteenth-century British office.
4. The 1911 attempt is noted in *MT*, (26 December 1919), p. 9. In 1914 the Associated Bank Clerks of Canada held a founding meeting in Toronto. See *Toronto Daily Star* and *Toronto Globe* on 5 March 1914. See also Buschlen, *Behind the Wicket*, pp. 256–64, for an autobiographical account of this organizing drive. After the First World War clerks reacted to their dramatic drop in living standards with discontent, sowing the seeds for yet another unionization drive. The Bank Employees Association, an affiliate of the American Federation of Labour, began organizing in 1919. The AFL's 1920 convention, held on 14 July in Montreal, voted to set up a $15,000 fund and hire organizers. The Canadian Trades and Labour Congress followed this up with a resolution at its 1920 convention to organize office and clerical employees (*Report of Proceedings*, 36th Annual Convention, Windsor, 13–18 September 1920, p. 183).
5. For a discussion of employee organization in the federal civil service see Hodgetts et al., *Biography*, chapter 8; and Anthony Thompson, 'The large and generous view: the debate on labour affiliation in the Canadian civil service, 1918–1928', *Labour/Le Travailleur*, 2 (1977), pp. 108–36.
6. Documentation is found in the CPR Archives, Montreal, 'Shaughnessy Letterbooks', correspondence for November 1912 to January 1913. These clerks soon after joined with other railway clerks to form the Canadian Brotherhood of Railway Employees.
7. Kocka, *White Collar Workers in America*, p. 178. Kocka contrasts the lack of

union activity among US clerks during this period to the concerted and successful actions of their German counterparts.

8. Recent union membership trends for the three countries are presented in George S. Bain and Robert Price, 'Union growth: dimensions, determinants, and destiny', in George S. Bain (ed.), *Industrial Relations in Britain* (Oxford, Basil Blackwell, 1983); Joseph B. Rose and Gary N. Chaison, 'The state of the unions: United States and Canada', *Journal of Labor Research*, 6 (1985), pp. 97–111. See Julie White, *Women and Unions* (Ottawa, Supply and Services Canada, 1980) for an analysis of trends and issues in female unionization in Canada.

9. For example, between 1970 and 1980 union membership in Canada increased 81.8 per cent for females and 25.4 per cent for males. Canada, *Corporation and Labour Unions Return Act, Report for 1970*, part II, Labour Unions (Ottawa, Statistics Canada, 1973), p. 13; Canada, *Women in the Labour Force*, part III (Ottawa, Labour Canada, Women's Bureau, 1983), p. 13.

10. Vipond, 'Image of women', p. ll8.

11. E. G. Gowdy, 'Women in the banking world', *JCBA*, (July 1916), p. 320.

12. Davies, *Women's Place*, p. 171.

13. This argument has been developed by a number of sociologists. Blackburn's study of British bank unions, *Union Character and Social Class*, documents how women's inferior market position inhibits unionization by fostering low job commitment. Kate Purcell's article, 'Militancy and acquiescence amongst women workers', in Sandra Burman (ed.), *Fit Women For Work* (London, Croom Helm, 1979), critically elaborates Blackburn's point, claiming that lower unionization reflects the lack of industrial bargaining power possessed by most women by virtue of the weak economic position of the industries in which they are concentrated. In short, industrial patterns of collective action are equally influential for both male and female workers. Empirical evidence from the United States lends support to this view. A statistical model of male–female unionization differences estimated that if both sexes had similar occupational and industrial characteristics there would be a 50 per cent increase in the number of female unionists. See Joseph R. Antos, Mark Chandler and Wesley Mellow, 'Sex differences in union membership', *Industrial and Labor Relations Review*, 33 (1980), pp. 168–9. Further, a study of union representation elections found that sex had no significant impact on vote outcome. See Henry S. Farber and Daniel H. Saks, 'Why workers want unions: the role of relative wages and job characteristics', *Journal of Political Economy*, 88 (1980), p. 365.

14. Overviews of union drives in retailing and banking are found in Eileen Sufrin, *The Eaton Drive – The Campaign to Organize Canada's Largest Department Store, 1948 to 1952* (Toronto, Fitzhenry and Whiteside, 1982); G. S. Lowe, 'Causes of unionization in Canadian banks', *Relations industrielles/Industrial Relations*, 36 (1981), pp. 865–92; A. Ponak and L. F. Moore, 'Canadian bank unionism: perspectives and issues', *Relations industrielles/Industrial Relations*, 36 (1981), pp. 1–31; and E. Beckett, *Unions and Bank Workers: Will the Twain Ever Meet?* (Ottawa, Labour Canada, Women's Bureau, 1984).

15. See Heron and Palmer, 'Through the prism of the strike', pp. 432–58. The virtual absence of overt conflict in the white-collar sector necessitates the use of different methodologies to analyse the reactions of clerks to changes in the administrative labour process.
16. See e.g. Rosemary Crompton, 'Trade unionism and the insurance clerks', *Sociology*, 13 (1979), pp. 402–26, and John Heritage, 'Feminization and unionization', in E. Gamarnikow et al. (eds), *Gender, Class and Work*.
17. These points are elaborated in Heidi Gottfried and David Fasenfest, 'Gender and class formation: female clerical workers', *Review of Radical Political Economics*, 16 (1984), pp. 89–103, and Roslyn Feldberg and Evelyn Nakano Glenn, 'Incipient workplace democracy among United States clerical workers', *Economic and Industrial Democracy*, 4 (1983), pp. 47–67.
18. Ruth Milkman, 'Female factory labour and industrial structure: control and conflict over "women's place" in auto and electrical manufacturing', *Politics and Society*, 12 (1983), pp. 159–203.
19. Ibid., p. 188
20. On the historical significance of the family wage see Jane Humphries, 'Class struggle and the persistence of the working-class family', *Cambridge Journal of Economics*, 1 (1977), pp. 241–58.
21. Organizational research has been roundly criticized for neglecting virtually all issues related to gender. See Hearn and Parkin, 'Gender and organizations'.
22. James N. Baron and William T. Bielby, 'Workers and machines: dimensions and determinants of technical relations in the workplace', *American Sociological Review*, 47 (1982), pp. 175–88.
23. This point is elaborated by Crompton and Jones in *White-Collar Proletariat*, p. 76–7.
24. Mann, 'A crisis in stratification theory', p. 47.
25. Ken Prandy, 'Similarities of life-style and occupations of women', in Crompton and Mann (eds), *Gender and Stratification*, p. 141.
26. Michael Burawoy, 'Towards a Marxist theory of the labour process: Braverman and beyond', *Politics and Society*, 8 (1978), p. 253.

Appendix

Table A1 Clerical workers distributed by major industry groups, by sex, Canada, 1901–31[a]*

	1901			1911			1921			1931		
	Total	Male	Female	Total	Male	Female	Total	Male	Female	Total	Male	Female
All industries	57,231	44,571	12,660	103,543	69,820	33,723	216,691	126,114	90,577	260,674	143,037	117,637
Agriculture							74	45	29	333	147	186
Forestry				256	243	13	621[f]	614	7	546[f]	483	63
Fishing												
Mining				350	302	48	1,195	1,051	144	1,282	1,015	267
Manufacturing	6,415	5,357	1,058	9,315	5,672	3,643	41,727	26,217	15,510	61,058	36,185	24,873
Electricity, gas & water							222	221	1	3,717	2,073	1,644
Construction				551	383	168	1,790	1,279	511	3,555	2,380	1,175
Transportation & communication	3,121	2,958	163	8,195	6,814	1,381	26,509	20,055	6,454	30,360	22,669	7,691
Trade (wholesale & retail)	20,286	15,687	4,599	25,654	14,813	10,841	25,480	11,133	14,347	49,066	23,087	25,979
Finance	2,884	2,861	23	16,604	13,928	2,676	31,911	17,130	14,781	47,937	24,184	23,753
Service	8,841	8,360	481	31,261	26,062	5,199	53,518	33,110	20,408	58,934	29,339	29,595
Community & business	304[b]	294	10	4,381[d]	2,233	2,148	9,096	2,559	6,537	17,069	3,942	13,127
Government	8,537	8,066	471	26,880	23,829	3,051	38,806	27,009	11,797	33,376	20,818	12,558
Recreation							646	285	361	1,577	639	938
Personal							4,970	3,257	1,713	6,912	3,940	2,972
Industry unspecified	15,684[c]	9,348	6,336	11,357[m]	1,603	9,754	33,644	15,259	18,385	3,886	1,475	2,411

Table A1 notes

*Data adjusted to 1951 census industry and occupation classifications.

[a] Includes persons ten years of age and over in 1901 and 1911; 14 years of age and over in 1921 and 1931. Prior to 1951, the 'gainfully occupied' concept, rather than the 'labour force' concept was used to define the country's total workforce. See Frank T. Denton and Sylvia Ostry, *Historical Estimates of the Canadian Labour Force* (Ottawa, Queen's Printer, 1967), pp. 1–8, for a discussion of these two concepts. Comparability between censuses has been achieved by rearranging data on clerical occupations for 1901, 1911, 1921, and 1931 on the basis of the 1951 census industry and occupation classifications. See *Occupational Classification Manual* (Ottawa, Queen's Printer, 1951), and *Standard Industrial Classification Manual* (Ottawa, Queen's Printer, 1951). See Meltz, *Manpower in Canada*, chapter II, for a discussion of the methodology involved.

[b] Clerks in law offices only.

[c] Includes a total of 4,336 stenographers and typists (905 males and 3,461 females).

[d] Includes stenographers in law offices.

[e] Stenographers and typists only.

[f] Clerks in forestry, fishing and trapping.

Sources: Computed from the following: 1901 Census of Canada, Census and Statistics, Bulletin I, *Wage-Earners by Occupations* (Ottawa, King's Printer, 1907) table II; 1901 Census of Canada, Census and Statistics, Bulletin XI, *Occupations of the People* (Ottawa, King's Printer, 1910), table II; 1911 Census of Canada, volume VI, tables I, III and IV; 1911 Census of Canada, volume IV, table 4; *Occupational Trends in Canada, 1891–1931*, table 5; Meltz, *Manpower in Canada*, section II, tables D-1, D-2, and D-3; unpublished working tables for the censuses of 1901, 1911 and 1921, showing occupations by industries, using 1951 census occupation classification.

Table A2 Percentage distribution of male and female clerical workers within major industry groups, Canada, 1901–31*

	1901 M	1901 F	1911 M	1911 F	1921 M	1921 F	1931 M	1931 F
All industries	77.9	22.1	67.4	32.6	58.2	41.8	54.9	45.1
Agriculture					60.8	39.2	44.1	55.9
Forestry			94.9	5.1	98.9	1.1	88.5	11.5
Fishing								
Mining			86.3	13.7	87.9	12.1	79.2	20.8
Manufacturing	83.5	16.5	60.9	39.1	62.8	37.2	59.3	40.7
Electricity, water & gas					99.5	0.5	54.8	44.2
Construction	94.8	5.2	69.5	30.5	71.5	28.5	66.9	33.1
Transportation & communication	77.3	22.7	83.1	16.9	75.7	24.3	74.7	25.3
Trade (wholesale & retail)			57.7	42.3	43.7	56.3	47.1	52.9
Finance	99.2	0.8	83.9	16.1	53.7	46.3	50.4	49.6
Service	94.6	5.4	83.4	16.6	61.9	38.1	49.8	50.2
Community & business	96.7	3.3	51.0	49.0	28.1	71.9	23.1	76.9
Government	94.5	5.5	88.6	11.4	69.6	30.4	62.4	37.6
Recreation					44.1	55.9	40.5	59.5
Personal					65.5	34.5	57.0	43.0
Industry unspecified	59.6	40.4	14.1	85.9	45.4	54.6	38.0	62.0

*Data adjusted to 1951 census industry and occupation classifications.
Source: Computed from table A1.

Table A3 Percentage distribution of clerical workers by major industry groups, by sex, Canada, 1901–31*

	1901			1911			1921			1931		
	T	M	F	T	M	F	T	M	F	T	M	F
All industries	100.0	100.0	100.0	100.0	100.0	100.0	100.0	100.0	100.0	100.0	100.0	100.0
Agriculture				0.2	0.3	+	+	+	+	0.1	0.1	0.2
Forestry							0.3	0.5	+	0.2	0.3	+
Fishing												
Mining				0.3	0.4	0.1	0.6	0.8	0.2	0.5	0.7	0.2
Manufacturing	11.2	12.0	8.4	9.0	8.1	10.8	19.3	20.8	17.1	23.4	25.3	21.1
Electricity, gas & water							0.1	0.2	+	1.4	1.4	1.4
Construction				0.5	0.6	0.5	0.8	1.0	0.6	1.4	1.7	1.0
Transportation & communication	5.5	6.6	1.3	7.9	9.8	4.1	12.2	15.9	7.1	11.7	15.8	6.5
Trade (wholesale & retail)	35.4	35.2	36.3	24.8	21.2	32.1	11.8	8.8	15.8	18.8	16.1	22.1
Finance	5.0	6.4	0.2	16.0	19.9	7.9	14.7	13.6	16.3	18.4	16.9	20.2
Service	15.4	18.8	3.8	30.2	37.3	15.4	24.7	26.3	22.5	22.6	20.5	25.2
Community & business	0.5	0.7	+	4.2	3.2	6.4	4.2	2.2	7.2	6.6	2.7	11.2
Government	14.9	18.1	3.7	26.0	34.1	9.0	17.9	21.4	13.0	12.8	14.6	10.7
Recreation							0.3	0.2	0.4	0.6	0.4	0.8
Personal							2.3	2.6	1.9	2.7	2.8	2.5
Industry unspecified	27.4	21.0	50.0	11.0	2.3	28.9	15.5	12.1	20.3	1.5	1.0	2.0

*Data adjusted to 1951 census industry and occupation classifications. Columns may not add because of rounding.
+Less than 1/10 of 1 per cent.
Source: Computed from table A1.

Table A4 Numerical growth and distribution of Bank of Nova Scotia employees, Ontario branches and General Office, by selected occupational groups and sex, 1911–31

	1911			1916			1921			1926			1931		
	T	M	F	T	M	F	T	M	F	T	M	F	T	M	F
1 Ontario branches and General Office combined															
Total staff[a]	151	142	9	417	295	122	922[h]	681	241	968	766	202	1102	863	239
Management[b]	40	40	0	101	100	1[k]	221	221	0	211	211	0	278	278	0
Total clerical[c]	105	96	9	280	166	114	627	401	226	688	499	189	738	514	224
Clerks[d]	100	96	4	248	165	83	587	400	187	613	499	114	655	514	141
Stenographers[e]	5	0	5	32	1	31	40	1	39	75	0	75	83	0	83
Miscellaneous[f]	6	6	0	36	29	7	71	59	12	69	56	13	81	67	14
Temporary and part-time[g]	0	0	0	0	0	0	3	0	(3)	0	0	0	5	4	1
2 Ontario branches[i]															
Total staff[a]	113	111	2[j]	326	245	81	741	575	166	807	666	141	883	716	167
Management[b]	28	28	0	81[h]	81	0	180	180	0	175	175	0	220	220	0
Total clerical[c]	81	79	2	236	155	81	530	365	165	599	459	140	624	457	167
Clerks[d]	79	79	0	214	155	59	508	364	144	540	459	81	561	457	104
Stenographers[e]	2	0	2	22	0	22	22	1	21	59	0	59	63	0	63
Miscellaneous[f]	4	4	0	9	9	0	31	30	1	33	32	1	39	39	0
Temporary and part-time[g]	0	0	0	0	0	0	0	0	0	0	0	0	0	0	0
3 General Office															
Total staff[a]	38	31	7	91	50	41	181	106	75	161	100	61	219	147	72
Management[b]	12	12	0	20	19	1[k]	41	41	0	36	36	0	58	58	0

Total clerical[c]	24	17	7	44	11	33	97	36	61	89	40	49	114	57	57
Clerks[d]	21	17	4[j]	34	10	24	79	36	43	73	40	33	94	57	37
Stenographers[e]	3	0	3	10	1	9	18	0	18	16	0	16	20	0	20
Miscellaneous[f]	2	2	0	27	20	7	40	29	11	36	24	12	42	28	14
Temporary and part-time[g]	0	0	0	0	0	0	3[m]	0	3	0	0	0	5[o]	4	1

a Includes all individuals employed permanently, temporarily and part-time by the bank as of 31 December in branches located in the province of Ontario and at the Toronto head office.

b Includes mainly branch managers; assistant managers; provisional and relieving managers; accountants; provisional, acting provisional, and assistant accountants; inspection staff; and General Office executives.

c Includes all clerical employees below the position of assistant accountant, excluding messengers, telegraph operators, office boys, and porters, all of whom are part of the 'miscellaneous' category. The definition of clerk used in compiling these tables conforms as closely as possible with that used in the 1951 census.

d Includes all clerical employees other than stenographers. This category consists of bookkeepers, juniors, chief clerks, tellers, ledger keepers, accounting clerks, office machine operators, filers, general manager's clerks, occasional provisional accountants, receptionists, switchboard operators, plus a large number of persons performing unspecified clerical tasks.

e This title was used throughout the 1911–31 period; the bank employed no typists, clerk-typists or secretaries. Several women were employed as 'stenographer and clerk'. They are classified as stenographers.

f Includes all non-clerical staff in the dining room, and stationery department, as well as maintenance workers, chauffeurs, messengers, porters, and telegraph operators.

g Includes only part-time or temporary workers, all occupations, in the bank's employ on 31 December. Temporary or part-time workers whose term of employment ended prior to this date are computed into the turnover rate.

h Includes many branches of the Bank of Ottawa, which merged with the Bank of Nova Scotia in 1919.

i Two stenographers, one at the Hamilton main branch and the other at the Toronto main branch. Both were hired in 1911. No other females were employed in Ontario branches at this time.

j Includes several bookkeepers.

k Manager of stationery department.

l Does not include sub-branches.

m Part-time dining room help.

n Includes the only managerial-level employee not internally recruited during the 1911–31 period. In 1916 the Barrie branch hired a provisional accountant at a salary of $800.

o Includes four men working part-time in the stationery factory, and a temporary female clerk.

Source: Calculated from 'Branch Staff Lists for 1911–31', Bank of Nova Scotia Archives

Table A5 Percentage change in the number of persons employed by the Bank of Nova Scotia in Ontario, over 5 year intervals, by selected occupational groups and sex, 1911–31

	1911–16	1916–21	1921–6	1926–31
1 Total				
Total Ontario staff[a]	176.2%	121.1%	5.0%	13.8%
General Office staff	139.5	98.9	−11.0	36.0
Ontario branches staff	188.5	127.3	8.9	9.4
Total clerical[b]	166.7	123.9	9.7	7.3
Stenographers	540.0	25.0	87.5	10.7
2 Male				
Total Ontario staff[d]	107.7%	130.8%	12.5%	12.7%
General Office staff	61.3	112.0	−5.7	47.0
Ontario branches staff	120.7	134.7	15.8	7.5
Total clerical[b]	72.9	141.6	24.4	3.0
Stenographers	−	−	−	−
3 Female				
Total Ontario staff[a]	1,225.6%	97.5%	−16.2%	18.3%
General Office staff	485.7	82.9	−18.6	18.0
Ontario branches staff	3,950.0	104.9	−15.1	18.4
Total clerical[b]	1,166.7	98.2	−16.4	18.5
Stenographers	520.0	25.8	92.3	10.7

[a] Includes all employees, General Office and Ontario branches.
[b] Includes clerks and stenographers. See footnote c, table A4.
Source: Computed from table A4.

Table A6 Numerical growth and distribution of Manufacturers Life Insurance Company employees, head office, by selected occupational groups and sex, 1911–31

	1911			1916			1921			1926			1931		
	T	M	F	T	M	F	T	M	F	T	M	F	T	M	F
Total staff[a]	93	58	35	105	50	55	200	105	96	290	150	140	445	227	218
Managers and professionals[f]	10	10	0	13	12	1[g]	14	14	0	21	20	1[g]	37	36	1[g]
Total clerical[b]	79	46	33	89	37	52	184	88	96	260	124	136	393	176	217
Clerks[c]	61	45	16	71	37	34	167	88	79	237	121	116	389	175	214
Stenographers and typists[d]	18	1	17	18	0	18	17	0	17	23	3	20	4[e]	1	3
Messengers and porters	1	1	0	1	1	0	1	1	0	3	3	0	4	4	0
Temporary and part-time[h]	3	1	2	2	0	2	1	1	0	6	3	3	11	11	0

a Includes all persons employed permanently, temporarily or part-time in the company's Toronto head office as of 31 December.

b Includes all clerical employees below the level of department head, excluding messengers and porters. The 1951 census definition of clerk is used to classify employees into this category.

c Includes all clerical employees other than stenographers and typists. This category consists of a large number of persons performing unspecified clerical tasks as well as fisher operators, addressograph clerks, multigraph operators, and other office machine operators; bookkeepers; card clerks; inquiry clerks; and switchboard operators.

d The 1911, 1916, and 1921 staff lists only refer to stenographers. The occupational title of typist appears on the 1926 staff list.

e The 1931 staff list is organized by department. Clerical occupations within each department are often not specified. This accounts for the apparent decrease in the number of stenographers and typists. Most of the employees in these occupations are classified as clerks in the table.

f Includes executives, department heads, cashiers, actuaries, accountants, translators, doctors (medical referees) and registered nurses.

g Registered nurses, 1916 and 1931; translator, 1916.

h See footnote g, table A4.

Source: Computed from Manufacturers Life Insurance Company Archives, head office salary books for 1911–31.

Index

stem can be influenced in various ways
on was concerned with the question of w.
can also be altered by means of intravenous ...
relationships of age and behavior of the blood
rious reaction-types were found, includ... a group
ator activity in diluted plasma followi... fat inft
ents of higher median age and with higher increase
ing fat infusion than in the other groups with unch
tor activity.